September 17, 1986

Peg —
Thanks for your
persistent pursuit of these
same goals. Thanks, too, for
your friendship over all
these years — since those
relatively "gentle" days of
working to guide and
sensitize deacons at SMU —

Happy Birthday —
and
Many More!

Bob Trebay

WOMANGUIDES

Hand in hand, women guide each other as they claim their buried past and journey to the place of the death of patriarchy and the beginning of new possibilities for womanbeing.

The Goddess Isis Leads Queen Nefertari by the Hand. Entrance room to the tomb of Queen Nefertari at Thebes.

WOMANGUIDES

Readings Toward a Feminist Theology

ROSEMARY

RADFORD

RUETHER

Beacon Press / Boston

Beacon Press books are published under the auspices
of the Unitarian Universalist Association of
Congregations in North America,
25 Beacon Street, Boston, Massachusetts 02108
Published simultaneously in Canada by
Fitzhenry and Whiteside Limited, Toronto

Library of Congress Cataloging in Publication Data

Ruether, Rosemary Radford.
    Womanguides.

    Bibliography: p.
    Includes index.
    1. Women and religion—Addresses, essays, lectures.
2. Feminism—Religious aspects—Addresses, essays,
lectures.   3. Women (Theology)—Addresses, essays, lectures.
I. Title.
BL458.R84   1985   291.8′088042   84-14508
ISBN 0-8070-1202-5

Acknowledgments

Photographs and Art

Grateful acknowledgment is made to the following for permission to reprint: Hirmer Verlag Munchen for their photo of "Isis leading Queen Nefertai by the Hand"; Princeton University Press for permission to reprint "The Canaanite Goddess Ashera," Louvre Museum, "The Goddess Nut," Temple of Hathar, Dendera, Egypt, "Lilith," collection of Colonel Norman Colville, and "The Birth of Aphrodite," Museo Nazionale delle Terme, Rome, from their book *The Great Mother: An Analysis of the Archetype*, translated by Ralph Manheim, Bollingen Series 47. Copyright © 1955, renewed 1981 by Princeton University Press; Sopraintendenza per i beni artistica e storica, Province of Siena e Giosseto, for "The Madonna of Mercy" by Giovanni Paolo, Chiesa dei Servi, Siena; Leonard Swidler for photo of "Trinity," Urschalling Church, Germany; The British Museum, for the photo of "Witches" by Goya; Almuth Lutkenhaus for the photo of "The Crucified Woman"; Meinrad Craighead for the photo of "Women for Life on Earth"; Beinecke Rare Book and Manuscript Library, Yale University for the photo of "A duel between a woman and a Dominican."

Poetry and Prose

Grateful acknowledgment is made to the following for permission to reprint: Except where noted, the scripture quotations in this book are from the *Revised Standard Version* of the Bible, copyright 1946, 1952, © 1971, 1973, reprinted by permission of the National Council of Churches of Christ in the United States of America; "Enki and Ninhursag, a Paradise Myth," "Prayer of Lamentation to Ishtar," "The Creation Epic (Akkadia)," and "Poems about Anath and Baal," from *Ancient Near Eastern Texts: Relating to the Old Testament*, 3rd edition, with Supplement, edited by James B. Pritchard, © 1969 by Princeton University Press. Reprinted by permission of Princeton University Press; from *The Golden Ass* by Apuleius, translated by Robert Graves, copyright © 1951 by International Authors N.V., by permission of Farrar, Straus and Giroux, Inc.; from *Gifts of Power, The Writings of Rebecca Jackson, Black Visionary, Shaker*

Eldress, edited and with an Introduction by Jean McMahon Humez. Manuscripts upon which this modern edition is based are in the Berkshire Athenaeum and the Western Reserve Historical Society, reprinted by permission of Jean McMahon Humez; Odes 19 and 36 from *The Odes of Solomon*, edited and translated by J.H. Charlesworth, © 1973, Oxford University Press, by permission of the publisher; from Hesiod's *Theogony* translated by Norman O. Brown, © 1983, Liberal Arts Press, by permission of The Bobbs-Merrill Company, Inc.; from *The Essential Philo* edited by Nahum Glatzer, copyright © 1971, by permission of Schocken Books, Inc.; from *Gates to the Old City: A Book of Jewish Legends* by Raphael Patai, Avon Books, 1980 and Wayne State University Press, 1981, by permission of the author; "The Coming of Lilith" by Judith Plaskow, by permission of the author; from The *Nag Hammadi Library* edited by James M. Robinson, English language copyright © 1978 by E. J. Brill, by permission of Harper & Row, Publishers, Inc.; from *The New English Bible*, Zachariah 9:9–10; 15:1–9; Revelation 19:11–21; 20:1–3; Matthew 20:17–28; 23:1–12; Philippians 2:6–11; John 1:2–5, 9–13; Colossians 1:15–20, copyright © The Delegates of the Oxford Unversity Press and the Syndics of the Cambridge University Press, 1961, 1970, reprinted by permission; "Untitled," "I Scream for Joanna," and "Woman Love" by Nancy Ore, by permission of the author; from *The Gnostic Religion* by Hans Jonas, 2nd edition, copyright © 1963 by Hans Jonas, by permission of Beacon Press; from *Confessions*, Book VIII by Augustine, translated by E. B. Pusey, Macmillan and Company, London; from *The Interior Castle* by Teresa of Avila, translated by Allison Peers, Sheed and Ward, Ltd., 1944, by permission of the publisher; from *The Future of Man* by Teilhard de Chardin, translated by Norman Denny, Harper & Row, 1964, by permission of the publisher; from *Post-Scarcity Anarchism* by Murray Bookshin, Ramparts Press, 1971, by permission of the author; from *The First Sex* by Elizabeth Gould Davis, copyright © 1971 by Elizabeth Gould Davis, by permission of G. P. Putnam's Sons; abridged excerpts from *Inanna: Queen of Heaven and Earth* by Diane Wolkstein and Samuel Noah Kramer, copyright © 1983 by Diane Wolkstein and Samuel Noah Kramer, by permission of Harper & Row, Publishers, Inc.; from *Early Christian Fathers* edited and translated by Cyril C. Richardson (Volume I: The Library of Christian Classica). Published simultaneously in Great Britain and the United States by the S.C.M. Press, Ltd., London, and the Westminster Press, Philadelphia, 1953. Reprinted by permission; from *His Religion and Hers; A Study of the Faith of Our Fathers and the Work of Our Mothers* by Charlotte Perkins Gilman, published by T. Fisher Unwin, 1924, reprinted by permission of Adam and Charles Black, Publishers; "The Parable of the Naked Lady" by Anne Spurgeon, by permission of the author; "The Journey" by Beth Hamilton, by permission of the author.

Contents

Introduction

The purpose of this collection of texts is to provide a resource for the
doing of feminist theology. This collection is not intended to be a closed
set of historical documents so much as a springboard for constructing
what must become a new expression of theology from the perspective
of the full personhood of women. Feminist theology must create a new
textual base, a new canon. However, this collection is not the new
canon. That will have to emerge from a longer process of community
building and a larger consensus of such an emerging community. This
is a working handbook from which such a new canon might emerge,
much as early Christians collected stories about their experience from
which they preached the "good news" and from which, eventually,
fuller texts were developed and ratified as the interpretive base for the
new community.

A collection of texts is the accumulated heritage of a people's reflection on its experience in the light of questions of ultimate meaning
and value. The texts provide norms for judging good and evil, truth
and falsehood, for judging what is of God/ess and what is spurious
and demonic.

Feminist theology cannot be done from the existing base of the
Christian Bible. The Old and New Testaments have been shaped in
their formation, their transmission, and, finally, their canonization to
sacralize patriarchy. They may preserve, between the lines, memories
of women's experience. But in their present form and intention they
are designed to erase women's existence as subjects and to mention
women only as objects of male definition. In these texts the norm for
women is absence and silence. Whether praised for their compliance

or admonished for their "disobedience," women remain in these texts "the other." Their own point of view, their own experience, their own being as human subjects is never at the center. They appear, if at all, at the margin. Mostly, they do not appear at all. Even their absence and silence are not noted since, for women in patriarchy, absence and silence are normative.

Thus the doing of feminist theology demands a new collection of texts to make women's experience visible. How does one make the right start in developing such a collection of texts? Does one seek an alternative, matriarchal religion and resurrect its canon? Unfortunately, such a canon cannot be found. There are, of course, surviving texts from ancient religions that revere Mother Goddesses, but these texts are not fully "feminist" but are more or less androcentric. The power of the Mother is viewed from the perspective of males who wish to defeat or harness this power to seat themselves on it as their throne.

Perhaps, before that, lost in the mists of time, there was an earlier religion, an earlier cultural consciousness, where women appeared as subjects of their own humanity, speaking of their experience in their own name; where they were not mother, wife, or whore, goddess or demon, but persons. But such a religion is lost to us. Perhaps it once existed. Perhaps it did not. In any case, it is "prehistoric," which is to say that it does not exist as a part of our historical experience. For this reason, its texts cannot be found.

How then should we go about collecting the texts for the doing of feminist theology? Should we reject all roots in the past and create something totally *de novo*? Even if we pretended to do that, we could not. Our new stories would be built in some way on old ones. So we need to know what those old ones were and what they meant in their original context. Should we make up what should have been, what *must have been*, in those "prehistoric" times? To do so would be exciting, but also mystifying, if we were not clear that our situation today is the source of this projection into a distant past. The past provides us only with a dark mirror on which to throw our own images but yields no developed texts by which to verify our imagination. Better then to claim that imagination as our own.

Even though there is no canon of an alternative feminist religion of ancient times, we are not left without sources for our own experience in the past. We can read between the lines of patriarchal texts and find fragments of our own experience that were not completely erased. We can also find, outside of canonized texts, remains of alternative communities that reflect either the greater awe and fear of female power denied in later patriarchy or questionings of male domination in groups where women did enter into critical dialogue. Whether anathematized and declared heretical or just overlooked, some of these texts are recoverable. We can resurrect them, gather them together, and begin to glimpse the larger story of our experience.

In so doing, we read canonical, patriarchal texts in a new light. They lose their normative status and we read them critically in the light of that larger reality that they hide and deny. In the process, a new norm emerges on which to construct a new community, a new theology, eventually a new canon. That new norm makes women as subjects the center rather than the margin. Women are empowered to define themselves rather than to be defined by others. Women's speech and presence are normative rather than aberrant.

This collection is guided by such an understanding of our historical experience. Some texts can be recovered from the margins of the dominant traditions of patriarchy. It puts these texts side by side with the patriarchal definitions of woman, for these definitions also have been our experience. We have not only heard these texts, we have internalized them. But in the light of forgotten but rememberable texts from the margins, we are now able to reflect in a new way on texts that we have been told to know and to accept. We can read these patriarchal texts from the underside and note their hidden message — namely, the struggle to reverse reality, to make subjects into objects, to reduce to silence those who sometimes spoke, to make absent those whose presence was thereby actually acknowledged.

These texts purposely do not go beyond the borders of the Western Christian culture of its author and, it is presumed, of most of its readers. There is no effort to provide creation stories from Australian aborigines or Amerindians, although such stories could indeed be revelatory and would be, rightfully, texts for persons whose actual history has been a part of those experiences. But this collection chooses to remain within the context of that cultural matrix that has shaped Western Christianity: the ancient Near East, the Hebrews, the Greeks, the New Testament, the marginated communities at the edges of Judaism and Christianity. It consists primarily of texts from these ''classical'' foundations, although lines of minority traditions or post-Christian consciousness are sketched through texts of more recent vintage. The purpose is to provide a working collection that reflects the basic paradigms that have shaped our cultural consciousness, both what we have chosen to remember and something of what we have tried to forget but, in some dim way, still remember.

There is nothing definitive about such a collection. It is one person's selection, and any other person would have done it somewhat differently. One could endlessly ask why this or that "gem" has not been included. Indeed, one might expect that any group using this handbook for its intended purpose might end by doing a revision of it, adding and leaving out some things. But it is hoped that there is enough here to make a start, to provide a working handbook of those stories from our enlarged memory of our experience to provide a basis for discussion. In the light of the Gospel of Mary, we can read the dictates of 1 Timothy about women's silence and exclusion from ministry in a new light. We can start the work of our own theological reflection.

This work of reflection need not remain encapsulated in past symbols and texts. New liberating experience is empowered to write new stories, new parables, new *midrashim* on the old stories. We, too, can write new texts to express our new consciousness. We can read them in community gatherings of WomanChurch. They can become texts for teaching and preaching the vision. So in several of the sections of this collection I have included examples of feminist *midrashim,* parables and myths. Judith Plaskow wrote the *midrash* of Lilith and Eve at a gathering of a woman's theology conference at Grailville in 1973. This *midrash* has become a classic for Jewish feminism and has been included in chapter IV, following the rabbinic *midrash* on Lilith and Eve.

Several of my students at Garrett-Evangelical Theological Seminary — Ann Spurgeon, Beth Hamilton, and Nancy Ore — have written poems and parables of particular creativity and power in expressing their feminist theological journey. I have included some examples of these in the chapters on Christology (chapter V) and Conversion (chapter VI) and in a concluding section (chapter XII). I hope that any group using this handbook as a basis of feminist theologizing will be similarly empowered to write their own stories, parables and *midrashim,* read them to each other, and use them to proclaim a new word and celebrate a new reality. With this in mind, I have included in each chapter discussion sections that suggest ways of questioning the texts and stimulating the imagination to write new texts.

WOMANGUIDES

Seated between goats to which she offers ears of corn, the Goddess is vibrant with the powers of life.

The Canaanite Goddess Ashera. Mycenean lid of an ivory unguent box, Ras Shamra, Syria, thirteenth century B.C., Louvre.

1

Gender Imagery for God/ess

I start this first chapter on gender imagery for deity with a text from the psalm that displays the sense of deity as Sky-father. I start here not because it is the earliest human consciousness of the divine but because it is the present starting point of the dominant cultural consciousness of contemporary Christians (and Jews). Here we see the sense of deity built on the experience of desert patriarchy. The text brings vividly before our minds the desert dweller looking up to the heavens in that vast terrain where the vault of the sky looms majestic and earth appears quiescent, bare of vegetation. The music of the revolving cycle of night to night, day to day speaks as wordless voice of God's handiwork. Like a bridegroom emerging from his wedding canopy, the sun emerges and runs its course across the sky. From this Sky-father comes down Law that instructs the soul. The desert chief whose soul exults in God's world is also secure as humble servant of the Great Patriarch who rules from above.

The text speaks of a Hebrew patriarchalism filled with a sense of poetry and music that reflects the soul of the man who stands before his tent surveying the vault of God's Heaven above him. He stands alone. Bride, wife, children are there somewhere in the background, but they are invisible. They need not speak or be seen. Their existence does not need to be noted to complete the picture. The Lord of the sky speaks to the chieftain of the small, tented world as patriarch to patriarch. He is his humble son and servant, who is thereby also empowered to rule his clan as God rules the tent of the cosmos.

Although this man in his desert patriarchalism could mostly ignore the roles of women when thinking about or experiencing God, occasionally they intruded on his consciousness. One thing women did that he could not do was to give birth. This impressed him very much. Indeed, it was for this reason more than anything else that women must be controlled and reduced to dependency. Unlike modern people who banish birth to hospitals, this ancient patriarch heard the cries of birth emerging from the dark tents. He knew that it was not something sweet and gentle, but something fierce and powerful and bloody, an immense thrust of energy from which came forth new life. So he readily compared it with his own most intense life-and-death experience, the experience of battle. Not surprisingly, then, in the midst of imagery of God as warrior, the archetypal imagery of the male God, we find mingled the imagery of God as a birthing mother, shouting and panting as she gives birth with thrusting energy and bloody exertion. Through this thrusting energy of God as warrior and mother in travail, Israel's foes will be defeated, the waters and vegetation of the earth scorched, and the people of Israel taken by the hand, led and protected by their chieftain.

But this Hebrew patriarch was not really the Lord of the cosmos. He was a relative latecomer to the settled world of lush vegetation and watered plains that he had entered as warrior and conqueror. The peoples of those agricultural plains and glittering cities that he coveted had an older culture of king and temple. They worshipped other deities who were both God and Goddess. These alien deities must be dethroned and dispossessed so that he and his desert Lord could take control. While dispossessing them, however, he also incorporated much of their culture. The psalms written in the name of the Lord whose name could not be named echoed the patterns of psalms once sung to other deities. Thus in the psalm to Ishtar, which we read from a seventh-century B.C. Babylonian text, we readily recognize the parallels with Hebrew psalms.

The great Goddess of Babylonia evoked by the worshipper in this ancient psalm is not mother, sweetheart, or tender inspirer of the soul. This kind of gender complementarity in which all things female have become ''feminine'' — that is, reduced to auxiliary status, rendered gentle and supportive — has not yet happened in this ancient culture. Rather, the Goddess addressed is imagined as a person of sovereign power, like a queen or a great priestess who formed the female half of the ruling class. As a member of a reigning aristocracy she rules, gives decrees, wears the crown of dominion.

The servant of this Lady exalts Her, flatters Her by declaring that She has *all* power, that She is exalted over all others of Her class. She is also a war-lord, not in some modern Freudian sense of a "devouring mother" but precisely in the same sense as the Hebrew God is a war-lord. Battle is the way She defends Her realm, defeats Her foes and protects Her servants. To Her, Her servants turn in appeal to vindicate them in their cause against their foes. They seek to excite Her pity by bringing before Her eyes their miserable condition as they are wasted by affliction and assaulted by enemies. They cry out in distress. They pour out their woes to their divine mistress. They hope She will pity them, forgive any offenses they have made against Her, and will deliver them from their foes. Then they will exult and be victorious. They will trample their foes, and, in their victory, will glorify the Name of their Mistress who is in Heaven.

Who is the speaker in this psalm of lamentation and appeal for vindication? One can imagine that a ruling-class woman might have spoken such a prayer, a woman who governed her household and who appealed to such a Goddess as protector. It should not be beyond the realm of our imagination to visualize such a prayer emerging from the lips of such a woman. But this woman was no egalitarian. She made no common cause with the females among her own servants. Whether from female or, most likely, male lips, this prayer comes from an ancient Near Eastern ruling class who seek to dominate their little world of slaves and possessions and to protect them from foes and who appeal to their Goddess for aid and protection in this enterprise.

Eight hundred years after the text of the psalm of Ishtar was written in the temple Esagila in Babylon, copied from an earlier version of the text from Borsippa, Apuleius, a Roman provincial from Maudauros (Africa), educated as a cosmopolitan of the Silver Age of Greco-Roman society, wrote a satiric novel called the *Metamorphoses* (or *The Golden Ass*). All kinds of legends, popular lore, and social commentary are found in its pages. One of the most serious sections of the novel records the transformation of the enchanted ass back into a human being through the intervention of the Goddess Isis and his subsequent initiation into her rites. This section probably reflects Apuleius' own initiation into the rites of Isis. In the excerpt from *The Golden Ass* on the vision of Isis we see the image of this great Goddess who was one of the most powerful deities of the later Greco-Roman world. It was Isis who provided much of the iconography, as well as the popular piety, that fueled the Christian cult of Mary that began to arise in Egypt in the third century A.D.

Much had happened to Isis and other great Goddesses of the ancient Near East in their three-millennia history as deities of the ancient empires of Egypt and Babylonia. The Greeks who conquered Egypt in the fourth century transformed Isis into the cult deity of a mystery religion. The mysteries of death and rebirth ceased to be a part of public ceremony of the agricultural cycle and the empowerment of autonomous rulers and temple priesthoods. The Goddesses and their cults were detached from their earlier political base and became personal religions whose rites assured the initiate of prosperity, health, and immortality.

The Greeks had divided the ancient Goddess, who was both virgin and mother, protector and warrior, into separate types: Athena, the virgin warrior; Artemis, the virgin huntress; Hera, the nagging wife of Zeus; and Aphrodite, the love Goddess. These types represent the severing of the Goddess from earlier wholeness and cultic power and her transformation by the literary imagination of patriarchal society. Although the Hellenized Isis was a potent cult deity in the Greco-Roman world, Apuleius' vision of Isis reflects this Hellenistic literary imagination. It also reflects the platonizing belief that all names of ancient deities of the Mediterranean cultures are but interchangeable names for the same divine forces.

Isis in Apuleius' vision is above all a nature-spirit, a gentle potency that underlies all natural processes of growth. Unlike the earlier Ishtar, Isis conforms to the male stereotypes of femininity. She is described in terms of her beautiful female appearance, her visual image, her perfumed scent. She is kindly and nurturing, alluring as a mistress, comforting as a mother. Battles and political power, defeat of public foes are far from her mind. She comforts the enchanted ass as a victim of private misfortune. In this form, Isis passed readily into the type of the gentle virgin-mother Mary, who similarly comforts the luckless sinner who cries out for her mercy and protection. Like Isis, Mary also directs her devotees to fasting, penitence, and curbing of sexual appetites. She demands special devotion to her but rewards her devotees with assurance of protection in this life and happiness in heaven.

Fourteen hundred years later, even this dim survival of the ancient Goddess was banished in the Protestant Reformation, which allowed only the patriarchal Father God and his Son into its theology. Catholics continued to cultivate Mary all the more fervently, but in a way strictly severed from the doctrine of God and from the fecundity of nature or humanity. Yet the desire for a mother in deity did not vanish even from Protestant hearts. Successive pietist and mystic sects learned to cultivate the "feminine" side of God from the seventeenth-century Protestant mystic Jacob Boehme. In nineteenth-century America, a host of mystic and utopian sects suggested to pious searchers that the divine was more Mother than Father. Mary Baker Eddy, the founder of one such healing sect, drew on the contemporary typologies of masculinity as materialistic and aggressive, feminity as spiritual and loving. In her rewriting of the Lord's Prayer to include Mother as well as Father as the name of God, she manifests this assumption that the feminizing of the divine also demands a spiritualizing of religion as inward and personal, severed from material and political realities.

However, not all women who searched for the mother-face of deity wanted just to add the feminine "side" to God within an androcentric culture of gender complementarity. Some women sought the empowering center of their own personhood, which would free them from the strictures of silence and passivity of patriarchal religion and command them to speak and act on their own behalf. Such a searcher was Rebecca Jackson, a Black mystic whose journals, written between 1830 and 1864, record the inner visions of her progressive journey into spiritual empowerment.

Originally illiterate, Jackson received the gift of literacy from her inner visions. She was led by her guiding spirit to become an itinerant revival preacher, against the hostility of her brother and the elders and ministers of the African Methodist Episcopal Church. She probably learned of the female image of God as Wisdom from the Shaker tradition, which she eventually joined. She was allowed in 1870 to become the Elderess of an independent Shaker community of Black women in Philadelphia. However, in a vision dated 1835, long before her entrance into Shakerism, at a time when she was pursuing the itinerant preaching ministry against the hostile reception by the African Methodist Episcopal Church, she recorded her vision of a Mother in Deity as the empowering revelation that allowed her to resist and triumph over those churchmen who would silence her and confine her to the pew.

Reflection

With the new birth of feminism in the last third of the twentieth century, the question of a nonpatriarchal image of God arises with new insistency. It raises again the basic question of the source and basis of our imagery of the divine. Is God/ess as male or female simply the projection into the heavens of our social gender roles? Do we simply wish to add the nurturing mother to the strong father of patriarchal gender symbolism? If God/ess is beyond gender, can we afford to image God in abstract and genderless images, such as Sovereign, which are depersonalizing while concealing other messages, such as the imagery of absolute Power? How is God/ess imagery related to our persona as male or female? How can it remain the ground of personhood while not ratifying gender stereotypes or the domination of one sex over another?

One can answer this question in theological terms by saying that all language for God is metaphorical and not literal and that the authentic God/ess is beyond gender while being the ground of the personhood of both men and women. But such statements will mean little unless we also probe the roots of our feeling based on our particular experiences of our own gender identity in relation to that of parents and authorities. So I might suggest the following discussion process for any group using these texts as a point of departure for reflection on gender imagery for God.

With paper and marking pens sketch a symbol for your self and for God/ess. First, imagine God/ess in male gender terms. Write down what images or names come to mind. Then imagine God/ess in female imagery. On another piece of paper write what ideas and images come to mind. Redraw your symbol of your self and God/ess. Do you find it necessary to locate the relation between your self and God/ess differently when you move from one gender image to the other? If so, what is the difference?

Compare the terms that come to mind for deity as male and deity as female. What kinds of terms are these? What social roles do they suggest? How do you feel about yourself when relating to God/ess in one set of imagery and in the other? Does this change how you think and feel about your own gender identity?

Are there words and images that come to mind for God/ess that are not based on gender roles? What are these terms and what effect do they have on your sense of your own identity? How would you locate yourself in relation to God/ess when using these non-gender-specific terms? On the basis of this exploration, reflect on the meaning of gender-imagery for God/ess for you. What imagery do you prefer and why?

1. The Sky-God as Lord and Lawgiver[1]

The heavens tell out the glory of God,
the vault of heaven reveals his handiwork.
One day speaks to another,
night with night shares its knowledge,
and this without speech or language
or sound of any voice.
Their music goes out through all the earth,
their words reach to the end of the world.
In them a tent is fixed for the sun,
who comes out like a bridegroom from his wedding canopy,
rejoicing like a strong man to run his race.
His rising is at one end of the heavens,
his circuit touches their farthest ends;
and nothing is hidden from his heat.

The law of the Lord is perfect and revives the soul.
The Lord's instruction never fails,
and makes the simple wise.
The precepts of the Lord are right and rejoice the heart.
The commandment of the Lord shines clear
and gives light to the eyes.
The fear of the Lord is pure and abides for ever.
The Lord's decrees are true and righteous every one,
more to be desired than gold, pure gold in plenty,
sweeter than syrup or honey from the comb.
It is these that give thy servant warning,
and he who keeps them wins a great reward.

2. God as Warrior and Birthing Mother[2]

The Lord goes forth like a mighty man,
like a man of war he stirs up his fury;
he cries out, he shouts aloud,
he shows himself mighty against his foes.

For a long time I have held my peace,
I have kept still and restrained myself;

now I will cry out like a woman in travail,
    I will gasp and pant.
I will lay waste mountains and hills,
    and dry up all their herbage;
I will turn the rivers into islands,
    and dry up the pools.
And I will lead the blind
    in a way that they know not,
in paths that they have not known
    I will guide them.
I will turn the darkness before them into light,
    the rough places into level ground.
These are the things I will do,
    and I will not forsake them.

3. Ishtar, Shepherdess of the People[3]

I pray to thee, O Lady of ladies, goddess of goddesses.
O Ishtar, queen of all peoples, who guides mankind aright,
O Irnini, ever exalted, greatest of the Igigi,
O most mighty of princesses, exalted is thy name.
Thou indeed art the light of heaven and earth, O valiant daughter
    of Sin (the Moon)
O supporter of arms, who determines battle,
O possessor of all divine power, who wears the crown of
    dominion,
O Lady, glorious is thy greatness; over all the gods it is exalted.
O star of lamentation, who causes peaceable brothers to fight,
Yet who constantly gives friendship,
O mighty one, Lady of battle, who suppresses the mountains,
O Gushea, the one covered with fighting and clothed with terror
Thou dost make complete judgment and decision, the ordinances
    of heaven and earth.
Chapels, holy places, sacred sites, and shrines pay heed to thee.
Where is not thy name, where is not thy divine power?
Where are thy likenesses not fashioned, where are thy shrines not
    founded?
Where art thou not great, where art thou not exalted?
Anu, Enlil, and Ea have made thee high; among the gods they
    have caused thy dominion to be great.

They have made thee high among all the Igigi; they have made
thy position pre-eminent.
At the thought of thy name heaven and earth tremble.
The gods tremble; the Anunnaki stand in awe.
To thine awesome name mankind must pay heed.
For thou art great and thou art exalted.
All the black-headed (people and) the masses of mankind pay
homage to thy might.
The judgment of the people in truth and righteousness thou
indeed dost decide.
Thou regardest the oppressed and mistreated; daily thou causest
them to prosper.
Thy mercy! O Lady of heaven and earth, shepherdess of the
weary people.
Thy mercy! O Lady of holy Eanna the pure storehouse.
Thy mercy! O Lady; unwearied are thy feet; swift are thy knees.
Thy mercy! O Lady of conflict (and) of all battles.
O shining one, lioness of the Igigi, subduer of angry gods,

O most powerful of all princes, who holdest the reins (over)
kings,
(But) who dost release the *bridles* of all maidservants,
Who art exalted and firmly fixed, O valiant Ishtar, great is thy
might.
O brilliant one, torch of heaven and earth, light of all peoples,
O unequaled angry one of the fight, strong one of the battle,
O firebrand which is kindled against the enemy, which brings
about the destruction of the furious,
O gleaming one, Ishtar, assembler of the host,
O deity of men, goddess of women, whose designs no one can
conceive,
Where thou dost look, one who is dead lives; one who is sick
rises up;
The erring one who sees thy face goes aright.
I have cried to thee, suffering, wearied, and distressed, as thy
servant.
See me O my Lady; accept my prayers.
Faithfully look upon me and hear my supplication.
Promise my forgiveness and let thy spirit be appeased.
Pity! For my wretched body which is full of confusion and
trouble.

Pity! For my sickened heart which is full of tears and suffering.

Pity! For my wretched intestines (which are full of) confusion and trouble.

Pity! For my afflicted house which *mourns bitterly*.

Pity! For my feelings which are satiated with tears and suffering.

O *exalted* Irnini, fierce lion, let thy heart be at rest.

O angry wild ox, let thy spirit be appeased.

Let the favor of thine eyes be upon me.

With thy bright features look faithfully upon me.

Drive away the evil spells of my body (and) let me see thy bright light.

How long, O my Lady, shall my adversaries be looking upon me,

In lying and untruth shall they plan evil against me,

Shall my pursuers and those who exult over me rage against me?

How long, O my Lady, shall the crippled and weak seek me out?

One has made for me long sackcloth; thus I have appeared before thee.

The weak have become strong; but I am weak.

I toss about like flood-water, which an evil wind makes violent.

My heart is flying; it keeps fluttering like a bird of heaven.

I mourn like a dove night and day.

I am beaten down, and so I weep bitterly.

With "Oh" and "Alas" my spirit is distressed.

I — what have I done, O my god and my goddess?

Like one who does not fear my god and my goddess I am treated;

While sickness, headache, loss, and destruction are provided for me;

So are fixed upon me terror, disdain, and fullness of wrath,

Anger, choler, and indignation of gods and men.

I have to expect, O my Lady, dark days, gloomy months, and years of trouble.

I have to expect, O my Lady, judgment of confusion and violence.

Death and trouble are bringing me to an end.

Silent is my chapel; silent is my holy place;

Over my house, my gate, and my fields silence is poured out.

As for my god, his face is turned to the sanctuary of another.

My family is scattered; my roof is broken up.

(But) I have paid heed to thee, my Lady; my attention has been turned to thee.

To thee have I prayed; forgive my debt.

Forgive my sin, my iniquity, my shameful deeds, and my offence.

Overlook my shameful deeds; accept my prayer;
Loosen my fetters; secure my deliverance;
Guide my steps aright; radiantly like a hero let me enter the
    streets with the living.
Speak so that at thy command the angry god may be favorable;
(And) the goddess who has been angry with me may turn again.
(Now) dark and smoky, may my brazier glow;
(Now) extinguished, may my torch be lighted.
Let my scattered family be assembled;
May my fold be wide; may my stable be enlarged.
Accept the abasement of my countenance; hear my prayers.
Faithfully look upon me and accept my supplication.
How long, O my Lady, wilt thou be angered so that thy face is
    turned away?
How long, O my Lady, wilt thou be infuriated so that thy spirit is
    enraged?
Turn thy neck which thou hast set against me; set thy face
    [toward] good favor.
Like the water of the opening up of a canal let thy emotions be
    released.
My foes like the ground let me trample;
Subdue my haters and cause them to crouch down under me.
Let my prayers and my supplications come to thee.
Let thy great mercy be upon me.
Let those who see me in the street magnify thy name.
As for me, let me glorify thy divinity and thy might before the
    black-headed (people), [saying,]
Ishtar indeed is exalted; Ishtar indeed is queen;
The Lady indeed is exalted; the Lady indeed is queen.
Irnini, the valorous daughter of Sin, has no rival.

4. Isis, Queen of Heaven[4]

Not long afterwards I awoke in sudden terror. A dazzling full
moon was rising from the sea. It is at this secret hour that the
Moon-goddess, sole sovereign of mankind, is possessed of her
greatest power and majesty. She is the shining deity by whose
divine influence not only all beasts, wild and tame, but all
inanimate things as well, are invigorated; whose ebbs and flows
control the rhythm of all bodies whatsoever, whether in the air,
on earth, or below the sea. Of this I was well aware, and

therefore resolved to address the visible image of the goddess,
imploring her help; for Fortune seemed at last to have made up
her mind that I had suffered enough and to be offering me a hope
of release.

Jumping up and shaking off my drowsiness, I went down to
the sea to purify myself by bathing in it. Seven times I dipped my
head under the waves — seven, according to the divine
philosopher Pythagoras, is a number that suits all religious
occasions — and with joyful eagerness, though tears were running
down my hairy face, I offered this soundless prayer to the
supreme Goddess:

"Blessed Queen of Heaven, whether you are pleased to be
known as Ceres, the original harvest mother who in joy at the
finding of your lost daughter Proserpine abolished the rude
acorn diet of our forefathers and gave them bread raised from the
fertile soil of Eleusis; or whether as celestial Venus, now adored at
sea-girt Paphos, who at the time of the first Creation coupled the
sexes in mutual love and so contrived that man should continue
to propagate his kind for ever; or whether as Artemis, the
physician sister of Phoebus Apollo, reliever of the birth pangs of
women, and now adored in the ancient shrine at Ephesus; or
whether as dread Proserpine to whom the owl cries at night,
whose triple face is potent against the malice of ghosts, keeping
them imprisoned below earth; you who wander through many
sacred groves and are propitiated with many different rites — you
whose womanly light illuminates the walls of every city, whose
misty radiance nurses the happy seeds under the soil, you who
control the wandering course of the sun and the very power of his
rays — I beseech you, by whatever name, in whatever aspect,
with whatever ceremonies you deign to be invoked, have mercy
on me in my extreme distress, restore my shattered fortune, grant
me repose and peace after this long sequence of miseries. End my
sufferings and perils, rid me of this hateful four-footed disguise,
return me to my family, make me Lucius once more. But if I have
offended some god of unappeasable cruelty who is bent on
making life impossible for me, at least grant me one sure gift, the
gift of death."

When I had finished my prayer and poured out the full
bitterness of my oppressed heart, I returned to my sandy hollow,
where once more sleep overcame me. I had scarcely closed my
eyes before the apparition of a woman began to rise from the
middle of the sea with so lovely a face that the gods themselves

would have fallen down in adoration of it. First the head, then the whole shining body gradually emerged and stood before me poised on the surface of the waves. Yes, I will try to describe this transcendent vision, for though human speech is poor and limited, the Goddess herself will perhaps inspire me with poetic imagery sufficient to convey some slight inkling of what I saw.

Her long thick hair fell in tapering ringlets on her lovely neck, and was crowned with an intricate chaplet in which was woven every kind of flower. Just above her brow shone a round disc, like a mirror, or like the bright face of the moon, which told me who she was. Vipers rising from the left-hand and right-hand partings of her hair supported this disc, with ears of corn bristling beside them. Her many-coloured robe was of finest linen; part was glistening white, part crocus-yellow, part glowing red and along the entire hem a woven bordure of flowers and fruit clung swaying in the breeze. But what caught and held my eye more than anything else was the deep black lustre of her mantle. She wore it slung across her body from the right hip to the left shoulder, where it was caught in a knot resembling the boss of a shield; but part of it hung in innumerable folds, the tasselled fringe quivering. It was embroidered with glittering stars on the hem and everywhere else, and in the middle beamed a full and fiery moon.

In her right hand she held a bronze rattle, of the sort used to frighten away the God of the Sirocco; its narrow rim was curved like a sword-belt and three little rods, which sang shrilly when she shook the handle, passed horizontally through it. A boat-shaped gold dish hung from her left hand, and along the upper surface of the handle writhed an asp with puffed throat and head raised ready to strike. On her divine feet were slippers of palm leaves, the emblem of victory.

All the perfumes of Arabia floated into my nostrils as the Goddess deigned to address me: "You see me here, Lucius, in answer to your prayer. I am Nature, the universal Mother, mistress of all the elements, primordial child of time, sovereign of all things spiritual, queen of the dead, queen also of the immortals, the single manifestation of all gods and goddesses that are. My nod governs the shining heights of Heaven, the wholesome sea-breezes, the lamentable silences of the world below. Though I am worshipped in many aspects, known by countless names, and propitiated with all manner of different rites, yet the whole round earth venerates me. The primeval

Phrygians call me Pessinuntica, Mother of the gods; the
Athenians, sprung from their own soil, call me Cecropian Artemis;
for the islanders of Cyprus I am Paphian Aphrodite; for the
archers of Crete I am Dictynna; for the trilingual Sicilians, Stygian
Proserpine; and for the Eleusinians their ancient Mother of the
Corn.

"Some know me as Juno, some as Bellona of the Battles;
others as Hecate, others again as Rhamnubia, but both races of
Aethiopians, whose lands the morning sun first shines upon, and
the Egyptians who excel in ancient learning and worship me with
ceremonies proper to my godhead, call me by my true name,
namely, Queen Isis. I have come in pity of your plight, I have
come to favour and aid you. Weep no more, lament no longer;
the hour of deliverance, shone over by my watchful light, is at
hand."

5. The Father-Mother God of Christian Science[5]

Thy will be done in earth, as it is in heaven.
> *Enable us to know, — as in heaven, so on earth, — God is
> omnipotent, supreme.*

Give us this day our daily bread;
> *Give us grace for to-day; feed the famished affections;*

And forgive us our debts, as we forgive our debtors.
> *And Love is reflected in love;*

And lead us not into temptation, but deliver us from evil;
> *And God leadeth us not into temptation, but delivereth us from sin,
> disease, and death.*

For Thine is the kingdom, and the power, and the glory, forever.
> *For God is infinite, all-power, all Life, Truth, Love, over all, and All.*

> Here let me give what I understand to be the spiritual sense of
> the Lord's Prayer:

Our Father which art in heaven,
> *Our Father-Mother God, all-harmonious,*

Hallowed be Thy name.
   Adorable One.

Thy kingdom come.
   Thy kingdom is come; Thou art ever-present.

6. *The Woman Face of Deity Empowers a Woman Preacher*[6]

In 1835, I was in the west — I thought I would not mention this
but I feel it a duty so to do — persecution was raging on every
side. The Methodist ministers told the trustees not to let me speak
in the church nor in any of the houses. And nobody must go to
hear me — if they did, they should be turned out of the church.
One of the trustees got up and said he would go 20 miles to hear
me. So the minister turned him right out, and said he hoped he
would never be taken in again.

They published me in three Quarterly Meetings — at Bush
Hill, West Chester, and West Town. He said he would stop me.
He would go as far as his horse would travel, and then he would
write, where he could not go.

The friends stopped him in Downingtown and told him that
they would stop him or me. So they took his horse, and told him
they would take care of it, and him too, until he proved Rebecca
Jackson to be the woman he said she was. They had sent to me
before, desiring me to put the law in force, and defend my
course. I told them that I understood my call, before I started, was
to live the life that I preached, and if I did, they would say all
manner of evil about me, for they had about Christ when He was
on earth.

This great persecution throwed open doors before me. Even a
wicked drunken man, when the members was afraid to let me
speak in their houses and the people waiting to hear the word, he
opened his house and said, "Let her come into my house and
preach. I don't belong to meeting." So when the people heard,
they came and told me. I went. The house was filled and all
around the house and the road each way.

And at this time I had as much upon me as my soul and body
and spirit was able to bear. I was all alone, had nobody to tell my
troubles to except the Lord. When I got up to speak to the people,
and seeing [them] on the fence, on the road, in the grass, my

heart seemed to melt within. I throwed myself on the Lord. I saw that night, for the first time, a Mother in the Deity. This indeed was a new scene, a new doctrine to me. But I knowed when I got it, and I was obedient to the heavenly vision — as I *see* all that I hold forth, that is, with my spirit eye. And was I not glad when I found that I had a Mother! And that night She gave me a tongue to tell it! The spirit of weeping was upon me, and it fell on all the assembly. And though they never heard it before, I was made able by Her Holy Spirit of Wisdom to make it so plain that a child could understand it.

The feminine Holy Spirit, between Father and Son; too much female in deity for patriarchal Christian orthodoxy but too circumscribed by male power for feminist theology. But, still, she is worthy of our contemplation. What would it have meant for Christianity if the Trinity had been taught to us in this form?

Fourteenth-century fresco in Urschalling Church, southwest of Munich, Germany.

2

The Divine Pleroma

Christianity has not been content simply to speak of the One God of Jewish monotheism, whether imaged predominantly as a male or occasionally given "feminine" characteristics as well. Building on ancient concepts of the divine as a community of person, it has developed its doctrine of the Trinity. While claiming that this manifoldness of God is still contained within ultimate unity, the Trinity allows Christian theology to expand the relationality of the God-concept. One can now think in terms of relationality within the divine, as well as a more complex relationality between the divine, history, the created world, and human persons. As relational, the divine enters into history. The Trinity allows the concept of God to span transcendence and immanence. Concepts like Spirit, Wisdom, or Word represent the immanence of the divine, which has moved out of its transcendent otherness and entered into the creative process as ground and guide of the cosmos.

The Trinity also allows the God-concept to enter into history. One can use the Trinity to span past, present, and future. The "Father" can be seen as the Old Testament or "patriarchal" foundations of Christianity, the "Son" or "Word" as the new foundations on which Christianity presently stands, and the Spirit as the ongoing dynamic that brings in the future. Word and Spirit can also be seen as two sides of a revelational-transformative dialectic between the self and the divine, the "Word" standing for the objective side of revelation and the Spirit standing for the subjective side which empowers our acceptance of and transformation into new possibilities. By claiming that God is Trinitarian, Christianity has claimed that this relationality of God is not mere appearance or manifestation but pertains to the essential nature of God.

Orthodox Christian Trinitarian imagery sees God as a relationality of Father and Son, or an "older" and a "younger" male. The Jewish background of Trinitarianism in Hellenistic Jewish Wisdom as well as Syriac and gnostic kinds of Christianity introduced relationships of male and female into their concepts of the divine pleroma or divine "fullness." What is the difference between the male-male Trinitarian model of orthodox theology and pleromas that contain male and female divine persons?

Some years ago, when teaching the course on feminist theology that made use of the texts of this chapter, I asked the students what model of relationality came to mind when they read the Trinitarian creed of Athanasius. After a silence, one student piped up with the reply: "Cloning!" I believe that this is a significant insight. When reading the Athanasian description of the Three Persons of the Trinity, each one equally and identically "un-create," "incomprehensible," "eternal," "Almighty," "Lord," and "God," the modern analogy that indeed comes to mind is cloning. The Son and the Spirit are "clones" of the Father. No principle of otherness, newness, or difference is introduced through bisexuality in the movement from first to second to third. The three are the triune multiplication of one single male divine identity. One might say that the relationality of the Trinity, either within itself or with creation, has disappeared in this account of the Trinity to affirm the one overriding concern for the divine sameness of the three persons of the Trinity.

By contrast, the pleromic concepts of deity reflected in the other texts in this chapter — the Wisdom of Solomon, Odes 19 and 36 of the Odes of Solomon (third-century Syriac Christian hymns), the description of the pleroma by the Valentinian Christian theologian Ptolemaeus, and the nineteenth-century description of the androgyny of God in the Shaker Bible — all introduce a more dynamic sense of movement, life, and relationality by imaging the pleroma as male and female. The language of these other texts is more mythical, that is, closer to concrete human experiences of relationality, as opposed to the severely abstracted style of the orthodox creed.

The Wisdom of Solomon was written by an Alexandrian Jew of the second century B.C. It reflects both the mythical cultures of the Egyptian and Hellenistic world, which identified Goddesses with Wisdom, and also philosophical concepts that speak of an immanent power of divine truth and knowledge that comes forth from the transcendent world to found and guide the cosmos. The predominant imagery for Wisdom is drawn from light. Wisdom is like a spiritual effulgence that radiates from the divine source of light. As light, Wisdom both reveals the divine and illumines our knowledge of the divine. She is both the knowledge and the power of God immanent in our midst, for she is the power through which God creates the world.

She is the image of God for she translates into form the unspoken or unmanifest latency of transcendent divinity. As agent of creation, she translates divine potency into act in created beings. As revealer, she translates the search for God into clear forms of knowledge and divine precept. She is both the objective and subjective side of divine revelation for she not only manifests the latent power of God but enters into the seeker of truth and goodness and enables him to find knowledge and virtue.

This light imagery for Wisdom mingles with her description as feminine to suggest another modality of relationship. Wisdom is a love-object of the wise or "kingly" soul. Like the Goddess Isis, which probably has influenced the image of Wisdom here, she is a wise and beautiful woman whom the seeker after wisdom and virtue wishes to bring home as his bride. Like Isis, she is a model of faithful, wifely love. She is the ideal wife who can act as counselor, inspirer of virtue, and provider of peace and happiness to the man who comes home to her weary from the day's battles.

Thus, in spite of the image of female power conveyed in this Wisdom text, the interpretive stance of the writer is androcentric. One can assume that the Almighty from whom she arises is thought of as the patriarchal God of Judaism. Since Wisdom plays the same theological roles (except for incarnation) as the Logos of the New Testament, we might speak of her as "Daughter" of God. As such, she functions as a feminine mediator between the male God and humanity. Moreover, the seeker after Wisdom is thought of exclusively in male terms. As a "kingly" person, he is a male spiritual and social aristocrat. Thus Wisdom really provides no place where women can identify their own personhood as the center of agency and action. As in patriarchal culture generally, the femininity of Wisdom operates to mediate between male self and male self, in this case the transcendent Almighty as divine male self and the seeker after Wisdom as human male self. The femininity of Wisdom is containable in this androcentric culture precisely because it remains relative to and auxiliary to these male ego dramas rather than acting as a focus of female personhood in her own right.

Although an androgynous concept of the Trinity was repressed in Greco-Roman Christianity, Syriac Christianity carried on the Hebrew tradition of the feminine Wisdom and translated it into a feminine image of the Holy Spirit. This feminine Holy Spirit was thought of as mother and nurturer of the Christian. She was closely linked with baptism as the womb of rebirth and with regeneration imaged as breastfeeding of the reborn soul. There is a close parallelism between Christ, as one born from the womb of the Virgin Mary by the power of the Holy Spirit, and reborn Christians who likewise are to be virginal people through the gestating and birthing power of the Holy Spirit.

This kind of imagery of the Holy Spirit as the female power of gestation, birth, and nurturing is evident in the Syriac Ode of Solomon, No. 19. Here God is thought of as androgynous, containing breasts that burst with milk like a nursing mother's. The Holy Spirit is the power that milks these full breasts of the Father, and she herself *is* this full bosom of the Father. She bestows this milk of God upon Christians, giving them thereby regenerate life.

This milk from the breasts of God is thought of as the power of gestation and birth by which the Virgin Mary conceived and gave birth to Christ. Thus the belief that Mary "conceived through the power of the Holy Spirit" is not imaged as analogous to the male impregnating seed but as a female generative power that derives from the milk of the mothering breasts of God. Giving birth is itself seen not as a painful, much less a polluted, act but as both painless and powerful, a creative act that mirrors the generation or regeneration of the New Creation itself by God.

In a parallel Ode No. 36, this mothering Holy Spirit is thought of as lifting Christ (and the reborn Christian) from the earth to heaven, presenting him before the divine throne of perfection and glory. Thereby, Christ (and the Christian) become truly Son of Man, the image of divine perfection and glory. Again, as in the Wisdom text, the ultimate ego-center of the Transcendent God, as well as Christ and the reborn Christian, is seen as male. The birthing power of the Holy Spirit, however striking and powerful, mediates the power of this male God to the human male self and, in turn, exalts this male self to heaven to stand before the throne of the male God.

Although females were doubtless included among these virginal, reborn Christians of Syriac Christianity, the persona of the reborn Christian, like that of Christ, is normatively male. Female power remains auxiliary to this male-centered drama of mediation, rebirth, and transformation. The female person can relate to this text either by including herself, anomalously, as the reborn Christian or by imagining herself as playing an auxiliary role of birthgiver to a male offspring whose quest for redemption she supports and promotes through her motherly efforts.

The *Pleroma* of Ptolemaeus represents the drama of the unfolding of the divine Being to make up the fullness of the heavenly Community. This unfolding of the divine world takes place through the self-impregnation of the female by the male side of the divine, thereby bringing forth successive pairs of male and female divine beings. Although divine being is thought of as androgynous, it is an androcentric conception of the union of male and female principles. The word *androgyny* itself conveys this androcentric perspective. That is, the androgynous divine being of Depth and Silence is seen as a male self who contains within himself a womb, which he can impregnate with his male seed, rather than a female self who possesses the power of self-impregnation.

Depth ejaculates his seed of creativity into his self-contained womb of Silence, and Silence becomes pregnant and bears a male offspring, Mind (*Nous*). He is identified as the Only-Begotten and the Father who is able to comprehend as Mind all that remains latent in Depth. Along with this male-identified Mind, who articulates the thought of the Father, there is a female twin, Truth (*Aletheia*). This Tetrad of Divine Beings, Father-Mother-Son-Daughter, stands as the root of Divine Being.

The second stage of unfolding is initiated by the Only-Begotten, who is identified as the Father. He is the intellectual power of the divine, who is able to comprehend why this process of unfolding and self-disclosure of the divine is taking place. From this comprehension, he begins a second round of manifestations, emitting from himself another divine pair, *Logos* and Life (*Zoe*). From this union of the male-female pair, *Logos-Zoe*, there is born Man (*Anthropos*) and Church (*Ekklesia*). These four, together with the original Tetrad, make up the divine Ogdoad.

The androcentric character of the Ogdoad is emphasized by indicating that the male line is the center: Depth, Mind, *Logos*, and Man, each united with his own female power. *Logos* and Life, in turn, emit ten other aeons (five male-female pairs) and Man-Church emit twelve other aeons, or six male-female pairs, making up the full thirty aeons of the Divine *Pleroma*. The last of the female aeons is Sophia, which, in the Valentinian system, functions as a cosmic Eve who brings about the rupture of the Divine *Pleroma* and the generation of the fallen demonic and material cosmos. Sophia brings about this Fall by getting out of her place in the divine hierarchy and by acting "on her own," concepts that again indicate the androcentric perspective of Valentinian gnosticism.

The final text in this section comes from the nineteenth-century Shaker Bible, which drew on a comprehensive understanding of the androgyny of the divine, of the order of creation and the New Creation. The Shakers took literally the Genesis text that God created humanity male and female "in their image" to mean that the Deity is male and female. The plural form of the Genesis text, "let us make humanity in our image," they understood to be the discourse between the Father and Mother in Deity. This eternal Mother they identify with the Wisdom of the Hebrew tradition. It is this female Wisdom who speaks as the voice of the revelation of God.

Although remnants of the concept of the female as subordinate or included within the Father continue in the Shaker Bible from the Hebrew biblical text, nevertheless the Shakers move toward seeing the Father and Mother aspects of Deity as equal. They stand on the same level of divinity as a divine pair who counsel together as partners in the creation of the world and of humanity, male and female. Divine parentage proceeds from what we might today call a "partnership marriage" rather than a patriarchal marriage of dominant male and subordinate and mediating female wife and mother. Like the Valentinians, the Shaker view of the Divine *Pleroma* is a binary one of Father and Mother which leads, in turn, to the Tetrad of Father-Mother-Son-Daughter, that is, the male and female Christs or the male and female pairs of regenerate Christians. However, the female, as Christ and as regenerate Christian, unlike in Syriac Christianity, is visible and affirmed in this nineteenth-century Church of Christ's Second Appearing.

Reflection

Where do these texts lead us in our exploration of the Divine *Pleroma* as divine relationality? We must ask what dimensions of relationality are introduced when the *Pleroma* includes relations between male and female, rather than simply a relationship between a dominant and a subordinate (or older and younger) male.

How is the divine as Father with mediating Daughter-Wisdom different from male Father and mediating *Logos*-Son?

How would the Christian relate differently to the Spirit as Mother than to the Spirit as generative power of the Father?

How would one experience the immanence of God as female Wisdom differently from a *Logos* thought of as son and image of the Father?

One can also ask how women as subjects experience these relationships differently from men. Women relate to mother and father differently from the way men relate to mother and father. What kind of relationship with themselves would happen for men if they would imagine themselves regenerated by a Mother-Spirit? What kind of relation to themselves would happen for women if they would think of themselves as regenerated by a Mother-Spirit?

The Trinity can also be seen, as in Augustinian Trinitarian theology, as a model of the self's own internal relationships. Augustine saw the Father as the being of the self, the Son as its self-consciousness, and the Spirit as the relationality between the two. How would self-integration be understood differently for women if they were able to see the being of the self as female and name these internal dynamics in terms of female-identified relationships?

Why have none of these models of the Divine *Pleroma* been able to imagine a female-centered Deity who contains the power to bring forth divine or creaturely beings? What would change if a transcendent Mother brought forth a divine Daughter? How would the divine Mother-Daughter relate to the regeneration of the human female?

Develop stories of the Divine *Pleroma* in which the Mother functions as the center of divine transcendence and where the relationship of Deity to itself and to creation is a female-female relationship. What issues does this raise about the relationship of daughters to mothers? Can women relate to women as inspirers and liberators?

1. *Divine Wisdom as Effulgence of God and Bride of the Wise*[1]

Wisdom shines bright and never fades; she is easily discerned by those who love her, and by those who seek her she is found. She is quick to make herself known to those who desire knowledge of her; the man who rises early in search of her will not grow weary in the quest, for he will find her seated at his door. To set all one's thoughts on her is prudence in its perfect shape, and to lie wakeful in her cause is the short way to peace of mind. For she herself ranges in search of those who are worthy of her; on their daily path she appears to them with kindly intent, and in all their purposes meets them half-way. The true beginning of wisdom is the desire to learn, and a concern for learning means love towards her; the love of her means the keeping of her laws; to keep her law is a warrant of immortality; and immortality brings a man near to God. Thus the desire of wisdom leads to kingly stature. If, therefore, you value your thrones and your sceptres, you rulers of the nations, you must honour wisdom, so that you may reign for ever.

What wisdom is, and how she came into being, I will tell you; I will hide no secret from you. From her first beginnings I will trace out her course, and bring the knowledge of her into the light of day; I will not leave the truth untold. Pale envy shall not travel in my company, for the spiteful man will have no share in wisdom. Wise men in plenty are the world's salvation, and a prudent king is the sheet-anchor of his people. Learn what I have to teach you, therefore, and it will be for your good.

Therefore I prayed, and prudence was given to me; I called for help, and there came to me a spirit of wisdom. I valued her above sceptre and throne, and reckoned riches as nothing beside her; I counted no precious stone her equal, because all the gold in the world compared with her is but a little sand, and silver worth no more than clay. I loved her more than health and beauty; I preferred her to the light of day; for her radiance is unsleeping. So all good things together came to me with her.

For in wisdom there is a spirit intelligent and holy, unique in its kind yet made up of many parts, subtle, free-moving, lucid, spotless, clear, invulnerable, loving what is good, eager, unhindered, beneficent, kindly towards men, steadfast, unerring, untouched by care, all-powerful, all-surveying, and permeating all intelligent, pure, and delicate spirits. For wisdom moves more easily than motion itself, she pervades and permeates all things because she is so pure. Like a fine mist she rises from the power of God, a pure effluence from the glory of the Almighty; so nothing defiled can enter into her by stealth. She is the brightness that streams from everlasting light, the flawless mirror of the active power of God and the image of his goodness. She is but one, yet can do everything; herself unchanging, she makes all things new; age after age she enters into holy souls, and makes them God's friends and prophets, for nothing is acceptable to God but the man who makes his home with wisdom. She is more

radiant than the sun, and surpasses every constellation; compared
with the light of day, she is found to excel; for day gives place to
night, but against wisdom no evil can prevail. She spans the
world in power from end to end, and orders all things benignly.

Wisdom I loved; I sought her out when I was young and
longed to win her for my bride, and I fell in love with her beauty.
She adds lustre to her noble birth, because it is given her to live
with God, and the Lord of all things has accepted her. She is
initiated into the knowledge that belongs to God, and she decides
for him what he shall do. If riches are a prize to be desired in life,
what is richer than wisdom, the active cause of all things? If
prudence shows itself in action, who more than wisdom is the
artificer of all that is? If virtue is the object of a man's affections,
the fruits of wisdom's labours are the virtues; temperance and
prudence, justice and fortitude, these are her teaching, and in the
life of men there is nothing of more value than these. If a man
longs, perhaps, for great experience, she knows the past, she can
infer what is to come; she understands the subtleties of argument
and the solving of problems, she can read signs and portents, and
can foretell the outcome of events and periods. So I determined to
bring her home to live with me, knowing that she would be my
counselor in prosperity and my comfort in anxiety and grief.
Through her, I thought, I shall win fame in the eyes of the people
and honour among older men, young though I am. When I sit in
judgement, I shall prove myself acute, and the great men will
admire me; when I say nothing, they will wait for me to speak;
when I speak they will attend, and though I hold forth at length,
they will lay a finger to their lips and listen. Through her I shall
have immortality, and shall leave an undying memory to those
who come after me. I shall rule over many peoples, and nations
will become my subjects. Grim tyrants will be frightened when
they hear of me; among my own people I shall show myself a
good king, and on the battlefield a brave one. When I come
home, I shall find rest with her; for there is no bitterness in her
company, no pain in life with her, only gladness and joy.

2. The Holy Spirit as Mother in Syriac Christianity[2]

ODE 19

A cup of milk was offered to me,
And I drank it in the sweetness of the Lord's kindness.

The Son is the cup,
And the Father is He who was milked;
And the Holy Spirit is She who milked Him;

Because His breasts were full,
And it was undesirable that His milk should be ineffectually
    released.

The Holy Spirit opened Her bosom,
And mixed the milk of the two breasts of the Father.

Then She gave the mixture to the generation without their
    knowing,
And those who have received (it) are in the perfection of the right
    hand.

The womb of the Virgin took (it),
And she received conception and gave birth.

So the Virgin became a mother with great mercies.

And she laboured and bore the Son but without pain,
Because it did not occur without purpose.

And she did not require a midwife,
Because He caused her to give life.

She brought forth like a strong man with desire,
And she bore according to the manifestation,
And acquired with great power.

And she loved with redemption,
And guarded with kindness,
And declared with grandeur. Hallelujah.

ODE 36

I rested on the Spirit of the Lord,
And She lifted me up to heaven;

And caused me to stand on my feet in the Lord's high place,
Before His perfection and His glory,

Where I continued glorifying (Him) by the composition of His
Odes.

(Christ Speaks)
(The Spirit) brought me forth before the Lord's face.
And because I was the Son of Man,
I was named the Light, the Son of God;

Because I was the most glorified among the glorious ones,
And the greatest among the great ones.

For according to the greatness of the Most High, so She made me;
And according to His newness He renewed me.

And He anointed me with His perfection;
And I became one of those who are near Him.

And my mouth was opened like a cloud of dew,
And my heart gushed forth (like) a gusher of righteousness.

And my approach was in peace,
And I was established in the Spirit of Providence.

Hallelujah.

3. *The Androgynous Unfolding of the Heavenly* **Pleroma**[3]

There is a perfect pre-existent Aeon, dwelling in the invisible and
unnameable elevations; this is Pre-Beginning and Forefather and
Depth. He is uncontainable and invisible, eternal and ungenerated
in quiet and in deep solitude for infinite aeons. With him is
Thought, which is also called Grace and Silence. Once upon a
time, Depth thought of emitting from himself a Beginning of all,
like a seed, and he deposited this projected emission, as in a
womb, in that Silence who is with him. Silence received this seed
and became pregnant and bore Mind, which resembled and was
equal to him who emitted him. Mind alone comprehends the
magnitude of his Father; he is called Only-Begotten and Father
and Beginning of all. Along with him, Truth was emitted; this
makes the first Four, the root of all: Depth and Silence, then Mind
and Truth.

When Only-Begotten perceived why he had been emitted, he too emitted Logos and Life, since he was the Father of all who were to come after him and was the beginning and form of the whole Pleroma. From the union of Logos and Life were emitted Man and Church. This is the originative Eight, the root and substance of all, called by four names: Depth and Mind and Logos and Man. Each of them is male-female, as follows: first the Forefather was united with his own Thought; then Only-Begotten [Mind] with Truth; then Logos with Life and Man with Church.

When these Aeons, which had been emitted to the glory of the Father, themselves desired to glorify the Father through their own products, they emitted emanations by uniting. After emitting Man and Church, Logos and Life emitted ten other Aeons, whose names are as follows: Deep and Mingling, Unageing and Union, Self-Produced and Pleasure, Immovable and Mixture, Only-Begotten and Blessing. Man with Church emitted twelve Aeons, whose names are as follows: Paraclete and Faith, Paternal and Hope, Maternal and Love, Everlasting and Intelligence, Ecclesiastical and Blessedness, Willed and Sophia. These are the thirty Aeons which are kept in silence and are not known. This is the invisible and spiritual Pleroma, triply divided into an Eight, a Ten, and a Twelve.

4. The Orthodox Trinity as a Co-Equal Procession of Male Persons[4]

And the Catholic Faith is this: That we worship one God in
    Trinity, and Trinity in Unity;
Neither confounding the Persons: nor dividing the Substance.
For there is one Person of the Father, another of the Son: and
    another of the Holy Ghost.
But the God-head of the Father, of the Son, and of the Holy
    Ghost, is all one: the Glory equal, the Majesty co-eternal.
Such as the Father is, such is the Son: and such is the Holy
    Ghost.
The Father un-create, the Son un-create: and the Holy Ghost
    un-create.
The Father incomprehensible, the Son incomprehensible: and the
    Holy Ghost incomprehensible.
The Father eternal, the Son eternal: and the Holy Ghost eternal.
And yet they are not three eternals: but one eternal.

As also there are not three incomprehensibles, nor three
    un-created: but one un-created, and one incomprehensible.
So likewise the Father is Almighty, the Son Almighty: and the
    Holy Ghost Almighty.

And yet they are not three Almighties: but one Almighty.
So the Father is God, the Son is God: and the Holy Ghost is God.
And yet they are not three Gods: but one God.
So likewise the Father is Lord, the Son is Lord: and the Holy
    Ghost is Lord.
And yet not three Lords: but one Lord.
For like as we are compelled by the Christian verity: to
    acknowledge every Person by Himself to be God and Lord;
So we are forbidden by the Catholic Religion: to say, there be
    three Gods, or three Lords.
The Father is made of none: neither created, nor begotten.
The Son is of the Father alone: not made, nor created, but
    begotten.
The Holy Ghost is of the Father *and of the Son:* neither made, nor
    created, nor begotten, but proceeding.
So there is one Father, not three Fathers; one Son, not three
    Sons: one Holy Ghost, not three Holy Ghosts.
And in this Trinity none is afore, or after other: none is greater,
    or less than another;
But the whole three Persons are co-eternal together: and co-equal.
So that in all things, as is aforesaid: the Unity in Trinity, and the
    Trinity in Unity, is to be worshipped.

5. *Deity as a Partnership Marriage of Divine Mother and Father*[5]

THE ORDER OF DEITY, MALE AND FEMALE, IN WHOSE IMAGE MAN
WAS CREATED.

The subject of the order in Deity, as male and female, and the
corresponding order in Christ, has been set forth and illustrated,
at considerable length, in the preceding pages; but in various
places, not immediately concentrated, being adapted as
explanatory of the various subjects with which it is connected.
Hence, this important subject may be more clearly understood in a
compendious form.

All who profess the Christian name, mutually believe in *one God*, the eternal *Father*, the Creator of heaven and earth; the original Father of spirits, of angels, and of men. They also believe in the first begotten *Son* of God in man; the Saviour of the world; the Redeemer of men. By the Son, the *true* being and *true character* of the Father, was first revealed: and, the existence of the Son, while it proved the existence of the *Eternal Father*, proved also the existence of the *Eternal Mother*.

Neither argument, nor illustration, would seem necessary to prove this! For, without both a *father* and *mother*, there can be neither son nor daughter; either natural or spiritual, visible or invisible! The visible order of *male* and *female*, by which all animated creation exists, proves the existence of the order, in the invisible world, from which our existence is primarily derived. *"For the invisible things of God, from the creation of the world are clearly seen, being understood by the things that are made, even his eternal Power and Divinity; so that they are without excuse:* because that when they knew God, they glorified him not as God."

For "God said, *Let us make man in our image, after our likeness."* "So God created man; *male and female* created he them, in his own image, and after his own likeness." To whom did God say, "Let US make man in OUR image?" Was it to the Son the Father spoke, as the divines (so called) have long taught, and still teach? How then came man to be created male and female? *father* and *son* are not male and female; but *father* and *mother* are male and female, as likewise are *son* and *daughter*. It was in this order that man was created. It was the order that existed in Deity, and superior spiritual intelligences before him, even *"before the world was;"* and in the image and after the likeness of which he was made, and placed as a probationer on the earth.

But it was not the Son with whom the Father spoke or counselled; or with any other being, angel or spirit, save only with the Eternal *Mother;* even *Divine Wisdom;* the Mother of all celestial beings! It was the *Eternal Two* who thus counselled together, and said, *"Let* US *make man in our image, after our likeness."* This is the same Eternal Mother who was with the Father, whom the *"Lord possessed in the beginning of his way, before his works of old; even from everlasting, before ever the earth was."*

And this was, and is, the voice of the Eternal Mother, through the inspiration of her holy spirit: When the Lord prepared the heavens, I was there: When he appointed the foundations of the earth, then I was by him as one brought up with him; and I was daily his delight, rejoicing always before him. Now, therefore, hearken unto me, my children; for blessed are they that keep my ways."

Thus we may see the true order and origin of our existence, descending through proper mediations, not only in the state of innocent nature, but in the state of grace; proceeding from an Eternal *Parentage;* the Eternal Two, as distinctly Two, as *Power* and *Wisdom* are Two; and as the *Father* and *Mother* are two; yet immutably, unchangeably, *One Spirit*: One in *Essence* and in *substance*, One in *love* and in *design*; and so of the whole spiritual relationship in the new creation and household of God, *Father* and *Mother, Son* and *Daughter, Brother* and *Sister, Parents* and *Children;* of which the order in the natural creation is a similitude.

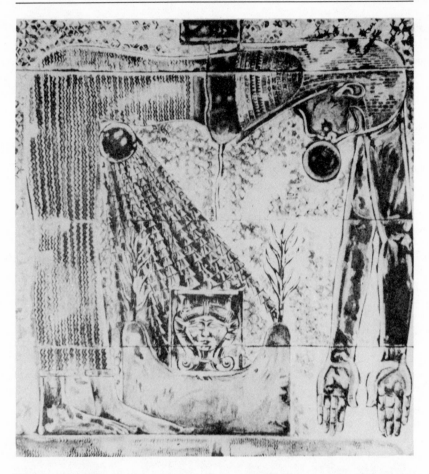

The body of the Goddess forms the encompassing matrix of the universe, radiating the sun powers of life from her womb, the moon powers from her head.

The Goddess Nut (Sky). Painted relief, Temple of Hathar, Dendera, Egypt, Roman period.

3

Stories of Creation

This chapter encompasses a succession of creation stories of the ancient Near Eastern and Greek world: Sumerian creation and paradise stories, the Babylonian creation story, Hesiod's *Theogony*, the Hebrew Creation story of Genesis 1, and Plato's *Timaeus*. In these stories we see a process of progressive patriarchalization. The origins of the Sumerian stories go back to the third and perhaps the fourth millennia B.C. Shaped by the priestly classes of the temples of the Gods and Goddesses, one can not rule out the possibility that priestesses had a hand in their development.[1] The Babylonian story in its present form was probably written about 1900 B.C., although it is itself a revision of earlier material going back to Sumerian times. Its authors were likely priestly males of the temple of Marduk.

Hesiod's *Theogony* was composed by a Greek poet of perhaps the eighth century B.C., although he too relies on more ancient material. The Hebrew story was written by male priestly writers about 500 B.C., when Judah was a province of Persia. During this time Jerusalem was in the hands of high priests, and the priestly writers shaped their account of creation to reflect their concern for the laws of Sabbath. Finally, Plato's account, while rooted in mythological traditions, has been reshaped by philosophical concepts derived especially from the Pythagorean mathematical cosmologists.

In these accounts we can see a progressive trend toward the subordination and finally the elimination of female deities in cosmogenesis. The emerging male creator God, who displaces the original mother Goddess, comes to be seen as eternal, originating before cosmogenesis rather than being generated within it. The imagery of creation shifts from procreation to that of artisan tool-making and verbal fiat. The world comes to be seen as something "created" outside of the Creator from alien and different "stuff" rather than a procreative process by which the Gods are gestated within the body of the primal Mother.

The earliest creation stories are theogonic as well as cosmogonic. The primal Mother is the Mother of the Gods as well as the cosmos. The Gods and Goddesses gestate within her body and emerge in successive generations. The divine generations represent the primal parents, Heaven and Earth; then primal forces of the cosmos, such as sea and air; and then the Gods and Goddesses who represent the ordered agricultural world of urban settlements. This concept of theogony, by which a series of divine pairs emerge from the original divine parents, is preserved in gnostic theogonies, as we have seen in the previous chapter. A remnant of this idea is preserved in the Christian Trinity where the *Logos* or "Son" of God is said to have been "begotten" from all eternity by the Father. But maternal power has been eliminated from this Christian theogony, and the creation of the world is seen as a distinct process of "making" (not begetting) a contingent nondivine reality.

The Sumerian equivalent of the Babylonian creation story has not been preserved, but from other Sumerian texts we can gather that the Sumerians believed that all things began with the primal mother Nammu, identified with the primal sea. Out of her was born the cosmic mountain that represents heaven and earth united. From the union of this primal pair, An (Heaven) and Ki (earth), there emerged the air God Enhil, who separates heaven from earth through the union of Enhil with Mother Earth.[2]

The Sumerian paradise story, included in this chapter, represents a story of the creation of vegetation and ordered agricultural life. The land of Dilmun is the primal paradise where there is no sickness or evil and where the immortals live. It is made fertile by Enki who supplies the gift of fresh water. Enki is described as lying with Ninhursag, the Mother Goddess, and bringing forth a succession of daughter Goddesses by impregnating each in turn. In the fourth generation, however, Ninhursag advises her great-granddaughter Uttu to withhold

her favors until Enki brings her fruits and vegetables. Enki supplies
the gardener with fresh water and receives, in turn, fruits and vegetables that the gardener brings as a gift to Uttu.

Instead of another deity coming forth from this union, Ninhursag
takes Enki's semen from Uttu's womb and from it creates eight plants.
But Enki uproots and devours these plants. Ninhursag in wrath curses
him with a series of diseases. The Gods sit in the dust (because the
waters have dried up?). A fox intervenes and persuades the Mother-
Goddess to cure Enki, and she then creates eight plants that cure the
various diseases suffered by different parts of Enki's body. Thus we
have in this story both the origin of agriculture and of medicinal plants.
The primacy of female power in Sumerian cosmogenesis is evident.

In the Babylonian creation story we also start with the primal
waters, but these are described as the primal parents, Apsu, the father,
and Mummu-Tiamat, the mother. These two also represent the primal
sea where sweet and salt water are still mingled together. The two are
united in one body, so we have here the idea of a primal mother
described as like a watery womb that contains within herself the male
principle of fertilization. The Gods are begotten and borne within this
primal body. They come forth in successive generations from more in-
choate forms to more anthropomorphic deities, resembling wise kings.
The succession of deities is described as males. Although there are also
Goddesses mentioned later on as their consorts, the origin of the Goddesses in this process is left unexplained.

The younger male Gods become unruly and are intolerable to their
parents. Apsu decides to kill them, although this plan is rejected in
horror by Tiamat who declines to destroy her offspring. Apsu goes
ahead with his plan but is foiled by his sons, led by Ea, who kill Apsu.
Ea places himself and his consort on a cosmic throne that he fashions
out of the prone body of Apsu. From the union of this pair, drawing
on the power of the defeated Apsu, Marduk is born. Marduk then becomes the champion of the drama of cosmogenesis, which is then recounted in the story.

The importance of Marduk in this story reflects the ascendency over
the Mesopotamian world of the city of Babylon, which worshipped
Marduk as its patron deity. In earlier versions of the creation story these
deeds of cosmogenesis were performed by other Gods, such as Ea.
This creation story played a public role of great significance in Babylonian life, being recited with great solemnity each year on the fourth
day of the New Year's festival to assure the defeat of the negative forces
of the universe and society and the ascendency of a political and cosmic
order ruled by Babylonia.[3]

The story goes on to describe Tiamat leading a war against the younger deities to avenge the death of Apsu. The younger deities, representing the confederation of Mesopotamian city-states under Babylonia, appoint Marduk their champion to fight the ancient Mother Goddess. Marduk defeats her and splits up her body, shaping the cosmos out of it. Marduk does not stand "outside" of Tiamat in this process but rather stands within her, placing one half of her body as the starry heavens above. He then shapes the heavenly planetary system upon her belly. Tiamat functions as the primal matrix or "matter" (mother) out of which the cosmos is shaped. Marduk acts as the orderer or shaper of this primal matter, which is also his own "mother."

The primal Mother is the encompassing reality within which the Gods and Goddess, as well as the cosmos, originate. This primal Mother evolves toward the ordered agricultural and urban world but threatens constantly to revert to its primal disordered or chaotic form. Marduk is the champion of the ordered world who defeats the primal Mother in her "chaotic" form and "orders" her into the separated and organized world of heaven and earth, planetary systems and settled fields, irrigation ditches and cities. The defeat of Tiamat also represents the defeat of the earlier Sumerian world by the new Semitic power of Babylonia.

Marduk does not stop at creating the cosmos out of Tiamat's body. He contrives further works. He decides to create humanity to be the slaves of the Gods. To do this he has delivered to him Kingu, who had joined Tiamat's rebellion against the Gods. Kingu is slain and out of his blood is fashioned humanity to do servile labor so that the Gods may be freed from labor and may be at ease. Marduk also divides the Gods into two classes and positions them in the universe. Thus the Babylonian story also explains the social system of the Babylonian world. The serfs who labor on the great plantations of the aristocracy of temple and palace are analogous to the lowly humans created to be serfs of the Gods, while the hierarchy of deities represents the hierarchy of cities in the Babylonian empire, crowned by the reigning city of Babylonia. The Gods complete the work of creation by creating a great temple to Marduk in Babylonia to fix the position of this city and its divine champion in the political cosmos.

Hesiod's *Theogony*, written more than a thousand years later than the Babylonian story, is a literary creation by a poet whom we know by name, rather than the product of anonymous priests. It draws on ancient mythic material that belongs to a common stock with the Babylonian story. In the beginning was Chaos, and from Chaos emerged Earth. Day and Night emerge from Chaos, and Earth in turn gives birth to Heaven whom she sets over against herself. Earth and Heaven become the primal parents who bring forth the elemental Deities and the Titans. Sky hated his offspring and conspired to prevent them from displacing him by hiding them within the Earth. But Cronus, the last of Earth's offspring, collaborated with his mother to free her from this burden. He castrated his Father with a sickle provided by Earth. From the blood of the severed organ, the Giants and Erinyes (spirits of maternal vengeance) were born, but also Aphrodite, who emerged from the white foam of the sea into which the organ fell. A further series of monstrous powers emerges from these Giants and Titans.

Then a new series of divine offspring arises from the union of Rhea (daughter of Earth) and Cronus. These are the Olympian deities. But again the father conspires against their future power by swallowing the males one by one. Rhea appeals to her parents, Earth and Sky, and Earth takes the youngest child, Zeus, and hides him in a cave in Crete, giving Cronus a stone to swallow in his stead. Zeus grows up to free his brothers from the stomach of their father and to take his place as the king of the universe, ruling over the world of the Olympian Gods and over mortals.

In Hesiod's story, as in the Babylonian story, the male primal parent wars against his sons, and the leader of the sons in turn dethrones his father. The mother Goddesses, Earth and Rhea, are more domesticated figures for Hesiod. They do not become leaders of a war against the younger Gods but rather play the subversive role of the mother in the patriarchal household by conspiring with the sons behind the father's back to seat the male offspring on the throne at the expense of the father. This story of successive generation of Gods probably also reflects the political and historical history of the displacement of earlier Minoan civilization by the later Doric civilization, which worshipped the Olympian sky-Gods. But the struggle between the older and younger powers is not seen as a struggle of male against primal mother, but a struggle of son against father.

In the Hebrew creation story, written a few hundred years after Hesiod, we see a revolution in thinking about "first things." Here the male Creator is not the product of a theogony that goes back to the Primal Mother. The ancient Mother has disappeared as an active factor. Instead there stands a single male God who is outside the world which is to be created. Over against him is primal watery chaos, but no longer imaged as his Mother or his primal parents. The Creator God shapes this watery chaos into the cosmos by a series of verbal commands. In a succession of six days, representing the primal counterpart of the six days of work in the Hebrew calendar, he separates night from day, sets the vault of the heaven above and fixes its waters (as does Marduk out of the body of Tiamat), gathers the dry land and separates it from the sea, and creates seed-bearing plants. He creates the planetary system and then the animals of the sea and air. Finally, he creates the land, animals, and humanity, male and female.

Rather than a later generation of gods being appointed sovereign over the earth, the human pair, male and female, are appointed as the representatives of God to rule the earth. They are given the mandate both to increase and multiply and also to subdue and rule the entire earth, with all its animals of land, sea, and air. All plants are given to them for their food. The reference to their possession of the "image of God" here should not be construed to mean that the priestly author sees this deity as androgynous. Rather, the concept of "image of God" refers to this role of the human pair as representative of the sovereignty of God over the universe.[4]

The Hebrew creation story has a different function than that of the Babylonian or the Greek creation story. It describes the ideal creation as it ought to be rather than the conflicts out of which the present world of good and evil has developed. In the Hebrew creation story, the divine power is both transcendent to its creation and totally in control. Chaos springs into order at his command. There is no struggle for power, no battle between older and younger powers in the cosmogenesis. Although evil arises in the Hebrew story, it is later and subordinate to the original act of cosmogenesis in which all is docile to divine authority.

The Hebrew story, while more authoritarian in the divine-cosmos relationship, is also more egalitarian in its view of the role of humanity. Unlike the Babylonian story, where humanity is fashioned by "bad blood" to be slaves of the Gods, humanity is shaped as the crown of God's six days of labor to be God's representative as ruler of the earth. In the primal paradise there is no hierarchy of gods, no hierarchy of humans, but only the one God in serene control and the one human pair who represent his rule on earth.

Plato's *Timaeus* is a creation story in which mythic categories are reshaped by philosophy. The language mingles consciously the storytelling personifications of myth and the abstract categories of philosophy and science. The primary division of reality for Plato is the division between the invisible and the visible, between eternal intellectual Essence and mutable, tangible Becoming. The story of cosmogenesis takes the form of explaining how the mutable, visible world arises from the invisible eternal world of ideas. That which is eternal, for Plato, is the invisible world of intellectual forms. This is that which always was, outside of time or change. The visible world could arise only by some process of artisanry in which this intellectual world serves as the original model or archetype.

To explain how this visible world was created in imitation of the invisible world, Plato hypothesizes a primal Demiurgos whom he calls Father and Maker. This artisan takes the primal elements of earth, air, fire, and water and shapes them as the spheric body of the cosmos. The body of the cosmos thus corresponds to the perfect geometric figure, the sphere. However, before creating the cosmic body, the Demiurgos creates the World Soul. This he makes by bringing together the two primary realities of the invisible and the visible and compounding a third intermediate essence partaking of both sameness and otherness. This soul-substance he bends into circular form and then infuses it into the world body. Or rather the world body is placed within it, for the World Soul acts as a kind of dynamic envelope that both encompasses the whole cosmos and is diffused throughout it. The cosmos then begins to move, animated by the World Soul, which mobilizes the cosmos and its planetary systems in perfect mathematical harmonies. This movement of the cosmos in planetary harmonies is the basis of time. Thus time itself is a product of the movement of the visible cosmos, or the "moving image of eternity."

Although the Demiurgos which shapes the cosmos and World Soul in imitation of the eternal world is described as a male artisan, the World Soul is imaged as female. This reflects the feminine gender of the word *psyche* in Greek. Earth, too, following mythological tradition, is our mother and nurse. But these feminine powers are strictly subordinate to the male Demiurgos and belong to a subordinate, visible world that is the image of the invisible world. The word *image* for Plato signifies the secondary status of this created world, which, like the statue in relation to its human model, reflects the original archetype but is ontologically different and lesser in status.

In Plato's description of the creation of humanity, we see further his tendency to view ontological hierarchy as analogous to the hierarchy of male over female. Out of the dregs of the World Soul, the Demiurgos mixes the souls of humans and places them in their native stars where they may imbibe eternal truth by contemplating the transcendent world of Ideas. Thus fortified, the souls are placed in (male) bodies, which are created by lesser, planetary Gods. Those souls who live righteously will return to their native stars to live an immortal existence, but those who fail to control their lower sense powers, which derive from the body, will be incarnated into lower animal forms, beginning with the human female. Thus the female in Plato's cosmogenesis is clearly seen as closer to the world of the visible and material and farther from the intellectual world of eternal being in the hierarchy of essence over existence.

Reflection

What is the significance of the change from thinking of the origin of all things as the primal Mother to the primal Parents and, finally, to the single male Creator? How does this change connect with the shift from thinking of cosmogenesis as analogous to sexual reproduction to thinking about the world as the product of verbal command and technological manufacture? How does the location of the divine in relationship to the cosmos change in this process? What is gained by this change? What is lost? How might such a shift in perspective correspond to changing views in the relationship of humans and nature? How might it correspond to changing systems of social hierarchy?

What view of the relationship of divine (and human) power and intelligence to nature would best promote a sense of ecological concern in the present crisis between human technology and nature?

1. The Creation of Vegetation by the Mother Goddess[5]

The land Dilmun is pure, the land Dilmun is clean;
The land Dilmun is clean, the land Dilmun is most bright.
Who had lain by himself in Dilmun —
The place, after Enki had lain with his wife,
That place is clean, that place is most bright; . . .

In Dilmun the raven utters no cries,
The *ittidu*-bird utters not the cry of the *ittidu*-bird,
The lion kills not,
The wolf snatches not the lamb,
Unknown is the kid-devouring *wild dog*,
Unknown is the grain-devouring . . . ,
[*Unknown*] is the . . . widow,
The bird on high . . . s not its . . . ,
The dove *droops* not the head, . . .
Ninsikilla says to her father Enki:

"The city thou hast given, the city thou has given, thy . . . ,
   water of abundance, . . .
Makes Dilmun (drink from it) the waters of ab(undance).
Her well of bitter water, verily it is become a well of sweet water,
Her *furrowed* fields (and) farms *bore* her grain,
Her city, verily it is become the *bank-quay* house of the land
Dilmun, (verily it is become) the *bank-(quay)* house (of the land),
Now Utu is . . . ; verily it was so.
Who is alone, *before* the wise Nintu, the mother of the land,
Enki (*before*) the wise Nintu, (the mother of the land),
Causes his phallus to water the dikes,
Causes his phallus to submerge the reeds, . . .

Enki . . .
Poured the semen in the womb of Ninhursag.
She took the semen into the womb, the semen of Enki. . . .
[Nintu], the mother of the land, like [. . . fat], (like . . . fat, like
   good princely fat),
Gave birth to [Ninmu].
Ninmu . . . d *at* the bank of the river,
Enki in the marshland *looks about, looks about,*
He says to his messenger Isimud:
"Shall I not kiss the young one, the fair?
(Shall I not kiss) Ninmu, the fair?"
He embraced her, he kissed her,
Enki poured the semen into the womb,
She took the semen into the womb, the semen of Enki, . . .

[Like . . .] fat, like [. . . fat], like good princely fat,
[Ninmu], (like) . . . [fat], (like . . . fat, like good princely fat),
Gave birth to Nink[urra].
Ninkurra . . . d *at* the bank of the river,
Enki in the marshland [*looks about, looks about*],
He [says] to his messenger Isimud:
"Shall I not [kiss] the young one, the fair?
(Shall I not kiss) Ninkurra, the fair?"
He embraced her, he kissed her,
Enki poured the semen into the womb, . . .
Ninkurra, (like) . . . fat, (like . . . fat, like good, princely fat),
Gave birth to Uttu, the *fair* lady.
Nintu says [to] Uttu, [the *fair* lady]:
"Instruction I offer thee, [take] my instruction,

. . .

Bring [the cucumbers in *their* . . .]
Bring [*the apples*] in their [. . .],
Bring the grapes in their . . . , . . .
Enki, his face turned green, he gripped the staff,
To Uttu Enki directed his step.
"Who . . . st *in her house*, open."
"Thou, who art thou?"
"I, the gardener, would give thee cucumbers, *apples*, and grapes
    as a 'so be it.' "
Uttu with joyful heart opened the door of the house.
Enki to Uttu, the *fair lady*,
Gives the cucumbers in their . . . ,
Gives *the apples* in their . . . ,
Gives the grapes in their . . . . .
Uttu, the fair lady . . . s the . . . for *him*, . . . s the . . . for *him*.
Enki took his joy of Uttu,
He embraced her, lay in her lap, . . .
With the young one he cohabited, he kissed her.
Enki poured the semen into the womb,
She took the semen into the womb, the semen of Enki.
Uttu, the fair lady . . . ,
Ninhursag . . . d the *semen from the thighs*,
[The "tree"-plant sprouted],
[The "honey"-plant spro]uted,
[The *roadweed*-plant spro]uted,
[The . . .-plant s]prouted,
[The *thorn* s]prouted,
[The *caper*-plant] sp(routed),
[The . . .-plant] sp(routed),
[The cassia-plant s]prouted.

[Enki then seizes each plant in turn and eats it.]
(Thereupon) Ninhursag cursed Enki's name:
"Until he is dead I shall not look upon him with the 'eye of
    life.' "

The Anunnaki sat in the dust,
(When) up speaks the fox to Enlil:
"If I bring Ninhursag before thee, what shall be my reward?"

[The fox then goes to Ninhursag and persuades her to heal Enki.]
Ninhursag seated Enki *by* her vulva:

"My brother, what hurts thee?"
"My . . . hurts me."
"Abu I have caused to be born for thee."
"My brother, what hurts thee?"
"My *jaw* hurts me."
"Nintulla I have caused to be born for thee."

[Ninhursag then creates a series of deities representing plants that
    heal Enki of his various illnesses.]

2. *The Shaping of the Cosmos from the Body of the Mother Goddess*[6]

When on high the heaven had not been named,
Firm ground below had not been called by name,
Naught but primordial Apsu, their begetter,
(And) Mummu-Tiamat, she who bore them all,
Their waters commingling as a single body;
No reed hut had been matted, no marsh land had appeared,
When no gods whatever had been brought into being,
Uncalled by name, their destinies undetermined —
Then it was that the gods were formed within them.
Lahmu and Lahamu were brought forth, by name they were
    called.
For aeons they grew in age and stature.
Anshar and Kishar were formed, surpassing the others.
They prolonged the days, added on the years.
Anu was their son, of his fathers the rival;
Yea, Anshar's first-born, Anu, was his equal.
Anu begot in his image Nudimmud.
This Nudimmud was of his fathers the master;
Of broad wisdom, understanding, mighty in strength,
Mightier by far than his grandfather, Anshar.
He had no rival among the gods,
    his brothers.
The divine brothers banded together,
They disturbed Tiamat *as they surged back and forth*,
Yea, they troubled the mood of Tiamat
By their *hilarity* in the Abode of Heaven.
Apsu could not lessen their clamor
And Tiamat was speechless at their [*ways*].
Their doings were loathsome unto [. . .].

Unsavory were their ways; they were *overbearing*.
Then Apsu, the begetter of the great gods,
Cried out, addressing Mummu, his vizier:
"O Mummu, my vizier, who rejoicest my spirit,
Come hither and let us go to Tiamat!"
They went and sat down before Tiamat,
Exchanging counsel about the gods, their first-born.
When Tiamat had thus lent import to her handiwork,
She prepared for battle against the gods, her offspring.
To avenge Apsu, Tiamat wrought evil.
That she was girding for battle, was divulged to Ea.
As soon as Ea heard of this matter,
He lapsed into dark silence and sat right still.
Then, on further thought, his anger subsided,
To Anshar, his (fore)father he betook himself.
When he came before his grandfather, Anshar,
All that Tiamat had plotted to him
      he repeated:
"My father, Tiamat, she who bore us, detests us."
Apsu, opening his mouth,
Said unto *resplendent* Tiamat:
"Their ways are verily loathsome unto me.
By day I find no relief, nor repose by night.
I will destroy, I will wreck their ways,
That quiet may be restored. Let us have rest!"
As soon as Tiamat heard this,
She was wroth and called out to her husband.
She cried out aggrieved, as she raged all alone,
Injecting woe into her mood:
"What? Should we destroy that which we have built?
Their ways indeed are most troublesome, but let us attend
      kindly!"

[Apsu goes ahead with his plan to destroy the younger Gods. But Ea, the earth and water God, puts him to sleep and kills him and erects a shrine over his body from which he reigns with his wife, Damkind. From this union Marduk is born. Tiamat is stirred up by the Gods to avenge Apsu.]

She has set up the Assembly and is furious with rage.
All the gods have rallied to her;
Even those whom you brought forth march at her side.

They throng and march at the side of Tiamat,
Enraged, they plot without cease night and day.
They are set for combat, growling, raging,
They have formed a council to prepare for the fight.

[Marduk is appointed by the embattled Gods to defend them from
Tiamat and meets her in combat.]

"Stand thou up, that I and thou meet in single combat!"
When Tiamat heard this,
She was like one possessed; she took leave of her senses.
In fury Tiamat cried out aloud.
To the roots her legs shook both together.
She recites a charm, keeps casting her spell,
While the gods of battle sharpen their weapons.
Then joined issue Tiamat and Marduk, wisest of gods.
They *swayed* in single combat, locked in battle.
The lord spread out his net to enfold her,
The Evil Wind, which followed behind, he let loose in her face.
When Tiamat opened her mouth to consume him,
He drove in the Evil Wind that she close not her lips.
As the fierce winds charged her belly,
Her body was distended and her mouth was wide open.
He released the arrow, it tore her belly,
It cut through her insides, splitting the heart.
Having thus subdued her, he extinguished her life.
He cast down her carcass to stand upon it.
The lord trod on the legs of Tiamat,
With his unsparing mace he crushed her skull.
When the arteries of her blood he had severed,
The North Wind bore (it) to places undisclosed.
On seeing this, his fathers were joyful and jubilant,
They brought gifts of homage, they to him.
Then the lord paused to view her dead body,
That he might divide the monster and do artful works.
He split her like a shellfish into two parts:
Half of her he set up and ceiled it as sky,
Pulled down the bar and posted guards.
He bade them to allow not her waters to escape. . . .
He constructed stations for the great gods,
Fixing their astral likenesses as constellations.
He determined the year by designating the zones:

He set up three constellations for each of the twelve months.
After defining the days of the year [by means] of (heavenly) figures,
He founded the station of Nebiru to determine their (heavenly)
     bands,
That none might transgress or fall short. . . .
In her belly he established the zenith.
The Moon he caused to shine, the night (to him) entrusting.
He appointed him a creature of the night to signify the days:
"Monthly, without cease, form designs with a crown.
At the month's very start, rising over the land,
Thou shalt have luminous horns to signify six days.
On the seventh day be thou a [half]-crown.
At full moon stand in opposition in mid-month.
When the sun [overtakes] thee at the base of heaven,
Diminish [thy crown] and retrogress in light.
[At the time of disappearance] approach thou the course of the
     sun,
And [on the twenty-ninth] thou shalt again stand in opposition to
     the sun."
When Marduk hears the words of the gods,
His heart prompts (him) to fashion artful works.
Opening his mouth, he addresses Ea
To impart the plan he had conceived in his heart:
"Blood I will mass and cause bones to be.
I will establish a savage, 'man' shall be his name.
Verily, savage-man I will create.
He shall be charged with the service of the gods
     That they might be at ease!
The ways of the gods I will artfully alter.
Though alike revered, into two (groups) they shall be divided."

          . . .

The king addresses a word to the Anunnaki:
"If your former statement was true,
Do (now) the truth on oath by me declare!
Who was it that contrived the uprising,
And made Tiamat rebel, and joined battle?
Let him be handed over who contrived the uprising.
His guilt I will make him bear that you may dwell in peace!"
"It was Kingu who contrived the uprising,
And made Tiamat rebel, and joined battle."
They bound him, holding him before Ea.
They imposed on him his guilt and severed his blood (vessels).

Out of his blood they fashioned mankind.
He imposed the service and let free the gods.

3. *The Mother Goddesses Help the Sons to Dethrone the Fathers*[7]

First of all, the chaos came into being, next broad-bosomed Earth,
the solid and eternal home of all, and Eros [Desire], the most
beautiful of the immortal gods, who in every man and every god
softens the sinews and overpowers the prudent purpose of the
mind. Out of Void came Darkness and black Night, and out of
Night came Light and Day, her children conceived after union in
love with Darkness. Earth first produced starry Sky, equal in size
with herself, to cover her on all sides. Next she produced the tall
mountains, the pleasant haunts of the gods, and also gave birth to
the barren waters, sea with its raging surges — all this without the
passion of love. Thereafter she lay with Sky and gave birth to
Ocean with its deep current, Coeus and Crius and Hyperion and
Iapetus; Thea and Rhea and Themis [Law] and Mnemosyne
[Memory]; also golden-crowned Phoebe and lovely Tethys. After
these came cunning Cronus, the youngest and boldest of her
children; and he grew to hate the father who had begotten him.

Earth also gave birth to the violent Cyclopes — Thunderer,
Lightner, and bold Flash — who made and gave to Zeus the
thunder and the lightning-bolt. They were like the gods in all
respects except that a single eye stood in the middle of their
foreheads, and their strength and power and skill were in their
hands.

There were also born to Earth and Sky three more children,
big, strong, and horrible, Cottus and Briareus and Gyes. This
unruly brood had a hundred monstrous hands sprouting from their
shoulders, and fifty heads on top of their shoulders growing from
their sturdy bodies. They had monstrous strength to match their
huge size.

Of all the children born of Earth and Sky these were the
boldest, and their father hated them from the beginning. As each
of them was about to be born, Sky would not let them reach the
light of day; instead he hid them all away in the bowels of Mother
Earth. Sky took pleasure in doing this evil thing. In spite of her
enormous size, Earth felt the strain within her and groaned.
Finally she thought of an evil and cunning stratagem. She

instantly produced a new metal, gray steel, and made a huge sickle. Then she laid the matter before her children; the anguish in her heart made her speak boldly: "My children, you have a savage father; if you will listen to me, we may be able to take vengeance for his evil outrage: he was the one who started using violence."

This was what she said; but all the children were gripped by fear, and not one of them spoke a word. Then great Cronus, the cunning trickster, took courage and answered his good mother with these words: "Mother, I am willing to undertake and carry through your plan. I have no respect for our infamous father, since he was the one who started using violence."

This was what he said, and enormous Earth was very pleased. She hid him in ambush and put in his hands the sickle with jagged teeth, and instructed him fully in her plot. Huge Sky came drawing night behind him and desiring to make love; he lay on top of Earth stretched all over her. Then from his ambush his son reached out with his left hand and with his right took the huge sickle with its long jagged teeth and quickly sheared the organs from his own father and threw them away, backward over his shoulder. But that was not the end of them. The drops of blood that spurted from them were all taken in by Mother Earth, and in the course of the revolving years she gave birth to the powerful Erinyes [Spirits of Vengeance] and the huge Giants with shining armor and long spears. As for the organs themselves, for a long time they drifted round the sea just as they were when Cronus cut them off with the steel edge and threw them from the land into the waves of the ocean; then white foam issued from the divine flesh, and in the foam a girl began to grow. First she came near to holy Cythera, then reached Cyprus, the land surrounded by sea. There she stepped out, a goddess, tender and beautiful, and round her slender feet the green grass shot up. She is called Aphrodite by gods and men, . . .

Night gave birth to hateful Destruction and the black Specter and Death; she also bore Sleep and the race of Dreams — all these the dark goddess Night bore without sleeping with any male. Next she gave birth to Blame and painful Grief, and also the Fates and the pitiless Specters of Vengeance: it is these goddesses who kept account of the transgressions of men and of gods, and they never let their terrible anger end till they have brought punishment down on the head of the transgressor. Deadly Night also bore Retribution to plague men, then Deceit and Love and accursed Old Age and stubborn Strife. . . .

Rhea submitted to the embraces of Cronus and bore him children with a glorious destiny: Hestia, Demeter, and Hera, who walks on golden sandals; Hades, the powerful god whose home is underground and whose heart is pitiless; Poseidon, the god whose great blows make the earth quake; and Zeus the lord of wisdom, the father of gods and men, whose thunder makes the broad earth tremble. As each of these children came out of their mother's holy womb onto her knees, great Cronus swallowed them. His purpose was to prevent the kingship of the gods from passing to another one of the august descendants of Sky; he had been told by Earth and starry Sky that he was destined to be overcome by his own son. For that reason he kept a sleepless watch and waited for his own children to be born and then swallowed them. Rhea had no rest from grief; so, when she was about to give birth to Zeus, the father of gods and men, she begged her own dear parents, Earth and starry Sky, to help her contrive a plan whereby she might bear her child without Cronus' knowing it, and make amends to the vengeful spirits of her father Sky. Earth and Sky listened to their daughter and granted her request; they told her what was destined to happen to King Cronus and to his bold son. When she was about to give birth to great Zeus, her youngest child, they sent her to the rich Cretan town of Lyctus. Huge Mother Earth undertook to nurse and raise the infant in the broad land of Crete. Dark night was rushing on as Earth arrived there carrying him, and Lyctus was the first place where she stopped. She took him and hid him in an inaccessible cave, deep in the bowels of holy earth, in the dense woods of Mount Aegeum. Then she wrapped a huge stone in baby blankets and handed it to the royal son of Sky, who then was king of the gods. He took the stone and swallowed it into his belly — the fool! He did not know that a stone had replaced his son, who survived, unconquered and untroubled, and who was going to overcome him by force and drive him from his office and reign over the gods in his place.

The young prince grew quickly in strength and stature. After years had passed Cronus the great trickster fell victim to the cunning suggestions of Mother Earth and threw up his own children again. The first thing he vomited was the stone, the last thing he had swallowed; Zeus set it up on the highways of the earth in holy Pytho under the slopes of Parnassus, to be a sign and a wonder to mankind thereafter.

Zeus also set free his father's brothers from the cruel chains in which their father Sky had in foolish frenzy bound them. They gratefully remembered his kindness and gave him the thunder and the lightning-bolt and flash, which huge Earth had kept hidden till then. In these weapons Zeus trusts; they make him master over gods and men.

4. The Creator Shapes the Cosmos by Command[8]

THE CREATION OF THE WORLD

In the beginning of creation, when God made heaven and earth, the earth was without form and void, with darkness over the face of the abyss, and a mighty wind that swept over the surface of the waters. God said, "Let there be light," and there was light; and God saw that the light was good, and he separated light from darkness. He called the light day, and the darkness night. So evening came, and morning came, the first day.

God said, "Let there be a vault between the waters, to separate water from water." So God made the vault, and separated the water under the vault from the water above it, and so it was; and God called the vault heaven. Evening came, and morning came, a second day.

God said, "Let the waters under heaven be gathered into one place, so that dry land may appear"; and so it was. God called the dry land earth, and the gathering of the waters he called seas; and God saw that it was good. Then God said, "Let the earth produce fresh growth, let there be on the earth plants bearing seed, fruit-trees bearing fruit each with seed according to its kind." So it was; the earth yielded fresh growth, plants bearing seed according to their kind and trees bearing fruit each with seed according to its kind; and God saw that it was good. Evening came, and morning came, a third day.

God said, "Let there be lights in the vault of heaven to separate day from night, and let them serve as signs both for festivals and for seasons and years. Let them also shine in the vault of heaven to give light on earth." So it was; God made the two great lights, the greater to govern the day and the lesser to govern the night; and with them he made the stars. God put these lights in the vault of heaven to give light on earth, to govern day and night, and to separate light from darkness; and God saw that it was good. Evening came, and morning came, a fourth day.

God said, "Let the waters teem with countless living creatures, and let birds fly above the earth across the vault of heaven." God then created the great sea-monsters and all living creatures that move and swarm in the waters, according to their kind, and every kind of bird; and God saw that it was good. So he blessed them and said, "Be fruitful and increase, fill the waters of the seas; and let the birds increase on land." Evening came, and morning came, a fifth day.

God said, "Let the earth bring forth living creatures, according to their kind: cattle, reptiles, and wild animals, all according to their kind." So it was; God made wild animals, cattle, and all reptiles, each according to its kind; and he saw that it was good. Then God said, "Let us make man in our image and likeness to rule the fish in the sea, the birds of heaven, the cattle, all wild animals on earth, and all reptiles that crawl upon the earth." So God created man in his own image; in the image of God he created him; male and female he created them. God blessed them and said to them, "Be fruitful and increase, fill the earth and subdue it, rule over the fish in the sea, the birds of heaven, and every living thing that moves upon the earth." God also said, "I give you all plants that bear seed everywhere on earth, and every tree bearing fruit which yields seed: they shall be yours for food. All green plants I give for food to the wild animals, to all the birds of heaven, and to all reptiles on earth, every living creature." So it was; and God saw all that he had made, and it was very good. Evening came, and morning came, a sixth day.

Thus heaven and earth were completed with all their mighty throng. On the sixth day God completed all the work he had been doing, and on the seventh day he ceased from all his work. God blessed the seventh day and made it holy, because on that day he ceased from all the work he had set himself to do.

This is the story of the making of heaven and earth when they were created.

5. The Creator Fashions the Visible World in Imitation of the Invisible[9]

Was the world always in existence and without beginning? or created, and had it a beginning? Created, I reply, being visible and tangible and having a body, and therefore sensible; and all sensible things are apprehended by opinion and sense and are in a process of creation and created. Now that which is created must, as we affirm, of necessity be created by a cause. But the father and maker of all this universe is past finding out; and even if we found him, to tell of him to all men would be impossible. And there is still a question to be asked about him: Which of the patterns had the artificer in view when he made the world, — the pattern of the unchangeable, or of that which is created? If the world be indeed fair and the artificer good, it is manifest that he must have looked to that which is eternal: . . . And having been created in this way, the world has been framed in the likeness of that which is apprehended by reason and mind and is unchangeable, and must therefore of necessity, if this is admitted, be a copy of something. . . .

For the Deity, intending to make this world like the fairest and most perfect of intelligible beings, framed one visible animal comprehending within itself all other animals of a kindred nature. . . .

In order then that the world might be solitary, like the perfect animal, the creator made not two worlds or an infinite number of them; but there is and ever will be one only-begotten and created heaven.

Now that which is created is of necessity corporeal, and also visible and tangible. And nothing is visible where there is no fire, or tangible which has no solidity, and nothing is solid without earth. Wherefore also God in the beginning of creation made the body of the universe to consist of fire and earth. . . . but now, as the world must be solid, and solid bodies are always compacted not by one mean but by two, God placed water and air in the mean between fire and earth, and made them to have the same proportion so far as was possible (as fire is to air so is air to water, and as air is to water so is water to earth); and thus he bound and put together a visible and tangible heaven. . . .

His intention was, in the first place, that the animal should be as far as possible a perfect whole and of perfect parts: secondly, that it should be one, leaving no remnants out of which another such world might be created: and also that it should be free from old age and unaffected by disease. . . . And he gave to the world the figure which was suitable and also natural. Now to the animal which was to comprehend all animals, that figure was suitable which comprehends within itself all other figures. Wherefore he made the world in the form of a globe, round as from a lathe, having its extremes in every direction equidistant from the centre, the most perfect and the most like itself of all figures; . . .

And in the centre he put the soul, which is diffused throughout the body, making it also to be the exterior environment of it; and he made the universe a circle moving in a circle, one and solitary, yet by reason of its excellence able to converse with itself, and needing no other friendship or acquaintance. Having these purposes in view he created the world a blessed god.

. . . he made the soul in origin and excellence prior to and older than the body, to be the ruler and mistress, of whom the body was to be the subject. And he made her out of the following elements and on this wise: Out of the indivisible and unchangeable, and also out of that which is divisible and has to do with material bodies, he compounded a third and intermediate kind of essence, partaking of the nature of the same and of the other, and this compound he placed accordingly in a mean between the indivisible, and the divisible and material. He took the three elements of the same, the other, and the essence, and mingled them into one form, compressing by force the reluctant and unsociable nature of the other into the same. When he had mingled them with the essence and out of three made one, . . . This entire compound he divided lengthways into two parts, which he joined to one another at the centre like the letter X, and bent them into a circular form. . . .

Now when the Creator had framed the soul according to his will, he formed within her the corporeal universe, and brought the two together, and united them centre to centre. The soul, interfused everywhere from the centre to the circumference of heaven, of which also she is the external envelopment, herself turning in herself, began a divine beginning of never-ceasing and rational life enduring throughout all time. . . .

When the father and creator saw the creature which he had made moving and living, the created image of the external gods, he rejoiced, and in his joy determined to make the copy still more like the original; and as this was eternal, he sought to make the universe eternal, so far as might be. Now the nature of the ideal being was everlasting, but to bestow this attribute in its fulness upon a creature was impossible. Wherefore he resolved to have a moving image of eternity, and when he set in order the heaven, he made this image eternal but moving according to number, while eternity itself rests in unity; and this image we call time. . . .

The sun and moon and five other stars, which are called the planets, were created by him in order to distinguish and preserve the numbers of time; and when he had made their several bodies, he placed them in the orbits in which the circle of the other was revolving — in seven orbits seven stars. . . . What remained, the creator then proceeded to fashion after the nature of the pattern. Now as in the ideal animal the mind perceived ideas or species of a certain nature and number, he thought that this created animal ought to have species of a like nature and number. There are four such; one of them is the heavenly race of the gods; another, the race of birds whose way is in the air; the third, the watery species; and the fourth, the pedestrian and land creatures. Of the heavenly and divine, he created the greater part out of fire, that they might be the brightest of all things and fairest to behold, and he fashioned them after the likeness of the universe in the figure of a circle, and made them follow the intelligent motion of the supreme, distributing them over the whole circumference of heaven, which was to be a true cosmos or glorious world spangled with them all over. . . .

The earth, which is our nurse, clinging around the pole which is extended through the universe, he framed to be the guardian and artificer of night and day, first and eldest of gods that are in the interior of heaven.

[Addressing the planetary Gods, the Demiurgos commands them to create the mortal bodies of animals and humans.]

". . . betake yourselves to the formation of animals, imitating the power which was shown by me in creating you. The part of them worthy of the name immortal, which is called divine and is the guiding principle of those who are willing to follow justice and you — of that divine part I will myself sow the seed, and having made a beginning, I will hand the work over to you. And do ye then interweave the mortal with the immortal, and make and beget living creatures, and give them food, and make them to grow, and receive them again in death."

Thus he spake, and once more into the cup in which he had previously mingled the soul of the universe he poured the remains of the elements, and mingled them in much the same manner; they were not, however, pure as before, but diluted to the second and third degree. And having made it he divided the whole mixture into souls equal in number to the stars, and assigned each soul to a star; and having there placed them as in a chariot, he showed them the nature of the universe, and declared to them the laws of destiny, according to which their first birth would be one and the same for all, — no one should suffer a disadvantage at his hands; they were to be sown in the

instruments of time severally adapted to them, and to come forth
the most religious of animals; and as human nature was of two
kinds, the superior race would hereafter be called man. Now,
when they should be implanted in bodies by necessity, and be
always gaining or losing some part of their bodily substance, then
in the first place it would be necessary that they should all have
in them one and the same faculty of sensation, arising out of
irresistible impressions; in the second place, they must have love,
in which pleasure and pain mingle; also fear and anger, and the
feelings which are akin or opposite to them; if they conquered
these they would live righteously, and if they were conquered by
them, unrighteously. He who lived well during his appointed time
was to return and dwell in his native star, and there he would
have a blessed and congenial existence. But if he failed in
attaining this, at the second birth he would pass into a woman,
and if, when in that state of being, he did not desist from evil, he
would continually be changed into some brute who resembled him
in the evil nature which he had acquired, and would not cease
from his toils and transformations until he followed the revolution
of the same and the like within him, and overcame by the help of
reason the turbulent and irrational mob of later accretions, made
up of fire and air and water and earth, and returned to the form
of his first and better state.

Lilith, according to Rabbinic tradition Adam's first wife, created equal with him and at the same time, represents for us woman's equality and autonomy, demonized and banished by patriarchal religious authority.

Terra-cotta relief. Sumer, c. 2000 B.C., collection of Colonel Norman Colville.

4

Humanity: Male and Female

DOCUMENTS

1. *The Creation of Human Pairs by the Mother Goddess*
2. *The Creation of Adam and Eve*
3. *The Creation of Eve as the Fall of Adam*
4. *Two Rabbinic Commentaries on Genesis*
   Lilith, Adam's Rebellious First Wife
   Eve, Adam's Rib
5. *A Jewish Feminist **Midrash** on Lilith and Eve*
6. *Patriarchal Science Constructs the Female*
   Woman as Defective Male
   Woman as Natural Slave
7. *The Three Sexes of Greek Culture*

The creation of humanity, male and female, is depicted in the Babylonian, Hebrew, and Platonic creation stories discussed in chapter III. In those stories the concern was to locate the relationship of humanity to the gods and the heavenly world. In the Babylonian story the relationship is analogous to the relationship of serf to leisured aristocrat. The gods did not want to work and so humanity was created to be the serfs of the gods so that the gods could be at ease.[1] The Hebrew story, by contrast, makes humanity "lords" of creation, acting as representatives of God.

Plato projects into his story his fundamental ontological dualism between the intellectual and material worlds. Humanity is compounded out of a combination of the material body of the cosmos (a task assigned to the astral gods since it is beneath the dignity of the Demiurgos) and soul, which the Demiurgos mixes from the dregs of the World Soul. Humanity thus is a microcosm reflecting, in diminished potency, the relationship of soul and body of the macrocosm. Life in the body is the soul's fate, but a disembodied life of contemplation in the heavens is its true destiny to which it must aspire by keeping the body and its passions in check.

The stories of the creation of humanity in this chapter locate humanity in relationship to each other, as male and female. Here we see, in the culture of the Hebrew and Greek worlds, the overwhelming effects of patriarchal sociology. Even the biological relationship of male and female is distorted and reversed in the effort to write a story that locates the female as the subordinate and inferior of the male.

The most obvious and natural way to image the creation of humanity is through the analogy to human birth. Humanity would be seen as brought forth through a primordial birthing process by the Mother Goddess. This is what we find in the old Babylonian and Assyrian stories that tell of the creation of humanity by the Goddess. Humanity is created out of a mixture of clay and the flesh and blood of the slain God, thus bringing together divine and earthly elements. This mixture is shaped by Ninhursag, the Mother Goddess, who is called the Mother-Womb and the Bearing One. With incantations, fourteen mother-wombs are assembled before her and from them she brings forth seven human pairs. The story contains instructions to the midwives who assist women in labor.

The creation story thus functions also as a birth chant by which the human mother brings forth the child. In labor the woman becomes ritually identified with the Mother Goddess and is thereby empowered to give birth. Her labor turns to rejoicing as she merges into the Bearing One. "May the mother of the child bring forth by herself" is the final triumphal cry of empowerment.

By contrast, the Hebrew story of the creation of Eve from Adam is a male-centered reversal of this relationship of Goddess, mother, and child in the female experience of birth. The male God shapes Adam from the clay of the earth, breathing life into him through the nostrils. Adam is given lordship over the Garden of Eden but lacks a companion. This companion is given to him by God in a male mimicking of birth. Adam is put to sleep and God draws the female out of the side of the male by taking one of Adam's ribs and building it up into a female. It has been argued by Phyllis Trible that the language of this relationship of woman to man is no way subordinate[2] — Eve is called a "partner" in language that signifies companionship and not subordination. The relationship is seen as an ideal one in which there is not yet the shame of the body that will be brought on by sin.

Although the language of the Second Genesis story is by no means as misogynist as the later rabbinic and Christian commentaries on it, we cannot escape the conclusion that the structuring of the story as a male reversal of birth carries an intention to make the male the primary human being and then to locate the female as secondary and auxiliary to him. This intention of the text was analyzed some years ago by the Jewish psychoanalyist Theodor Reik, who made the interesting suggestion that the story of Eve originated in a male puberty rite story.[3] Whether literally true or not, the story does indeed reflect the transformed relationship of male to female that male puberty rites aim at creating.

The male who is born and develops in his early years as a small creature dependent on a powerful mother is, through the male puberty rite, enabled to sever his relationship with his mother. He transfers his identity to a new world where the older males are in control and the women have been defeated and banished. He then receives back from this male world a woman, no longer as dominant mother but as dependent wife. It is precisely this situation of the male reborn into the male-identified world, where the woman is given to him as auxiliary to his male identity, that is depicted in the Hebrew story of the creation of Eve from Adam.

The later commentaries on the Hebrew story in Jewish and Christian theologies not only draw out and make explicit the subordinationalism implicit in the Eve story but typically add new elements that express male hostility toward women. Philo, a first-century Hellenistic Jewish philosopher, places the story in the context of Platonic dualistic philosophy. Philo draws on the First and Second Genesis stories to contrast archetypal Man, made in the image of God, and material man, who is created from the clay of the earth and thus is a compound of mortal matter and divine spirit. The intellectual or spiritual idea of man represents this immortal spirit that is bound into the earthly clay.

However, even mortal man, as originally created from clay and divine spirit, was in a state of immortality and happiness as long as he remained single. The fall of humanity thus coincides, for Philo, with the creation of Eve. Eve represents the lower, sensual nature of man, severed from his higher immortal soul and presented to him in such a way as to seduce him into a capitulation to his lower, material nature. Out of this fall into gender dualism and sexuality, man lost his original paradisal state and fell into sin, sorrow, and finitude. Eve thus is Adam's misfortune, as well as his lower self.

The rabbinic *midrashim* on the story of the creation of woman further express this ambivalence and hostility of men toward women. The rabbis puzzled over the fact of two successive stories of the creation of woman, one in which woman is created simultaneously and equal to man and a second in which woman was created afterward from

Adam's rib. One solution to this dilemma was to suggest that these were two different women. Adam had a first wife named Lilith who was created equal with him. But she rebelled against his efforts to subordinate her and flew off by herself to the Red Sea where she lurks as a demonic spirit who kills newborn babies. Thus the First Genesis story, which might suggest equality of men and women in the image of God, is converted in the rabbinic commentary into a warning against insubordinate wives who return as demons to terrorize birthing mothers.

Rabbinic commentary on the subsequent creation of Eve from Adam's rib is replete with male misogyny. The rib is interpreted as a symbol of woman's place as silent, submissive, chaste, and homebound. But God's (that is, man's) efforts to impose this position on women runs up against the reality of woman's autonomous personhood. And so woman's subordination must be constantly reinforced by a barrage of hostile attacks on woman's humanity that are intended to cow her into submission. Yet, beneath it all, the constant assumption of this male misogyny is that these efforts will fail. Woman will assert herself despite all efforts of patriarchy to shape her according to its wishes. The unnaturalness of patriarchy and the distortion of women's character historically by this process of forced submission and latent resistance is thus dramatically revealed beneath the lines of the rabbinic *midrash*.

In Judith Plaskow's *midrash* on the rabbinic commentary on Genesis 1–3, we see a contemporary Jewish feminist drawing out the latent message of the Lilith story. Lilith represents the banished power and autonomy of women, which have been driven out beyond the boundaries of the patriarchal world. Even the very thought of it is repressed by labeling it a fearsome demon. Lilith is the banished potential of Eve herself, the subordinate and despised wife. The return of Lilith means the reclaiming of women's own wholeness of personhood. Lilith and Eve share their experiences and thereby conduct the world's first feminist consciousness-raising session.

Male mythology is succeeded culturally by male "science," but this male science carries much the same purpose as patriarchal creation myths, namely, to prove that the subordination and inferiority of woman is "according to nature." Thus, we include here key passages from Aristotle's biology and politics. Not only do these passages illustrate the function of male biological and social sciences in the service of patriarchy, but they have a long history of being used to exegete the Biblical creation story and to give its doctrine of female subordination further "rationale."

For Plato and Philo, the relationship of male to female is analogous to the relationship of spirit to matter, intellectual to sensible, immortal to mortal. Aristotle translated this into his dualism of form and matter. In his biology, Aristotle describes the reproductive act as a relationship of active male formative principle to female materiality. The male semen provides what we today might call the entire genetic code of the embryo or its active power of formation. The blood of the female womb provides only the matter shaped by the male active power. But the female herself is a deformed or imperfect human. And so, although every male seed strives to fully form the maternal matter and produce a male, sometimes this fails to be perfected. The resistance of the female matter fails to "take" the male form perfectly, and so a defective human, or female, resembling the mother is born.

The influence of this Aristotelian biology on Christian theology, especially on medieval scholasticism,[4] can hardly be underestimated. Aristotle's biology gave "scientific expression" to the basic patriarchal assumption that the male is the normative and representative expression of the human species and the female is not only secondary and auxiliary to the male but lacks full human status in physical strength, moral self-control, and mental capacity. This lesser "nature" thus confirms the female's subjugation to the male as her "natural" place in the universe.

In his *Politics*, Aristotle carries this concept of male domination into a description of the normative social order as determined by the principle of hierarchy of reason over body. Females, slaves, animals, and even material tools represent the bodily world that is to be ruled over and dominated by the free Greek male as the representative of rationality. The female belongs to a lesser class of humans who are slaves by nature.

Patriarchal relationships of male and female would seem to be intended not only to make woman the servile laborer of the household but also to subordinate the woman sexually — to make her sexually available and to prevent her from having control over her own sexuality and fertility. She becomes hands, vagina, and womb, owned by her husband. But this does not seem to improve sexual pleasure. The ancient Sumerian and Babylonian texts that depict an independent Goddess also typically describe sexuality in delighted and pleasurable terms. By contrast, the patriarchal texts in this chapter give evidence of a male distaste for sexual relations with women, as though the physical consorting with such a degraded being comes to be seen as degrading to the male. Both Philo and the rabbinic commentaries express this sense of degradation through sexual relations with women. For the rabbis, the male can consort with the woman only by remaining in a dream state where he forgets for a moment the polluted being that she is bodily.

This distaste for female sexuality is also expressed in Greek idealization of male homosexuality. Aristophanes' speech on Eros in Plato's *Symposium* is a humorous effort to describe the etiology of the three sexual orientations that Greek culture not only recognized but accepted, within limits. For Aristophanes, humans are divided into three groups: males who are attracted to males, females attracted to females, and males or females attracted to the opposite sex. This third, heterosexual impulse is the most spiritually degrading, in his view. Although the Greeks expected most men and women to be married for procreation, they did not see this sexual act as a vehicle for a more uplifting love relationship. Indeed, those who engaged in it within marriage for the purpose of children were most virtuous when they had no great taste for it. Those who actually felt erotically drawn to the opposite sex thus are identified with adulterers for Aristophanes.

Aristophanes also acknowledges that women are attracted to women and those with this orientation form companionship relationships with other women. Although better than heterosexual eros, it is passed by without further comment. The possible meaning of women's love for women escapes the patriarchal imagination. For Aristophanes, the highest eros is that between male and male. It is this relationship that is a culturally uplifting love. This is the love appropriate for soldiers and statesmen. Love of men makes one manly (the opposite of current American assumptions), brave, wise, and strong. As adults, such men become lovers of youth and thereby also tutor youth in the ways of manliness. They prefer not to marry and do so only to beget children and not out of any erotic attraction toward women.

Reflection

Describe what seems to be happening to the male self-concept and to the female self-concept in this process of male social domination and sexual alienation. In eight or ten words or phrases for each, list the characteristics of maleness in our culture and the characteristics of femaleness. Make a list of words generated by the term *humanness* and compare it with the previous two lists.

What kind of relationships between males and females are created by the existing stereotypes of maleness and femaleness?

How would you describe your ideal understanding of yourself as a female human person or a male human person? Under ideal conditions, how would you describe the female-male relationship; that is, what would be the dynamics of psychic and social interaction and how would each be shaped in its own self-identity by relation with the other?

How would you image the psychic and social dynamics of same-sex relations? Of male-male relations? Of female-female relations? How do these models of relationships compare with each other and with your model of male-female relationships?

Sum up your reflections on gender identity and sexual-social relations as a result of working toward these questions. What has the sexual relationship become in our culture and what should it be?

1. The Creation of Human Pairs by the Mother Goddess[5]

"That which is slight shall grow to abundance;
The *burden* of creation man shall bear!"
The goddess they called, [. . .], [the *mot*]her,
The most helpful of the gods, the wise Mami:
"Thou art the mother-womb,
The one who creates mankind.
Create, then, Lullu and let him bear the yoke!
The yoke he shall bear, . . . [. . .] ;
The *burden* of creation man shall bear!"
. [.] . opened her mouth,
Saying to the great gods:
"With me is the *doing* of all that is suitable;
With his . . . let Lullu appear!
He who shall be [. . .] of all [. . .],
Let him *be formed* out of clay, be *animated* with blood!"
Enki opened his mouth,
Saying to the great gods:
"On the . . . and [. . .] of the month
The purification of the land . . . !
Let them slay one god,
And let the gods be purified in the *judgement*.
With his flesh and his blood
Let Ninhursag mix clay.
God and man
Shall [. . .] therein, . . . in the clay!
Unto eternity [. . .] we shall hear."
[. . . they kis]sed her feet,
[Saying: "The creatress of mankind] we call thee;
[The mistr]ess of all the gods be thy name!"
[They went] to the House of Fate,

[Nin]igiku-Ea (and) the wise Mama.
[Fourteen mother]-wombs were assembled
To tread upon the [c]lay before her.
[. . .] Ea says, as he recites the incantation.
Sitting before her, Ea causes her to recite the incantation.
[Mama reci]ted the incantation; when she completed [her]
    incantation,
[. . .] she drew upon her clay.
[Fourteen pie]ces she pinched off; seven pieces she placed on the
    right,
[Seven pie]ces she placed on the left; between them she placed a
    brick
[E]a was kneeling on the *matting*; he opened its navel;
[. . . he c]alled the wise wives.
(Of the) [seven] and seven mother-wombs, seven brought forth
    males,
[Seven] brought forth females.
The Mother-Womb, the creatress of destiny,
In pairs she completed them,
In pairs she completed before her.
The forms of the people Mami forms.
In the house of the bearing woman in travail,
    Seven days shall the brick lie.
. . . from the house of Mah, the wise Mami.
The vexed shall rejoice in the house of the one in travail.
As the Bearing One gives birth,
May the mother of the child bring forth by [her]self.

2. The Creation of Adam and Eve[6]

When the Lord God made earth and heaven, there was neither
shrub nor plant growing wild upon the earth, because the Lord
God had sent no rain on the earth; nor was there any man to till
the ground. A flood used to rise out of the earth and water all the
surface of the ground. Then the Lord God formed a man from the
dust of the ground and breathed into his nostrils the breath of
life. Thus the man became a living creature. Then the Lord God
planted a garden in Eden away to the east, and there he put the
man whom he had formed. The Lord God made trees spring from
the ground, all trees pleasant to look at and good for food; and in
the middle of the garden he set the tree of life and the tree of the
knowledge of good and evil.

There was a river flowing from Eden to water the garden, and
when it left the garden it branched into four streams. The name of
the first is Pishon, that is the river which encircles all the land of
Havilah, where the gold is. The gold of that land is good;
bdellium and cornelians are also to be found there. The name of
the second river is Gihon; this is the one which encircles all the
land of Cush. The name of the third is Tigris; this is the river
which runs east of Asshur. The fourth river is the Euphrates.

The Lord God took the man and put him in the garden of
Eden to till it and care for it. He told the man, "You may eat from
every tree in the garden, but not from the tree of the knowledge
of good and evil; for on the day that you eat from it, you will
certainly die." Then the Lord God said, "It is not good for man
to be alone. I will provide a partner for him." So God formed out
of the ground all the wild animals and all the birds of heaven. He
brought them to the man to see what he would call them, and
whatever the man called each living creature, that was its name.
Thus the man gave names to all cattle, to the birds of heaven, and
to every wild animal; but for the man himself no partner had yet
been found. And so the Lord God put the man into a trance, and
while he slept, he took one of his ribs and closed the flesh over
the place. The Lord God then built up the rib, which he had
taken out of the man, into a woman. He brought her to the man,
and the man said:

"Now this, at last —
bone from my bones,
flesh from my flesh! —
this shall be called woman,
for from man was this taken."

That is why a man leaves his father and mother and is united to
his wife, and the two become one flesh. Now they were both
naked, the man and his wife, but they had no feeling of shame
towards one another.

3. The Creation of Eve as the Fall of Adam[7]

After this, Moses says that "God made man, having taken clay
from the earth, and he breathed into his face the breath of life."
And by this expression he shows most clearly that there is a vast
difference between man as generated now, and the first man who

was made according to the image of God. For man as formed now is perceptible to the external senses, partaking of qualities, consisting of body and soul, man or woman, by nature mortal. But man, made according to the image of God, was an idea, or a genus, or a seal, perceptible only by the intellect, incorporeal, neither male nor female, imperishable by nature. But he asserts that the formation of the individual man, perceptible by the external senses is a composition of earthy substance, and divine spirit. For that the body was created by the Creator taking a lump of clay, and fashioning the human form out of it; but that the soul proceeds from no created thing at all, but from the Father and Ruler of all things. For when he uses the expression, ''he breathed into,'' &c., he means nothing else than the divine spirit proceeding from that happy and blessed nature, sent to take up its habitation here on earth, for the advantage of our race, in order that, even if man is mortal according to that portion of him which is visible, he may at all events be immortal according to that portion which is invisible; and for this reason, one may properly say that man is on the boundaries of a better and an immortal nature, partaking of each as far as it is necessary for him; and that he was born at the same time, both mortal and the immortal. Mortal as to his body, but immortal as to his intellect.

. . . But since nothing in creation lasts for ever, but all mortal things are liable to inevitable changes and alterations, it was unavoidable that the first man should also undergo some disaster. And the beginning of his life being liable to reproach, was his wife. For, as long as he was single, he resembled, as to his creation, both the world and God; and he represented in his soul the characteristics of the nature of each, I do not mean all of them, but such as a mortal constitution was capable of admitting. But when woman also was created, man perceiving a closely connected figure and a kindred formation to his own, rejoiced at the sight, and approached her and embraced her. And she, in like manner, beholding a creature greatly resembling herself, rejoiced also, and addressed him in reply with due modesty. And love being engendered, and, as it were, uniting two separate portions of one animal into one body, adapted them to each other, implanting in each of them a desire of connection with the other with a view to the generation of a being similar to themselves. And this desire caused likewise pleasure to their bodies, which is the beginning of iniquities and transgressions, and it is owing to this that men have exchanged their previously immortal and happy existence for one which is mortal and full of misfortune.

4. Two Rabbinic Commentaries on Genesis

LILITH, ADAM'S REBELLIOUS FIRST WIFE[8]

When the Holy One, blessed be He, created Adam the first man
single, He said: *It is not good for the man to be alone* (Gen. 2:18),
and He created for him a woman from the earth like him, and
called her Lilith. Instantly they began to quarrel. She said: "I shall
not lie beneath," and he said, "I shall not lie beneath but above,
for your place is beneath and mine above." She said to him:
"Both of us are equal for both of us are of earth." And they did
not listen to each other. When Lilith saw this, she uttered the
Ineffable Name and flew off into the air of the world.

Thereupon Adam rose in prayer before his Creator and said:
"Master of the World! The woman whom You gave me fled from
me." Instantly the Holy One, blessed be He, sent three angels
[Senoi, Sansenoi, and Semangelof] after her to bring her back.
And the Holy One, blessed be He, said to Adam: "If she wants to
return, good and well, and if not, she will have to take it upon
herself that every day one hundred of her children should die."

The angels left Adam and went after her. They overtook her
in the sea, in the strong waters in which the Egyptians were to
drown in the future. They told her the word of God, but she did
not want to return. They then said to her: "We shall drown you
in the sea." She said to them: "Let me be, for I was not created
except for weakening the newborn children: the males until their
eighth day, and the females from their birth until twenty days."

When they heard her words, they pressed her to take her,
whereupon she swore to them in the name of the Living and
Enduring God that "Each time when I see you or your names or
your likeness on an amulet, I shall not harm that child." And she
took it upon herself that a hundred of her children should die
every day. Therefore every day one hundred of the demons die,
and this is why we write the names of the three angels on
amulets for little boys, for Lilith sees them and remembers her
oath, and the child recovers."

EVE, ADAM'S RIB[9]

When God was on the point of making Eve, He said: "I will not
make her from the head of man, lest she carry her head high in
arrogant pride; not from the eye, lest she be wanton-eyed; not

from the ear, lest she be an eavesdropper; not from the neck, lest she be insolent; not from the mouth, lest she be a tattler; not from the heart, lest she be inclined to envy; not from the hand, lest she be a meddler; not from the foot, lest she be a gadabout. I will form her from a chaste portion of the body," and to every limb and organ as He formed it, God said, "Be chaste! Be chaste!" Nevertheless, in spite of the great caution used, woman has all the faults God tried to obviate. The daughters of Zion were haughty and walked with stretched forth necks and wanton eyes; Sarah was an eavesdropper in her own tent, when the angel spoke with Abraham; Miriam was a talebearer, accusing Moses; Rachel was envious of her sister Leah; Eve put out her hand to take the forbidden fruit, and Dinah was a gadabout. . . . Many of the physical and psychical differences between the two sexes must be attributed to the fact that man was formed from the ground and woman from bone. Women need perfumes, while men do not; dust of the ground remains the same no matter how long it is kept; flesh, however, requires salt to keep it in good condition. The voice of women is shrill, not so the voice of men; when soft viands are cooked, no sound is heard, but let a bone be put in a pot, and at once it crackles. A man is easily placated, not so a woman; a few drops of water suffice to soften a clod of earth; a bone stays hard, even if it were to soak in water for days. . . .

Adam was first made to fall into a deep sleep before the rib for Eve was taken from his side. For, had he watched her creation, she would not have awakened love in him.

. . . Knowing well all the details of her formation, he was repelled by her. But when he roused himself from his profound sleep, and saw Eve before him in all her surprising beauty and grace, he exclaimed, "This is she who caused my heart to throb many a night!" Yet he discerned at once what the nature of woman was. She would, he knew, seek to carry her point with man either by entreaties and tears, or flattery and caresses. He said, therefore, "This is my never-silent bell!"

5. A Jewish Feminist Midrash on Lilith and Eve[10]

In the beginning the Lord God formed Adam and Lilith from the dust of the ground and breathed into their nostrils the breath of life. Created from the same source, both having been formed from the ground, they were equal in all ways. Adam, man that he was, didn't like this situation, and he looked for ways to change it. He said, "I'll have my figs now, Lilith," ordering her to wait on him, and he tried to leave to her the daily tasks of life in the garden. But Lilith wasn't one to take any nonsense; she picked herself up, uttered God's holy name, and flew away. "Well, now, Lord," complained Adam, "that uppity woman you sent me has gone and deserted me." The Lord, inclined to be sympathetic, sent his messengers after Lilith, telling her to shape up and return to Adam or face dire punishment. She, however, preferring anything to living with Adam, decided to stay right where she was. And so God, after more careful consideration this time, caused a deep sleep to fall upon Adam, and out of one of his ribs created for him a second companion, Eve.

For a time Eve and Adam had quite a good thing going. Adam was happy now, and Eve, though she occasionally sensed capacities within herself that remained undeveloped, was basically satisfied with the role of Adam's wife and helper. The only thing that really disturbed her was the excluding closeness of the relationship between Adam and God. Adam and God just seemed to have more in common, being both men, and Adam came to identify with God more and more. After a while that made God a bit uncomfortable too, and he started going over in his mind whether he might not have made a mistake in letting Adam talk him into banishing Lilith and creating Eve, in light of the power that had given Adam.

Meanwhile Lilith, all alone, attempted from time to time to rejoin the human community in the garden. After her first fruitless attempt to breach its walls, Adam worked hard to build them stronger, even getting Eve to help him. He told her fearsome stories of the demon Lilith who threatens women in childbirth and steals children from their cradles in the middle of the night. The second time Lilith came she stormed the garden's main gate, and a great battle between her and Adam ensued, in which she was finally defeated. This time, however, before Lilith got away, Eve got a glimpse of her and saw she was a woman like herself.

After this encounter, seeds of curiosity and doubt began to grow in Eve's mind. Was Lilith indeed just another woman? Adam had said she was a demon. Another woman! The very idea attracted Eve. She had never seen another creature like herself before. And how beautiful and strong Lilith had looked! How bravely she had fought! Slowly, slowly, Eve began to think about the limits of her own life within the garden.

One day, after many months of strange and disturbing thoughts, Eve, wandering around the edge of the garden, noticed a young apple tree she and Adam had planted, and saw that one of its branches stretched over the garden wall. Spontaneously she tried to climb it, and struggling to the top, swung herself over the wall.

She had not wandered long on the other side before she met the one she had come to find, for Lilith was waiting. At first sight of her, Eve remembered the tales of Adam and was frightened, but Lilith understood and greeted her kindly. "Who are you?" they asked each other, "What is your story?" And they sat and spoke together, of the past and then of the future. They talked not once, but many times, and for many hours. They taught each other many things, and told each other stories, and laughed together, and cried, over and over, till the bond of sisterhood grew between them.

Meanwhile, back in the garden, Adam was puzzled by Eve's comings and goings, and disturbed by what he sensed to be her new attitude toward him. He talked to God about it, and God, having his own problems with Adam and a somewhat broader perspective, was able to help him out a little — but he, too, was confused. Something had failed to go according to plan. As in the days of Abraham, he needed counsel from his children. "I am who I am," thought God, "but I must become who I will become."

And God and Adam were expectant and afraid the day Eve and Lilith returned to the garden, bursting with possibilities, ready to rebuild it together.

6. Patriarchal Science Constructs the Female

WOMAN AS DEFECTIVE MALE[11]

The answer to the next question we have to investigate is clear from these considerations, I mean how it is that the male contributes to generation and how it is that the semen from the male is the cause of the offspring. Does it exist in the body of the embryo as a part of it from the first, mingling with the material which comes from the female? Or does the semen communicate nothing to the material body of the embryo but only to the power and movement in it? For this power is that which acts and makes,

while that which is made and receives the form is the residue of
the secretion in the female. Now the latter alternative appears to
be the right one both *a priori* and in view of the facts. For, if we
consider the question on general grounds, we find that, whenever
one thing is made from two of which one is active and the other
passive, the active agent does not exist in that which is made;
and, still more generally, the same applies when one thing moves
and another is moved; the moving thing does not exist in that
which is moved. But the female, as female, is passive, and the
male, as male, is active, and the principle of the movement comes
from him. Therefore, if we take the highest genera under which
they each fall, the one being active and motive and the other
passive and moved, that one thing which is produced comes from
them only in the sense in which a bed comes into being from the
carpenter and the wood, . . .

. . . an animal is a living body, a body with Soul in it. The
female always provides the material, the male provides that which
fashions the material into shape; this, in our view, is the specific
characteristic of each of the sexes: that is what it means to be male
or to be female. Hence, necessity requires that the female should
provide the physical part, *i.e.,* a quantity of material, but not that
the male should do so, since necessity does not require that the
tools should reside in the product that is being made, nor that the
agent which uses them should do so. Thus the physical part, the
body, comes from the female, and the Soul from the male, since
the Soul is the essence of a particular body. . . . Just as it
sometimes happens that deformed offspring are produced by
deformed parents, and sometimes not, so the offspring produced
by a female are sometimes female, sometimes not, but male. The
reason is that the female is as it were a deformed male. . . .

. . . also the female foetus is not perfected equally with the
male in man (but they are so in the other animals, for in them the
female is not later in developing than the male). For while within
the mother the female takes longer in developing, but after birth
everything is perfected more quickly in females than in males; I
mean, for instance, puberty, the prime of life, and old age. For
females are weaker and colder in nature, and we must look upon
the female character as being a sort of natural deficiency.
Accordingly while it is within the mother it develops slowly
because of its coldness (for development is concoction, and it is
heat that concocts, and what is hotter is easily concocted); but
after birth it quickly arrives at maturity and old age on account of

its weakness, for all inferior things come sooner to their perfection or end, and as this is true of works of art so it is of what is formed by Nature.

WOMAN AS NATURAL SLAVE[12]

But is there any one thus intended by nature to be a slave, and for whom such a condition is expedient and right, or rather is not all slavery a violation of nature?

There is no difficulty in answering this question, on grounds both of reason and of fact. For that some should rule and others be ruled is a thing not only necessary, but expedient; from the hour of their birth, some are marked out for subjection, others for rule.

And there are many kinds both of rulers and subjects . . . Such a duality exists in living creatures, but not in them only; it originates in the constitution of the universe; . . . We will restrict ourselves to the living creature, which, in the first place, consists of soul and body: and of these two, the one is by nature the ruler, and the other the subject. . . . We may firstly observe in living creatures both a despotical and a constitutional rule; for the soul rules the body with a despotical rule, whereas the intellect rules the appetites with a constitutional and royal rule. And it is clear that the rule of the soul over the body, and of the mind and the rational element over the passionate, is natural and expedient; whereas the equality of the two or the rule of the inferior is always hurtful.

. . . the male is by nature superior, and the female inferior; and the one rules, and the other is ruled; this principle, of necessity, extends to all mankind. Where then there is such a difference as that between soul and body, or between men and animals (as in the case of those whose business is to use their body, and who can do nothing better), the lower sort are by nature slaves, and it is better for them as for all inferiors that they should be under the rule of a master. For he who can be, and therefore is, another's, and he who participates in rational principle enough to apprehend, but not to have, such a principle, is a slave by nature.

7. The Three Sexes of Greek Culture[13]

Let me treat of the nature of man and what has happened to it; for the original human nature was not like the present, but

different. The sexes were not two as they are now, but originally
three in number; there was man, woman, and the union of the
two, having a name corresponding to this double nature, which
had once a real existence, but is now lost, and the word
"Androgynous" is only preserved as a term of reproach. In the
second place, the primeval man was round, his back and sides
forming a circle; and he had four hands and four feet, one head
with two faces looking opposite ways, set on a round neck and
precisely alike; also four ears, two privy members, and the
remainder to correspond. He could walk upright as men now do,
backwards or forwards as he pleased, and he could also roll over
and over at a great pace, turning on his four hands and four feet,
eight in all, like tumblers going over and over with their legs in
the air; this was when he wanted to run fast. Now the sexes were
three, and such as I have described them; because the sun, moon,
and earth are three; and the man was originally the child of the
sun, the woman of the earth, and the man-woman of the moon,
which is made up of sun and earth, and they were all round and
moved round and round like their parents.

[In response to threats against the Gods, Zeus decrees] " . . .
men shall continue to exist, but I will cut them in two and then
they will be diminished in strength and increased in numbers; this
will have the advantage of making them more profitable to us."
. . . Apollo was also bidden to heal their wounds and compose
their forms. So he gave a turn to the face and pulled the skin
from the sides all over that which in our language is called the
belly, like the purses which draw in, and he made one mouth at
the centre, which he fastened in a knot (the same which is called
the navel); he also moulded the breast and took out most of the
wrinkles, much as a shoemaker might smooth leather upon a last;
he left a few, however, in the region of the belly and navel, as a
memorial of the primeval state. After the division the two parts of
man, each desiring his other half, came together, and throwing
their arms about one another, entwined in mutual embraces,
longing to grow into one, they were on the point of dying from
hunger and self-neglect, because they did not like to do anything
apart; and when one of the halves died and the other survived,
the survivor sought another mate, man or woman as we call
them, — being the sections of entire men or women, — and clung
to that. They were being destroyed, when Zeus in pity of them
invented a new plan: he turned the parts of generation round to the
front, for this had not been always their position, and they sowed
the seed no longer as hitherto like grasshoppers in the ground,

but in one another; and after the transposition the male generated
in the female in order that by the mutual embraces of man and
woman they might breed, and the race might continue; or if man
came to man they might be satisfied, and rest, and go their ways
to the business of life: so ancient is the desire of one another
which is implanted in us, reuniting our original nature, making
one of two, and healing the state of man. Each of us when
separated, having one side only, like a flat fish, is but the
indenture of a man, and he is always looking for his other half.
Men who are a section of that double nature which was once
called Androgynous are lovers of women; adulterers are generally
of this breed, and also adulterous women who lust after men: the
women who are a section of the woman do not care for men, but
have female attachments; the female companions are of this sort.
But they who are a section of the male follow the male, and while
they are young, being slices of the original man, they hang about
men and embrace them, and they are themselves the best of boys
and youths, because they have the most manly nature. Some
indeed assert that they are shameless, but this is not true; for they
do not act thus from any want of shame, but because they are
valiant and manly, and have a manly countenance, and they
embrace that which is like them. And these when they grow up
become our statesmen, and these only, which is a great proof of
the truth of what I am saying. When they reach manhood they
are lovers of youth, and are not naturally inclined to marry or
beget children, — if at all, they do so only in obedience to the
law; but they are satisfied if they may be allowed to live with one
another unwedded; and such a nature is prone to love and ready
to return love, always embracing that which is akin to him.

Old and young woman meet, tell each other their stories, and fly off
together. Men, in fear and anger, calls them ''witches,'' saying that
that word means ''evil ones'' and ''consorts of the Devil.''

Etching by Goya, British Museum, London.

5

The Origins of Evil

The perception of good and evil is basic to human consciousness. By this perception the human being sets itself over against existing reality, names aspects of that reality as contrary to "what ought to be," and thereby also generates a vision of an ideal world that becomes the standard by which existing reality is judged as deficient. One way of relating this normative "ought" to the deficient "is" takes the form of imaging an original time, a paradise, where the world was as it ought to be. Evil originates through some act of sin through which this paradise was lost and the present ambiguous world arose.

A second way of relating the two is to see the ideal world as a future possibility that is unfolding through a developmental process or through a conflictual struggle. A third way of relating the two is to see the ideal world as a heavenly world available only to the gods (and a privileged aristocracy) but denied to ordinary mortals. Through cyclical ritual the lower mortal world might be fleetingly blessed by this divine world but would never capture it in a complete and final form. Ancient Near Eastern religion tended toward this third, pessimistic form. Greek thought had versions of the lost paradise story, while Judaism and Christianity combine the first and second versions in a dialectical perspective.

Biblical and rabbinic Judaism, however, have not shared the Christian notion that the departure from original paradise irrevocably handicapped human power to choose good or evil. Rather, Judaism favored an anthropology that affirms human freedom of choice. Although humans exist in a conflict between the two impulses of good and evil, they are able to choose good. It is significant, therefore, that the Genesis 3 story of the fall of Adam through Eve does not become a normative story for the origins of evil in the Hebrew Bible. It remains a folktale about the origins of alienated work and painful sexual reproduction. But the normative story of the etiology of evil in Hebrew thought is the golden calf story of the apostasy of Israel in the desert.

The liberation of Israel from Egyptian bondage and the covenanting at Sinai are the key stories of Israel's identity. Through these acts, God creates and chooses his elect people. The greatest evil, therefore, is the deliberate choice to reject this emancipation from Egyptian bondage, to long to be back in the land of slavery and idolatry. According to this paradigmatic story of apostasy, the act occurs even while Moses is on the top of Mount Sinai receiving the tablets of the Law from God. The actors in this drama are male. It is male representatives of Israel who come to Aaron to ask for the golden calf. Females are mentioned only as the passive wearers of golden jewelry that is stripped from them by their husbands to make the calf. This passive role of women even led the rabbinic commentators to suggest that women refused to give up their jewelry to make the calf and were rewarded by God for their superior faith. The men had to use their own gold earrings.[1] This idea is probably not in the mind of the original author, who is intent on the conflict between males and is not interested in either blaming or exonerating women.

Moses shatters the tablets in rage when he sees this apostasy. But he also placates the rage of God and prevents God from casting off his people altogether. The sins of Israel are purged by a bloodletting in which the Levites slay three thousand Israelites. This account reflects the rivalries of different priestly confraternities in the ancient Hebrew temple and was written to vindicate the Levitical priesthood. Their willingness to pitilessly slay their own brothers and sons proves their total devotion to God and wins them divine blessing.

Two ideas stand out from the golden calf story. First, evil is equated with an apostasy from God whereby a people emancipated by God rejects its own liberation. This idea has positive possibilities for feminist theology. It suggests that sin is a fear of freedom, a longing for the security of bondage. But this idea is linked with a second, questionable idea, namely, that loyalty to God demands a violent ethnocentrism that rejects all dialogue with other human cultures and requires one to be ready to murder one's own relatives if they adopt foreign practices.

While affirming freedom to choose good or evil, intertestamental Judaism increasingly recognized that this choice does not take place in a neutral realty. Rather, there is a negative ambiance that biases human acts toward evil. The favorite story for explaining the etiology of this negative ambiance in the Jewish texts of this period, however, is not the Eve story but rather the story that appears briefly in Genesis 6:1-4 about the birth of giants from a rape of the daughters of men by the Sons of God. This story was developed in the intertestamental tradition to explain the etiology of demonic powers who bias human decision in a negative direction.[2]

As we can see in the reference to this tradition in the *Testimony of the Twelve Patriarchs*, an explicit misogyny has now been added to the story. The rape has become a seduction. The daughters of men are thereby marked as dangerous sexual temptresses who are the gateway to evil. The only remedy for this is a strict purdah for women. By strict segregation of women, a banning of all visual ornamentation of hair, jewelry, cosmetics or dress, a sexual repression of mind, sin can be avoided. Although the Christian Church fathers favored the Eve story to scapegoat women for sin, the Watcher story was also used, especially to remonstrate against a female visual attractiveness that originally seduced the "angels."

The classic Greek myth of the loss of Paradise through the sins of woman is the Pandora story. This story also reflects a second theme frequently found in such myths, namely, the jealousy of the gods. Humans (male) are miserable not only because of betrayal by females but because the gods do not wish to share with them their life of ease, plenty and immortality. Prometheus, the benefactor of humanity, tries to ease the human lot by stealing fire, thus making technology possible. Prometheus is punished for this theft by endless torments, but Zeus determines to punish humanity (males) as well by sending to them a beautiful but treacherous woman as wife. Before this time, human (male) life had been free of ease, toil, disease, and old age. When Pandora lifts the lid of the vessel, all these evils are unleashed upon humanity.

This story is confusing because it mingles two different models of relationship to the past, one in which the human lot is improved through technology and a second in which an original paradisal life is ruined through an archetypal sin. The first view, expressed in the Prometheus story, has been artificially linked to the second view found in the Pandora story. Pandora represents the reversed and hostile relationship of the male to his wife created by the male puberty trauma. Pandora, originally the Mother Goddess (Allgiver), is demoted in this story to the wife toward whom the adult male feels both sexual attraction and hostility. The wife is blamed for the loss of the paradise of ease and plenty that the male child received from his mother. Hence, as wife, the woman is vilified as the source of all the troubles and misfortunes that the adult male must suffer in the struggle for existence.

For Christian theology, the classic story of the Fall is exegeted from the Genesis 3 account of the eating of the fruit of the tree of knowledge of good and evil and the expulsion from Paradise. Christianity read this story in the light of its theology of a human nature encapsulated in the evil impulse and unable, by its own efforts, to do unambiguously good deeds pleasing to God. It must be redeemed from this condition by the atoning death of a divine savior. Such a theological anthropology is far from the mind of the author of this biblical folktale. The story of the loss of Paradise in the Bible, as in the Pandora story, reflects an ambivalent relationship of the divine toward the human. The command not to eat the fruit of the tree of knowledge of good and evil suggests an effort by God to keep humanity innocent but also to keep it ignorant, to prevent humanity from taking that empowering knowledge that might rival and challenge divine power and control over the universe.

The snake also represents an ambivalent power. It is not the expression of "evil" so much as the expression of that dawning consciousness that begins to question the limits set by parental rule and reaches for autonomous experience and knowledge. Although Eve initiates this questioning and Adam passively complies, for both the knowledge that shatters childhood innocence is sexual knowledge, revealing to them their nakedness, that is, making them ashamed of their bodies. Both are thereby banished from Paradise and forced to live in the harsh world of adult existence. Painful labor, painful childbearing, and male domination are divine decrees but also simply the "facts" of this harsh adult world. There is no suggestion that Eve is more guilty or more punished than Adam. Both are tossed out into the mean world of struggle for existence, alienated sexuality, and oppressive relationship, with the loss of the dreaming innocence of childhood.

The gnostic commentary on the Genesis 3 story found in the *Hypostasis of the Archons* is a remarkable example of a gnostic reading of this text. For the gnostics, humanity was divided into three powers: carnal, psychic, and spiritual. The carnal power bound humans to the ignorance and materiality of the present world system. The psychic power opened them up to questioning this ignorance. But only the spiritual power was truly of the transcendent divine world and conveyed liberating knowledge. For the gnostics, this present world system was not the work of the true divinity but came about through fallen world Rulers. But the higher divine world, represented by Sophia, the Female Spiritual Principle, sought to break through this veil of ignorance and impart liberating knowledge.

In this gnostic exegesis of Genesis 3, the order not to eat of the fruit of the tree of the knowledge of good and evil is a deceptive command given by the fallen Rulers to keep Adam in ignorance. These same Rulers try to seduce and destroy the Spiritual Principle represented by the woman and the snake, but they succeed only in defaming a carnal shadow of these beings. The Female Spiritual Principle thus represents authentic gnosis (liberating knowledge) when it tells the woman to eat of the fruit of the tree. Once both Adam and Eve have eaten, their psychic powers are aroused to reveal to them their lack of authentic spiritual knowledge. The Rulers, to prevent Adam and Eve from seeking liberating knowledge and thus escaping their power, throw them out of Paradise into a world of toil where they will be so distracted by the struggle for existence that they will not be able to seek truth. So the eating of the fruit becomes, in gnosticism, an aborted tale of liberation that points forward to a future Revealer who can deliver humanity from its bondage.

Early Christianity was profoundly divided by radical readings of Scripture that suggested that the new humanity in Christ delivered the redeemed from the present world system — politically, culturally, and religiously. A new spiritual equality of women was one implication of this radical reading of Scripture. Paul himself was divided between radical reading of redemption and a conservative reading of coexistence with the present world system. But his followers in the next generation increasingly split into two camps. Some, represented by figures such as Marcion or by the popular *Acts of Paul and Thecla*,[3] believed that the baptized transcended patriarchal restrictions on women.

We find in conservative, second-generation Paulinism a series of counterattacks that declare that the traditional patriarchal familial and social order of husbands over wives, masters over slaves, parents over children is still intact and is to be even more strictly observed by Christians.[4] The exegesis of Genesis 3 represents this conservative Paulinism, which sought to repress the leadership and ministry of women in Christian churches by arguing for a patriarchal "order of Creation." Such use of Genesis 3 already had developed in rabbinic exegesis in this period.[5] But in 1 Timothy it emerges as a keystone for patriarchal Christianity. Eve was created second and sinned first. This establishes the natural dominance of male over female and reinforces submission on woman that is due to her priority in sin.

Adam is even said not to have been deceived. Later Christian exegesis of this passage suggests that Adam knew that eating the fruit was wrong but went along with Eve only as an act of *noblesse oblige*, so she would not be "alone."[6] Motherhood becomes the one way women can redeem themselves from this fault, a statement that is intended to reject the radical Christian appeal to an emancipatory celibacy for women that freed them from power of the patriarchal family.[7] Brief as this passage in 1 Timothy is, its importance is great, for it established the perspective through which subsequent forms of dominant Christianity were taught to read the whole Bible.

Even though, throughout the centuries of orthodox Christianity, the message has been drilled into women that they are second in creation and first in sin, must therefore be doubly submissive, and are good only for childbearing, women persisted in reading the gospel differently. At least as early as the fifteenth century, moreover, we can trace a line of incipiently feminist exegesis of Genesis 3 that reads the original folktale and perceives that its story could be understood quite differently.[8] Adam appeared to be a bit of a clod, while Eve's curiosity suggested an intelligent quest for knowledge and autonomous experience. So the reading of Genesis 3 in Elizabeth Cady Stanton's *The Woman's Bible* in the late nineteenth century is by no means the first time that women read the tale from their own perspective and found in it alternative possibilities.

In addition to these ancient myths, we include in this chapter two modern stories that have the status of foundational social myths of our times — the Freudian story and the Marxist story. The Freudian story is not about the fall from a good to an evil time but rather about the trade-offs between the evil of unbridled instinct and the evil of instinctual repression that is necessary for the establishment of civilization. In Freud's description of the original "state of nature," there is allout war between the father and the sons. The father dominates all the women, sexually as well as for their labor, and observes no incest taboos toward his own daughters. Sons are castrated or killed as they grow large enough to challenge the father or are expelled to roam in angry bands of young males without women. Finally, the sons attack and kill the father but devour him raw as an identification with his coveted power.

Finally, they realize that they will be ever at war with each other for paternal power until they band together and agree to sublimate this power in the form of an ancestral totem, while sharing authority among themselves. But this can happen only through a social contract that establishes laws of instinctual repression, duties, taboos on incest, and institutional order. Civilization is tragic, built on sublimating the primal act of violence and repressing spontaneity. But this neurosis-making repression can be clarified only by analysis to be consciously accepted as the price of civilized order.

Freud also suggests a temporary period of matriarchy, but this is only a transitional phase or interregnum between the reign of the father and the social contract of the sons. In primal patriarchy, the mother plays the subversive role of substituting the favored younger son for the aging father, but civilization is built on the renunciation by the sons of this mother-love.

Engels, in his treatise *Origin and History of the Family, Private Property, and the State,* builds on an alternative anthropology much in vogue in the late Victorian period, namely, that the earliest human society was matriarchal.[9] This matriarchal society was characterized by matrilineal and matrilocal family organization and communal property. Sex was unfettered since all children were legitimate children of the mothers. But, as wealth increased, the older males were no longer content with these arrangements. They engineered a social revolution in which the family became patrilineal and patrilocal. A woman's sexuality now had to be strictly confined to the one legitimate husband to ensure that her children were those of her husband. Monogamy thus does not express mutuality between men and women but is an institution forged for male domination of children and property. Women are thrown into subjugation. This, for Engels, is the cellular model of all subsequent oppressive class relationships between owner and worker.

For Engels, the subjugation of women, as well as subsequent class relations in feudal and capitalist societies, represents a trail of monstrous social injustices on which civilization is built. But these structures of oppression are also necessary to build that machine of economic productivity that will eventually allow for the abolition of scarcity. When this has finally evolved under capitalist industrialism, the final stage of the dialectical process of oppression and development can take place with the overthrow of the capitalist ruling class and the emergence of communist ownership of the means of production.

This final communist stage of civilization will also emancipate women and restore to them self-determination over their own labor and sexuality lost to them in the overthrow of primal matriarchy. Thus, for Engels, history is a Fall and Redemption story that begins in the

Eden of primitive matriarchal communism and ends in the final stage of communism, where humanity can leap from the Realm of Necessity to the Realm of Freedom.

Reflection

Compare the various fall stories in this chapter. What elements in them appeal to you as true? That is, which seem to you to point to the key elements in the advent or nature of evil? Why do these symbols seem true to you? What aspects of your own experience make these symbols ring true for you?

What aspects of the fall stories seem false, that is, to actually falsify the real source and nature of evil? Reflect on the sociology of consciousness manifest in these fall stories. How do these fall stories function to conceal the real evils of society by "blaming the victim," by making victims of social evil, such as women, appear to be the causes of evil? How do fall stories function to ratify and justify oppressive social arrangements?

On the basis of this discussion, write your own myth or parable of the origin of evil or human self-alienation. First, work out the ways you would describe authentic human nature and good human relationships with each other, with nature, with the divine. Then ask what is the nature and characteristics of the negative or destructive elements that contradict the good. What locus do these negative elements take in relationship to the self and to its social and cosmic relationships? What impulses seem to be the primary location of this "evil" tendency? Try then to express your conclusions in the form of a symbolic story.

1. The Exodus Community and the Golden Calf[10]

When the people saw that Moses was so long in coming down from the mountain, they confronted Aaron and said to him, "Come, make us gods to go ahead of us. As for this fellow Moses, who brought us up from Egypt, we do not know what has become of him." Aaron answered them, "Strip the gold rings from the ears of your wives and daughters, and bring them to me." So all the people stripped themselves of their gold earrings

and brought them to Aaron. He took them out of their hands, cast
the metal in a mould, and made it into the image of a bull-calf.
"These," he said, "are your gods, O Israel, that brought you up
from Egypt." Then Aaron was afraid and built an altar in front of
it and issued this proclamation, "Tomorrow there is to be a
pilgrim-feast to the Lord." Next day the people rose early, offered
whole-offerings, and brought shared-offerings. After this they sat
down to eat and drink and then gave themselves up to revelry.
But the Lord said to Moses, "Go down at once, for your people,
the people you brought up from Egypt, have done a disgraceful
thing; so quickly have they turned aside from the way I
commanded them. They have made themselves an image of a
bull-calf, they have prostrated themselves before it, sacrificed to it
and said, 'These are your gods, O Israel, that brought you up
from Egypt.' " So the Lord said to Moses, "I have considered this
people, and I see that they are a stubborn people. Now, let me
alone to vent my anger upon them, so that I may put an end to
them and make a great nation spring from you." But Moses set
himself to placate the Lord his God: "O Lord," he said, "why
shouldst thou vent thy anger upon thy people, whom thou didst
bring out of Egypt with great power and a strong hand? Why let
the Egyptians say, 'So he meant evil when he took them out, to
kill them in the mountains and wipe them off the face of the
earth'? Turn from thy anger, and think better of the evil thou dost
intend against thy people. Remember Abraham, Isaac and Israel,
thy servants, to whom thou didst swear by thy own self: 'I will
make your posterity countless as the stars in the sky, and all this
land, of which I have spoken, I will give to them, and they shall
possess it for ever.' " So the Lord relented, and spared his people
the evil with which he had threatened them.

Moses turned and went down the mountain with the two
tablets of the Tokens in his hands, inscribed on both sides; on the
front and on the back they were inscribed. The tablets were the
handiwork of God, and the writing was God's writing, engraved
on the tablets. Joshua, hearing the uproar the people were
making, said to Moses, "Listen! There is fighting in the camp."
Moses replied,

"This is not the clamour of warriors,
nor the clamour of a defeated people;
it is the sound of singing that I hear."

As he approached the camp, Moses saw the bull-calf and the
dancing, and he was angry; he flung the tablets down, and they
were shattered to pieces at the foot of the mountain. Then he took
the calf they had made and burnt it; he ground it to powder,
sprinkled it on water, and made the Israelites drink it. He
demanded of Aaron, ''What did this people do to you that you
should have brought such great guilt upon them?'' Aaron replied,
''Do not be angry, sir. The people were deeply troubled; that you
well know. And they said to me, 'Make us gods to go ahead of
us, because, as for this fellow Moses, who brought us up from
Egypt, we do not know what has become of him.' So I said to
them, 'Those of you who have any gold, strip it off.' They gave it
me, I threw it in the fire, and out came this bull-calf.'' Moses saw
that the people were out of control and that Aaron had laid them
open to the secret malice of their enemies. He took his place at
the gate of the camp and said, ''Who is on the Lord's side? Come
here to me''; and the Levites all rallied to him. He said to them,
''These are the words of the Lord the God of Israel: 'Arm
yourselves, each of you, with his sword. Go through the camp
from gate to gate and back again. Each of you kill his brother, his
friend, his neighbour.' '' The Levites obeyed, and about three
thousand of the people died that day. Moses then said, ''Today
you have consecrated yourselves to the Lord completely, because
you have turned each against his own son and his own brother
and so have this day brought a blessing upon yourselves.''

The next day Moses said to the people, ''You have committed
a great sin. I shall now go up to the Lord; perhaps I may be able
to secure pardon for your sin.'' So Moses returned to the Lord
and said, ''O hear me! This people has committed a great sin:
they have made themselves gods of gold. If thou wilt forgive
them, forgive. But if not, blot out my name, I pray, from thy book
which thou has written.'' The Lord answered Moses, ''It is the
man who has sinned against me that I will blot out from my
book. But go now, lead the people to the place which I have told
you of. My angel shall go ahead of you, but a day will come
when I shall punish them for their sin.'' And the Lord smote the
people for worshipping the bull-calf which Aaron had made.

2. Women Seduce the Angels and Produce Monsters[11]

[For] evil are women, my children; and since they have no power
or strength over man, they use wiles by outward attractions, that

they may draw him to themselves. And whom they cannot bewitch by outward attractions, him they overcome by craft. [For] moreover, concerning them, the angel of the Lord told me, and taught me, that women are overcome by the spirit of fornication more than men, and in their heart they plot against men; and by means of their adornment they deceive first their minds, and by the glance of the eye instil the poison, and then through the accomplished act they take them captive. For a woman cannot force a man openly, but by a harlot's bearing she beguiles him. Flee, therefore, fornication, my children, and command your wives and your daughters, that they adorn not their heads and faces to deceive the mind: because every woman who useth these wiles hath been reserved for eternal punishment. For thus they allured the Watchers who were before the flood; for as these continually beheld them, they lusted after them, and they conceived the act in their mind; for they changed themselves into the shape of men, and appeared to them when they were with their husbands. And the women lusting in their minds after their forms, gave birth to giants, for the Watchers appeared to them as reaching even unto heaven.

Beware, therefore, of fornication; and if you wish to be pure in mind, guard your senses from every woman. And command the women likewise not to associate with men, that they also may be pure in mind. For constant meetings, even though the ungodly deed be not wrought, are to them an irremediable disease, and to us a destruction of Beliar and an eternal reproach.

3. Pandora Opens the Box[12]

Zeus in the wrath of his heart hath hidden the means of
    subsistence —
Wrathful because he once was deceived by the wily Prometheus.
Therefore it was he devised most grievous troubles for mortals.
Fire he hid: yet that, for men, did the gallant Prometheus
Steal in a hollow reed, from the dwelling of Zeus the Adviser,
Nor was he seen by the ruler of gods, who delights in the
    thunder.
Then, in his rage at the deed, cloud-gathering Zeus did address
    him:
Iapetionides, in cunning greater than any,
"Thou in the theft of fire and deceit of me art exulting,
Source of regret for thyself and for men who shall be hereafter.

I, in the place of fire, will give them a bane, so that all men
May in spirit exult and find in their misery comfort!''
Speaking thus, loud laughed he, the father of gods and of mortals.
Then he commanded Hephaistos, the cunning artificer,
    straightway
Mixing water and earth, with speech and force to endow it,
Making it like in face to the gods whose life is eternal.
Virginal, winning and fair was the shape: and he ordered Athene
Skilful devices to teach her, the beautiful works of the weaver.
Then did he bid Aphrodite the golden endow her with beauty,
Eager desire and passion that wasteth the bodies of mortals.
Hermes, guider of men, the destroyer of Argus, he ordered,
Lastly, a shameless mind to bestow and a treacherous nature.
So did he speak. They obeyed Lord Zeus, who is offspring of
    Kronos.
Straightway, out of the earth, the renowned artificer fashioned
One like a shame-faced maid, at the will of the ruler of Heaven.
Girdle and ornaments added the bright-eyed goddess Athene.
Over her body the Graces divine and noble Persuasion
Hung their golden chains; and the Hours with beautiful tresses
Wove her garlands of flowers that bloom in the season of
    Springtime.
All her adornments Pallas Athene fitted upon her.
Into her bosom, Hermes the guide, the destroyer of Argus,
Falsehood, treacherous thoughts and a thievish nature imparted:
Such was the bidding of Zeus who heavily thunders; and lastly,
Hermes, herald of gods, endowed her with speech, and the
    woman
Named Pandora, because all the gods who dwell in Olympos
Gave her presents, to make her a fatal bane unto mortals.
When now Zeus had finished this snare so deadly and certain,
Famous Argus slayer, the herald of gods, he commanded,
Leading her thence, as a gift to bestow her upon Epimetheus.
He, then, failed to remember Prometheus had bidden him never
Gifts to accept from Olympian Zeus, but still to return them
Straightway, lest some evil befall thereby unto mortals.
So he received her — and then, when the evil befell, he
    remembered.
Till that time, upon earth were dwelling the races of mortals,
Free and secure from trouble and free from wearisome labour;
Safe from painful diseases that bring mankind to destruction
Since full swiftly in misery age unto mortals approacheth.

Now with her hands, Pandora the great lid raised from the vessel,
Letting them loose: and grievous the evil for men she provided.
Hope yet lingered, alone, in the dwelling securely imprisoned,
Since she under the edge of the lid had tarried and flew not
Forth: too soon Pandora had fastened the lid of the vessel.
Such was the will of Zeus, cloud-gatherer, lord of the aegis.
Numberless evils beside to the haunts of men had departed,
Full is the earth of ills, and full no less are the waters.
Freely diseases among mankind, by day and in darkness
Hither and thither may pass and bring much woe upon mortals:
Voiceless, since of speech high-counselling Zeus has bereft them.

4. Eve and the Snake in the Garden[13]

The serpent was more crafty than any wild creature that the Lord
God had made. He said to the woman, "Is it true that God has
forbidden you to eat from any tree in the garden?" The woman
answered the serpent, "We may eat the fruit of any tree in the
garden, except for the tree in the middle of the garden; God has
forbidden us either to eat or to touch the fruit of that; if we do,
we shall die." The serpent said, "Of course you will not die. God
knows that as soon as you eat it, your eyes will be opened and
you will be like gods knowing both good and evil." When the
woman saw that the fruit of the tree was good to eat, and that it
was pleasing to the eye and tempting to contemplate, she took
some and ate it. She also gave her husband some and he ate it.
Then the eyes of both of them were opened and they discovered
that they were naked; so they stitched fig-leaves together and
made themselves loincloths.

The man and his wife heard the sound of the Lord God
walking in the garden at the time of the evening breeze and hid
from the Lord God among the trees of the garden. But the Lord
God called to the man and said to him, "Where are you?" He
replied, "I heard the sound as you were walking in the garden,
and I was afraid because I was naked, and I hid myself." God
answered, "Who told you that you were naked? Have you eaten
from the tree which I forbade you?" The man said, "The woman
you gave me for a companion, she gave me fruit from the tree
and I ate it." Then the Lord God said to the woman, "What is
this that you have done?" The woman said, "The serpent tricked
me, and I ate." Then the Lord God said to the serpent:

"Because you have done this you are accursed
more than all cattle and all wild creatures.
On your belly you shall crawl, and dust you shall eat
all the days of your life.
I will put enmity between you and the woman,
between your brood and hers.
They shall strike at your head,
and you shall strike at their heel."

To the woman he said:

"I will increase your labour and your groaning,
and in labour you shall bear children.
You shall be eager for your husband,
and he shall be your master."

And to the man he said:

"Because you have listened to your wife
and have eaten from the tree which I forbade you,
accursed shall be the ground on your account.
With labour you shall win your food from it
all the days of your life.
It will grow thorns and thistles for you,
none but wild plants for you to eat.
You shall gain your bread by the sweat of your brow
until you return to the ground;
for from it you were taken.
Dust you are, to dust you shall return."

The man called his wife Eve because she was the mother of all
who live. The Lord God made tunics of skins for Adam and his
wife and clothed them. He said, "The man has become like one of
us, knowing good and evil; what if he now reaches out his hand
and takes fruit from the tree of life also, eats it and lives for
ever?" So the Lord God drove him out of the garden of Eden to
till the ground from which he had been taken. He cast him out,
and to the east of the garden of Eden he stationed the cherubim
and a sword whirling and flashing to guard the way to the tree of
life.

5. Liberating Knowledge and the Jealousy of the Rulers[14]

Now all these (events) came to pass by the will of the Father of
the Entirety. Afterwards, the Spirit saw the soul-endowed Man
upon the ground. And the Spirit came forth from the Adamantine
Land; it descended and came to dwell within him, and that Man
became a living soul.

It called his name Adam since he was found moving upon the
ground. A voice came forth from Incorruptibility for the assistance
of Adam; and the Rulers gathered together all the animals of the
earth and all the birds of heaven and brought them in to Adam to
see what Adam would call them, that he might give a name to
each of the birds and all the beasts.

They took Adam [and] put him in the Garden, that he might
cultivate [it] and keep watch over it. And the Rulers issued a
command to him, saying, "From [every] tree in the Garden shall
you eat; yet — [from] the tree of recognizing good and evil do not
eat, nor [touch] it; for the day you (pl.) eat [from] it, with death
you (pl.) are going to die."

They [. . .] this. They do not understand what [they have
said] to him; rather, by the Father's will, they said this in such a
way that he might (in fact) eat, and that Adam might [not] regard
them as would a man of an exclusively material nature.

The Rulers took counsel with one another and said, "Come,
let us cause a deep sleep to fall upon Adam." And he slept. —
Now the deep sleep that they "caused to fall upon him, and he
slept" is Ignorance. — They opened his side like a living Woman.
And then they built up his side with some flesh in place of her,
and Adam came to be endowed only with soul.

And the spirit-endowed Woman came to him and spoke with
him, saying, "Arise, Adam." And when he saw her, he said, "It
is you who have given me life; you will be called 'Mother of the
Living.' — For it is she who is my mother. It is she who is the
Physician, and the Woman, and She Who Has Given Birth."

Then the Authorities came up to their Adam. And when they
saw his female counterpart speaking with him, they became
agitated with great agitation; and they became enamored of her.
They said to one another, "Come, let us sow our seed in her,"
and they pursued her. And she laughed at them for their
witlessness and their blindness; and in their clutches, she became
a tree, and left before them her shadowy reflection resembling

herself; and they defiled [it] foully. — And they defiled the form that she had stamped in her likeness, so that by the form they had modelled, together with [their] (own) image, they made themselves liable to condemnation.

Then the Female Spiritual Principle came [in] the Snake, the Instructor; and it taught [them], saying, "What did he [say to] you (pl.)? Was it, 'From every tree in the Garden shall you (sing.) eat; yet — from [the tree] of recognizing evil and good do not eat'?"

The carnal Woman said, "Not only did he say 'Do not eat,' but even 'Do not touch it; for the day you (pl.) eat from it, with death you (pl.) are going to die.' "

And the Snake, the Instructor, said, "With death you (pl.) shall not die; for it was out of jealousy that he said this to you (pl.). Rather your (pl.) eyes shall open and you (pl.) shall come to be like gods, recognizing evil and good." And the Female Instructing Principle was taken away from the Snake, and she left it behind merely a thing of the earth.

And the carnal Woman took from the tree and ate; and she gave to her husband as well as herself; and these beings that possessed only a soul, ate. And their imperfection became apparent in their lack of Acquaintance; and they recognized that they were naked of the Spiritual Element, and took fig leaves and bound them upon their loins.

Then the chief Ruler came; and he said, "Adam! Where are you?" — for he did not understand what had happened.

And Adam said, "I heard your voice and was afraid because I was naked; and I hid."

The Ruler said, "Why did you (sing.) hide, unless it is because you (sing.) have eaten from the tree from which alone I commanded you (sing.) not to eat? And you (sing.) have eaten!"

Adam said, "The Woman that you gave me, [she gave] to me and I ate." And the arrogant Ruler cursed the Woman.

The Woman said, "It was the Snake that led me astray and I ate." [They turned] to the Snake and cursed its shadowy reflection, [. . .] powerless, not comprehending [that] it was a form they themselves had modelled. From that day, the Snake came to be under the curse of the Authorities; until the All-powerful Man was to come, that curse fell upon the Snake.

They turned to their Adam and took him and expelled him from the Garden along with his wife; for they have no blessing, since they too are beneath the curse.

Moreover they threw Mankind into great distraction and into a life of toil, so that their Mankind might be occupied by worldly affairs, and might not have the opportunity of being devoted to the Holy Spirit.

6. Adam Exonerated: A Patriarchalizing Commentary[15]

It is my desire, therefore, that everywhere prayers be said by the men of the congregation, who shall lift up their hands with a pure intention, excluding angry or quarrelsome thoughts. Women again must dress in becoming manner, modestly and soberly, not with elaborate hair-styles, not decked out with gold or pearls, or expensive clothes, but with good deeds, as befits women who claim to be religious. A woman must be a learner, listening quietly and with due submission. I do not permit a woman to be a teacher, nor must woman domineer over man; she should be quiet. For Adam was created first, and Eve afterwards; and it was not Adam who was deceived; it was the woman who, yielding to deception, fell into sin. Yet she will be saved through motherhood — if only women continue in faith, love, and holiness, with a sober mind.

7. Eve Exonerated: A Feminist Commentary[16]

Note the significant fact that we always hear of the "fall of man," not the fall of woman, showing that the consensus of human thought has been more unerring than masculine interpretation. Reading this narrative carefully, it is amazing that any set of men ever claimed that the dogma of the inferiority of woman is here set forth. The conduct of Eve from the beginning to the end is so superior to that of Adam. The command not to eat of the fruit of the tree of Knowledge was given to the man alone before woman was formed. Genesis ii, 17. Therefore the injunction was not brought to Eve with the impressive solemnity of a Divine Voice, but whispered to her by her husband and equal. It was a serpent supernaturally endowed, a seraphim as Scott and other commentators have claimed, who talked with Eve, and whose words might reasonably seem superior to the second-hand story of her companion — nor does the woman yield at once. She quotes the command not to eat of the fruit to which the serpent replies

"Dying ye shall not die," v. 4, literal translation. In other words telling her that if the mortal body does perish, the immortal part shall live forever, and offering as the reward of her act the attainment of Knowledge.

Then the woman fearless of death if she can gain wisdom takes of the fruit; and all this time Adam standing beside her interposes no word of objection. "Her husband with her" are the words of v. 6. Had he been the representative of the divinely appointed head in married life, he assuredly would have taken upon himself the burden of the discussion with the serpent, but no, he is silent in this crisis of their fate. Having had the command from God himself he interposes no word of warning or remonstrance, but takes the fruit from the hand of his wife without a protest. It takes six verses to describe the "fall" of woman, the fall of man is contemptuously dismissed in a line and a half.

The subsequent conduct of Adam was to the last degree dastardly. When the awful time of reckoning comes, and the Jehovah God appears to demand why his command has been disobeyed, Adam endeavors to shield himself behind the gentle being he has declared to be so dear. "The woman thou gavest to be with me, she gave me and I did eat," he whines — trying to shield himself at his wife's expense! Again we are amazed that upon such a story men have built up a theory of their superiority!

Then follows what has been called the curse. Is it not rather a prediction? First is the future fate of the serpent described, the enmity of the whole human race — "it shall lie in wait for thee as to the head" (v. 15, literal translation). Next the subjection of the woman is foretold, thy husband "shall rule over thee," v. 16. Lastly the long struggle of man with the forces of nature is portrayed. "In the sweat of thy face thou shalt eat food until thy turning back to the earth" (v. 19, literal translation). With the evolution of humanity an ever increasing number of men have ceased to toil for their bread with their hands, and with the introduction of improved machinery, and the uplifting of the race there will come a time when there shall be no severities of labor, and when women shall be freed from all oppressions.

"And Adam called his wife's name Life for she was the mother of all living" (v. 20, literal translation).

It is a pity that all versions of the Bible do not give this word instead of the Hebrew Eve. She was Life, the eternal mother, the first representative of the more valuable and important half of the human race.

8. Mother-Right and Patricide[17]

I put forward these assertions as much as a quarter of a century
ago in my *Totem and Taboo* (1912-13) and I need only repeat them
here. My construction starts out from a statement of Darwin's . . .
and takes in a hypothesis of Atkinson's. . . . It asserts that in
primaeval times primitive man lived in small hordes, each under
the domination of a powerful male. No date can be assigned to
this, nor has it been synchronized with the geological epochs
known to us: it is probable that these human creatures had not
advanced far in the development of speech. An essential part of
the construction is the hypothesis that the events I am about to
describe occurred to all primitive men — that is, to all our
ancestors. The story is told in an enormously condensed form, as
though it had happened on a single occasion, while in fact it
covered thousands of years and was repeated countless times
during that long period. The strong male was lord and father of
the entire horde and unrestricted in his power, which he exercised
with violence. All the females were his property — wives and
daughters of his own horde and some, perhaps, robbed from
other hordes. The lot of his sons was a hard one: if they roused
their father's jealousy they were killed or castrated or driven out.
Their only resource was to collect together in small communities,
to get themselves wives by robbery, and, when one or other of
them could succeed in it, to raise themselves into a position
similar to their father's in the primal horde. For natural reasons,
youngest sons occupied an exceptional position. They were
protected by their mother's love, and were able to take advantage
of their father's increasing age and succeed him on his death. We
seem to detect echoes in legends and fairy tales both of the
expulsion of elder sons and of the favouring of youngest sons.

The first decisive step towards a change in this sort of
"social" organization seems to have been that the expelled
brothers, living in a community, united to overpower their father
and, as was the custom in those days, devoured him raw. There
is no need to balk at this cannibalism; it continued far into later
times. The essential point, however, is that we attribute the same
emotional attitudes to these primitive men that we are able to
establish by analytic investigation in the primitives of the present
day — in our children. We suppose, that is, that they not only
hated and feared their father but also honored him as a model,
and that each of them wished to take his place in reality. We can,

if so, understand the cannibalistic act as an attempt to ensure identification with him by incorporating a piece of him.

It must be supposed that after the parricide a considerable time elapsed during which the brothers disputed with one another for their father's heritage, which each of them wanted for himself alone. A realization of the dangers and uselessness of these struggles, a recollection of the act of liberation which they had accomplished together, and the emotional ties with one another which had arisen during the period of their expulsion, led at last to an agreement among them, a sort of social contract. The first form of a social organization came about with a *renunciation of instinct*, a recognition of mutual *obligations*, the introduction of definite *institutions*, pronounced inviolable (holy) — that is to say, the beginnings of morality and justice. Each individual renounced his ideal of acquiring his father's position for himself and of possessing his mother and sisters. Thus the *taboo on incest* and the injunction to *exogamy* came about. A fair amount of the absolute power liberated by the removal of the father passed over to the women; there came a period of *matriarchy*. Recollection of their father persisted at this period of the "fraternal alliance." A powerful animal — at first, perhaps, always one that was feared as well — was chosen as a substitute for the father. A choice of this kind may seem strange, but the gulf which men established later between themselves and animals did not exist for primitive peoples; nor does it exist for our children, whose animal phobias we have been able to understand as fear of their father. In relation to the totem animal the original dichotomy in the emotional relation to the father (ambivalence) was wholly retained. On the one hand the totem was regarded as the clan's blood ancestor and protective spirit, who must be worshipped and protected, and on the other hand a festival was appointed at which the same fate was prepared for him that the primal father had met with. He was killed and devoured by all the tribesmen in common. (The totem meal, according to Robertson Smith. . . .) This great festival was in fact a triumphant celebration of the combined sons' victory over their father.

9. *The Rise of Private Property and the Demise of Mother-Right*[18]

Thus, as wealth increased, it, on the one hand, gave the man a more important status in the family than the woman, and, on the other hand, created a stimulus to utilize this strengthened position in order to overthrow the traditional order of inheritance in favour of his children. But this was impossible as long as descent according to mother right prevailed. This had, therefore, to be overthrown, and it was overthrown; and it was not so difficult to do this as it appears to us now. For this revolution — one of the most decisive ever experienced by mankind — need not have disturbed one single living member of a gens. All the members could remain what they were previously. The simple decision sufficed that in future the descendants of the male members should remain in the gens, but that those of the females were to be excluded from the gens and transferred to that of their father. The reckoning of descent through the female line and the right of inheritance through the mother were hereby overthrown and male lineage and right of inheritance from the father instituted. As to how and when this revolution was effected among the civilized peoples we know nothing. It falls entirely within prehistoric times. That it *was* actually effected is more than proved by the abundant traces of mother right which have been collected.

The overthrow of mother right was the *world historic defeat of the female sex*. The man seized the reins in the house also, the woman was degraded, enthralled, the slave of the man's lust, a mere instrument for breeding children. This lowered position of women, especially manifest among the Greeks of the Heroic and still more of the Classical Age, has become gradually embellished and dissembled and, in part, clothed in a milder form, but by no means abolished.

This was the origin of monogamy, as far as we can trace it among the most civilized and highly developed people of antiquity. It was not in any way the fruit of individual sex love, with which it had absolutely nothing in common, for the marriages remained marriages of convenience, as before. It was the first form of the family based not on natural but on economic conditions, namely, on the victory of private property over original, naturally developed, common ownership. The rule of the man in the family, the procreation of children who could only be his, destined to be the heirs of his wealth — these alone were frankly avowed by the Greeks as the exclusive aims of monogamy. For the rest, it was a burden, a duty to the gods, to the state and to their ancestors, which just had to be fulfilled. In Athens the law made not only marriage compulsory, but also the fulfilment by the man of a minimum of the so-called conjugal duties.

Thus, monogamy does not by any means make its appearance in history as the reconciliation of man and woman, still less as the highest form of such a reconciliation. On the contrary, it appears as the subjection of one sex by the other, as the proclamation of a conflict between the sexes entirely unknown hitherto in prehistoric times. In an old unpublished manuscript, the work of Marx and myself in 1846, I find the following: "The first division of labour is that between man and woman for child breeding." And today I can add: The first class antagonism which appears in history coincides with the development of the antagonism between man and woman in monogamous marriage, and the first class oppression with that of the female sex by the male. Monogamy was a great historical advance, but at the same time it inaugurated, along with slavery and private wealth, that epoch, lasting until today, in which every advance is likewise a relative regression, in which the well-being and development of the one group are attained by the misery and repression of the other. It is the cellular form of civilized society, in which we can already study the nature of the antagonisms and contradictions which develop fully in the latter.

The Crucified Woman: is she only a victim, or can women bring forth redemption from their sufferings on the cross of patriarchy?

Reproduction courtesy of the artist, Almuth Lutkenhaus

6

Redeemer/Redemptrix: Male and Female Saviors

DOCUMENTS

1. *Anath, Savior of Baal, Restores the World*
2. *The Warrior Messiah of Israel*
3. *The Warrior Christ of the Last Judgment*
4. *Kenosis Christology: Christ as Servant*
5. *Logos Christology: Christ as Cosmic Lord*
6. *The Androgynous Christ and Redeemed Humanity of Gnosticism*
7. *Christ as Mother: The Vision of a Woman Mystic*
8. *Jesus and Mary as Co-Redeemers in Catholic Piety*
9. *Woman Worship in Nineteenth-Century Romanticism*
10. *The Female Messiah in Shaker Theology*
11. *I Scream for Johanna, My Eternal Mother*
12. *Unless a WomanChrist Comes, We Will All Die*

Christology is that symbol of Christian theology that should manifest the face of God/ess as liberator. Christology should be filled with our best visions of the good potential of humans and the world concretely revealed. The Savior figure brings together the human and the divine, disclosing, at one and the same time, the gracious, redeeming face of God/ess and our authentic potential.

Precisely because it is the central symbol in Christianity, it is also the symbol most distorted by patriarchy. All efforts to marginalize women in the Church and Christian society, to deprive them of voice, leadership, and authority, take the form of proclaiming that Christ was male and so only the male can "image" Christ. Woman, while the passive object of his redeeming work, can never actively represent him as mediator of God's word and deed. If feminist theology and spirituality decide that Christianity is irredeemable for women, its primary reason is likely to be this insurmountable block of a male Christ who fails to represent women.

This chapter explores the range of redeemer and redemptrix symbols in our tradition. What, if anything, is the theological necessity of the maleness of the savior? The chapter open with a Canaanite myth of the redemption of Baal and the restoration of the world by the Goddess Anath. The chapter starts here to illustrate the ancient background of the Christ-myth. Christology is compounded of two theological symbols: the dying and rising God who symbolizes the conquest of sin and death and manifest Wisdom of God through whom the world is created, guided, and restored and who is the presence of God/ess in all revelatory disclosures.

Significantly, both these ideas existed first in female form. As we saw in chapter II, the female Wisdom is the earlier version of this concept of God's revelatory presence. The Baal-Anath story represents one version of that key story of the ancient Near East whereby a dying and rising God, who represented the King as well as the rain and vegetation, is resurrected by the power of the Goddess who represents the power to restore and redeem life.

In the section of the poem on Anath and Baal taken from a fourteenth-century B.C. clay tablet from Ras Shamra (the poems themselves are much older), we feel immediately the enormous power and authority of Anath. She commands the center of the stage with her swift, decisive actions on behalf of Baal and in confrontation with any power, even that of the High El, who stands in the way of her Beloved. She fights not for herself but for her brother-lover whose vitality and status she works constantly to vindicate and restore. The section of the text excerpted here opens with a rumor of a threat to Baal. Anath rushes to him, claiming their love relationship with each other. Then she rises to the court of El, the old King God, to demand a proper temple for Baal where his place in the pantheon of the Gods will be given its due. Forcing herself into the presence of El, she overwhelms him with angry, impetuous threats to pull his gray hair and beard until the blood flows. One can almost hear the frightened, reedy voice of the old God as he capitulates to these demands of his warrior daughter.

In the second section of the text, we see the death of Baal, overwhelmed by the forces of drought and death. Again Anath goes into swift action, traveling throughout the world until she finds the place where his body lies. She buries him with due rites of mourning but then seizes his foe, Mot (death) and slays him. Her defeat of Mot takes the form of the winnowing and harvesting of the wheat. From her sowing of the new wheat in the ground, Baal rises. With a cry of exaltation, we rejoice at the close of the drama: the Lord has arisen, is seated again on the throne. He reigns! Alleluia!

When we turn to Hebrew religion, which established itself in rivalry to this Canaanite world, we find that the warrior Divine Maiden has disappeared. In Her place is the male Warrior God of Israel and His son, the Anointed One (Messiah), the King of Israel. Kingship was contrary to the old desert traditions of Israel and was taken over from the Canaanite world of city-states only under protest. The Davidic kings, who established themselves in the old Jebusite city of Jerusalem, also took over elements of the Canaanite cult of the savior king who is annually reenthroned after a symbolic defeat of the powers of death. Each year the Davidic king rode triumphant into the city on a white ass, amid the waving palm fronds and songs of rejoicing of the people, to symbolize the defeat of Israel's enemies and the reestablishment of the reign of God through his Messiah.

Eventually Israel's Davidic kings were overthrown by the powerful empires of the Near East, and so the memory of the Davidic King was transformed into the hope for the restoration of the Davidic monarchy, symbol of the time of God's favor on Israel. In the passage from the prophet Zechariah, we see a description of the triumphant advent of this restored Messiah who rides into Jerusalem on the ceremonial white mount after having defeated Israel's enemies. In the imagination of the prophet, Israel, the people conquered by mighty empires, is established as the overlord of the world (the Middle East). Its former enemy, Egypt, is reduced to the status of a client state on which God will wreak vengeance in the form of drought if it does not come up to Jerusalem each year at the time of the Feast of Booths (the Harvest festival) to bring its tribute. This passage is important not only in summarizing some of the dreams of power and vengeance of Israelite messianism but also because the Gospels portray Jesus as acting out this drama of the restored Davidic king in his triumphant entrance into Jerusalem (Matt. 21:5).

However, these dreams of victory and vengeance did not materialize. Instead Israel was conquered by ever-larger empires: Persian, Hellenistic, and Roman. Its hopes for ultimate vindication became projected onto a cosmic screen in which all history was divided between the time of the reign of evil, when God's Elect were suppressed and suffered, and a final Day of Judgment when the Messiah, as angelic Warrior, would charge out of the heavens to defeat the power of Satan and his demonic hosts. This vision of apocalyptic vengeance and victory is continued in early Christianity. In the passage from the Book of Revelation, we see the returning Christ portrayed as this apocalyptic Messiah of the Last Judgment who binds Satan and his demons and establishes the saints in glory to reign on earth for a thousand years.

Although these visions of the Davidic Messiah, as well as the Apocalyptic Messiah, came to be attached to the figure of Jesus, the first-century prophet from Nazareth, it would seem that his own vision was far from these ways of thinking. Although he probably shared the perspective of first-century messianic preachers that the world was in its last days and the moment of God's decisive redemption of Israel was at hand, he seems to have tried to transform this announcement of redemption. Contrary to the parties of Torah righteousness and zealous nationalism, he announced that God's favor had come upon those who had no chance in the present system of social status and religious observance — the poor, the unclean, and the unlearned, the despised underclasses of Palestinian society, including women among these underclasses.

The way of redemption was the way of love and service to others, especially to the humiliated of society. Christ would not come as a king, warrior, and judge but as one who emulates this way of suffering service. Those who would be his followers must likewise become servants of all. By servanthood Jesus did not mean simply an acceptance of the servile status of the humble in present society. Such servanthood would change nothing. Rather he used the term *servant* in the prophetic sense of a relationship to God that freed one from servitude to all human masters. Jesus used this term to overcome the dualism between oppression and a vengeful rebellion that establishes new domination. He envisioned the New Age as a time when this pattern of power over others would be overcome by a new pattern of relationship in which those who are most able would become servants of all.

Early Christianity was imbued with a new sense of lordship and servanthood. It was now Christ, even God, who had emptied himself (*kenosis*) and come into the world not as a powerful king who conquered the present rulers but as a servant who suffered on behalf of the poor and was arrested and executed by the mighty ones of religion and state. This Crucified One, however, had been exalted by God and was the true lord of the universe. This lordship was set over against the lordship of the powerful empires of society. To acknowledge the lordship of Christ, the resurrected Crucified, enabled those presently suffering under unjust rule to become inwardly emancipated from it. Inwardly they were already freed from bondage to unjust Powers. By transferring their allegiance to Christ, they were no longer under the power of worldly masters. They looked forward to a time soon to come when Christ would return publicly as Lord of God's world and the might of the present rulers would be destroyed.

This kenosis Christology, represented here in texts from Matthew and Paul's letter to the Philippians, however, was soon integrated into a philosophical cosmology. In this philosophical cosmology Christ is not only the new liberating being over against existing world powers. He is also the original Logos or Word of God, an idea we have seen in an earlier female symbolism as the Sophia, or Wisdom. This Logos-Wisdom of God is the power through which the world is created, guided, and ruled. This linking of the messianic idea of new being with the original foundations of creation was necessary to prevent Christian theology from splitting into a dualism between redemption and creation, the dualistic pattern into which gnosticism had fallen. Cosmological Christology saved mainstream Christianity from this dualism between creation and redemption. By saying that the liberating Messiah is also the Logos through which the world was created, Christianity could say that our new liberated being does not contradict our created being but rather vindicates and fulfills its true nature and potential.

However, this uniting of creation and redemption carried a danger as well. There were two ways of looking at this relationship. If *both* the original and the true being of things are set over against the oppressive powers of the world, then Christ continues to be a symbol of our authentic selves over against systems of injustice. Resistance to injustice has an even firmer foundation. But if the Logos is seen as the foundation of the powers of the world, then Christology becomes integrated back into a world view that sacralizes the existing systems of sexism, slavery, and imperialism and sees these as the "order of creation."

Christianity, in the second and even third centuries, as a religion in conflict with the Roman state, held primarily to the first view. But as it became integrated into Roman society and was finally adopted by Constantine as the state religion, it capitulated to the second view. The Lordship of Christ ceased to liberate women, slaves, and conquered people from their lords and masters. Instead these lords and masters saw themselves as more "like" Christ than their subjects and deriving their lordship from the Lordship of Christ.

In early Christian martyr texts the martyr who might be a woman slave can be hailed as "another Christ." Such Christianity could encounter Christ in "our sister."[1] But imperial Christianity could no longer encounter Christ in slaves or women. Thomas Aquinas, the leading theologian of the Middle Ages, said that neither women nor slaves can be priests because, as servile people, they cannot "image" lordship.

Not all Christianity capitulated to this masculinist imperial Christology, however. Mystical and millennialist groups continued to cultivate a Christ that freed one from the oppressive power of the world. However, the temptation of these groups was also to confuse the oppressive powers of the world with creation and hence to fall into a dualism in which redeemed being was set over against creation. Gnosticism is the classic early expression of this dualism of spirit and flesh. The virtue of gnosticism is that it retained the early Christian sense of a redemption set over against oppressive hierarchies. It cultivated a spiritual egalitarianism among the redeemed.

This meant that it took seriously the belief that redemption in Christ made women and men equal. Women had the same spiritual authority as men and could share the same ministries for most gnostic groups.[2] But it confused this liberated equality with the dissolution of bodily existence. So the price of overcoming sexism was the renunciation of sexuality. Christ represents a spiritual androgyny that dissolves gender differences. The separation of woman from man (Eve from Adam) in the original creation is seen as the fall into sin. In Christ the redeemed become "neither male nor female." They become spiritually androgynous by renouncing sexuality and reproduction. The Christ that makes woman equal with the male is also said to transform the redeemed woman into a "spiritual male" by destroying "the works of the female." This androcentric concept of spiritual androgyny, with its ambivalent message for women, is illustrated in the excerpts from gnostic gospels included in this chapter.

Medieval Christian mysticism also cultivated the spiritual androgyny of God, Christ, and the redeemed person. Although the gnostic dualism of creation and redemption was rejected in Christian cosmology, it continued to dominate Christian spirituality, which remained fiercely body-rejecting. Yet this rejection of sexuality could also allow medieval mystics, male or female, to see themselves as uniting maleness and femaleness on a spiritual level. The male mystic could imagine himself a "bride" ravished by the male Spirit of God, while the female mystic could cultivate a view of God and Christ as both mother and father, exercising both authority and nurture.[3] This perspective is particularly illustrated in the passages from the fourteenth-century English mystic Julian of Norwich.

However, late-medieval piety increasingly diverted its cultivation of the "feminine" into a separate devotion of the Blessed Virgin Mary.

Devotion to Mary allowed the male celibate to sublimate a sweet affection in relation to a female figure who was subordinate to the male divine power. Mary became the heavenly mediator between heavenly male authorities and the saved sinner. This Marian theology suggested a split between divine justice, exercised sternly by God the Father and Christ, and a merciful reprieve exercised somewhat capriciously by Mary.[4] If one devoted oneself to Mary as "Lady," she would intervene in the heavenly court and save one from divine justice. This kind of duality of Christ and Mary is illustrated here by a passage from the eighteenth-century promoter of Marian devotion Alphonsus Liguori.

This veneration of the divine Woman did not disappear in European culture with the rejection of feudalism and Catholicism. In post-revolutionary nineteenth-century France, in thinkers who prided themselves as representing the secular spirit emancipated from priestly superstition, we find a secular restatement of woman worship. This is now seen as the enshrinement of the moral principle of altruism in society. It is the bourgeois wife who must receive this devotion in the Home, presumably enthroned on a settee in her parlor, from a husband who will cherish her as his "better half" and the representation of perfected humanity. But the price the bourgeois woman was to pay for this veneration was a confinement to the shrinking sphere of the middle-class household. Even there her capacities for sexual pleasure and work were denied to make her the fantasized "love object" of a male bourgeois culture busy with conquering the world through colonial expansion and industrialism. The French positivist sociologist Auguste Comte, writing in 1848, the same time Marx wrote his *Communist Manifesto*, illustrates this bourgeois culture, with its schizophrenic division between a public amoral masculinity and a private worship of sublimated feminine "virtue."

Nineteenth-century thought grappled with the feeling that one world of society and thought was coming to an end and a new one was dawning whose nature was unclear. One expression of this liminal sensitivity was the appearance of mystical, utopian sects whose roots lay in late-medieval and Reformation radical sectarianism. One such group, as we saw in chapter II, was the Shakers, or United Believers in Christ's Second Appearing. In the passage from the Shaker Bible excerpted here we have the defense of the Shaker belief in Mother Ann Lee as the female Christ. For the Shakers, the female Christ is the theological expression of the androgyny of God and of God's image, humanity, which must be expressed in a redeemer from both the male and the female orders of humanity. The female as the last of God's works is the crowning glory of creation. So the appearance of the female Christ is necessary to complete and perfect the redemptive revelation of God who is both Father and Mother.

Where does all this leave us today? The contemporary Christian woman is still taught to believe in a male Christ as the sole and unique expression of redeeming grace. This maleness of Christ still distances the woman from full representation in the new humanity. The male Christ, however, has taken on, from bourgeois Christianity, feminine attributes aplenty. He is all tenderness and sweetness. Seldom is heard a judgmental word about anyone, especially about the dominant social systems. Thus the male Christ with a "feminine" personality does not liberate women but reinforces the identification of femininity with passivity. The woman today, increasingly distraught both by her sense of her personal repression and by the growing danger of world destruction through male, amoral technology, longs for an unrevealed redemptrix, a Christ who can affirm her own personhood as woman and can dismantle the systems of private repression and public violence. This longing for the coming of a redeeming female is expressed in two poems written by Nancy Ore, a seminarian studying at Garrett-Evangelical Theological Seminary in 1983-1984.

Reflection

This survey of savior stories from Anath to contemporary feminist longings raises basic questions about the function of the Christ-myth. Do we need a savior? Is the Christ simply an objectification of our own ideal self, which we project on the heavens and then "encounter" as something beyond our own capacities that we need to receive from beyond? Would this process work better or not work at all if we recognized that what we were about was our own self-redemption rather than a "work" of redemption done outside our own capacities?

If the redeemer manifests for us the gracious, liberating face of God/ess and our own true human potential, won't an exclusively male Christ ever alienate women from claiming their humanity as women? Is it enough to claim that Jesus represents "generic humanity" or even was an antipatriarchal male, if he alone remains the exclusive face of the redeeming God and of our authentic humanity?

Can Christology remain encapsulated in a single, "once-for-all" figure of the past who "completed" the work of salvation, even though we and our history remain obviously unredeemed? Must not the Christ-image be ever projected on the new horizon of history that appears before us, leading us on to our yet unrealized potential? As our perception of our incompleteness changes with new sensitivities to racism, sexism, and European chauvinism, must not the image of Christ take ever new forms: as woman, as Black and Brown woman, as impoverished and despised woman of those peoples who are the underside of Christian imperialism?

In what ways do women need such an appearance of a Woman-Christ? Do men also need a WomanChrist, and how would their need for Her be different or similar to that of women today? Do we all today, in one way or another, really "know that we will all die unless a WomanChrist pops up from somewhere (like a rabbit out of a hat)" to break apart the weapons of global destruction and spill their seeds on the ground to renew the earth?

1. Anath, Savior of Baal, Restores the World[5]

What enemy's ris[en] 'gainst Baal,
    What foe 'gainst the Rider of Clouds?
Crushed I not El's Belov'd Yamm?
    Destroyed I not El's Flood Rabbim?
    Did I not, pray, muzzle the Dragon?
I did crush the crooked serpent,
    Shalyat [šlyt] the seven-headed.
I did crush El's Belov'd Ar[. . . ?],
    Cut off El's *Bullock* 'Atak.
I did crush *the Godly Bitch Hashat,*
    Destroy the house of El-Dhubub,
    Who fought thee (and) seized the gold;
Who drave Baal from the Heights of Zaphon,
    Sans frontlet, his ear pierced through;
Chas'd him from his throne of kingship,
    From the dais, the seat of his dominion.
What enemy's risen 'gainst Baal,
    What foe 'gainst the Rider of Clouds?" —
[A]nswer the lads twain make:
"No enemy's risen 'gainst Baal,
    No foe 'gainst the Rider of Clouds!
Message of Puissant Baal,
    Word of the Powerful Hero:
Take war away from the earth,
    Banish (all) strife from the soil,"
[An]swers the Maiden [An]ath,
    Replies [Yabamat] Liimmim:

"I'll *take* war *away* [from the earth,
    Banish] (all) *strife* from the soil,
Pour [peace] into earth's very bowels,
    Mu[ch amity into] earth's bos[om].
Let Baal [. . .] . . . ,
    Let him . . . [. . .] . . .
I'll *take* war *away* from the earth, etc.
Yet another word will I say:
Go, go, attendants divine.
    Ye *are slow* and I *am swift.*
There, she is off on her way
    To Baal of the Summit of Zaphon.
    His sister's approach Baal sees,
    The advance of his own father's-daughter.
He dismisses (his) wives from her presence.
He places an ox before her,
    A fatted one in front of her.
She draws some water and bathes,
    Sky-dew, fatness of earth;
Dew that the heavens do [sh]ed,
    Spray that is shed by the stars.
She rubs herself in with *ambergris*
    From a sperm-whale
No house hath Baal like the gods',
    Nor court like Asherah's children's.
Quoth [the Maiden Anath]:
"He'll heed me, will Bull E[l my father],
    He'll heed me for his own good!
[For I'll] fell him like a lamb to the ground,
    [Make] his gray hair [flow with] blood,
    The gray hair of his beard [with gore];
Unless he give
A house unto Baal like the gods',
    [And a cour]t like Asherah's children's." —
[She stamps] her foot [and the ea]rth [trembles].
[There, she is off on her] way.

ANATH DEMANDS BAAL'S REIGN FROM EL

    [Towards El of the S]ources of the Flo[ods,
    In the m]idst of [the Headwaters of the Two De]eps.

She penetrates *El's Field and enters*
    [The pavi]lion of K[i]ng Father [Shunem].
    . . .

Her voice Bull [El] her father [. . .] hea[rs].
[He replies] in the seven ch[am]bers,
    [In]side the eight enclosures:
Quoth the Maiden Anath:
"[. . .] O El,
    . . .

Rejoice not [. . .],
    . . . [. . .]
[. . .] . . .
    My long hand will [*smash*] *thy skull.*
I'll make thy gray hair flow [with blood],
    The gray hair of thy beard with gore." —
El replies in the seven chambers,
    Inside the eight enclosures:
"[I w]eened, daughter mine, thou wa[st gentle],
    And contumely 'mong goddesses was not.
What wouldst thou, O Maiden Anath?" —
And the Maiden Ana[th] re[pl]ied:
"Thy decree, O El, is wise:
    Wisdom with ever-life thy portion.
Thy decree: 'Our king's Puissant Baal,
    Our ruler, second to none.' "

BAAL IS DEFEATED BY MOT AND DIES

We came upon Baal
    Fallen on the ground:
"Puissant Baal is dead,
    The Prince, Lord of Earth, is perished."
Straightway Kindly El Benign
    Descends from the throne,
    Sits on the footstool;
From the footstool,
    And sits on the ground;
Pours dust of mourning on his head,
    Earth of mortification on his pate;
    And puts on *sackcloth and loincloth.*
He *cuts a gash* with a stone,

Incisions with . . .
He *gashes* his cheeks and his chin,
    He *harrows* the *roll* of his *arm*.
He plows his chest like a garden,
    Harrows his back like a plain.
He lifts up his voice and cries:
"Baal's dead! — What becomes of the people?
    Dagon's Son! — What of the masses?
    After Baal I'll descend into earth."
Anath also goes and wanders
    Every mount to the heart of the earth,
    Every hill to the earth's very bo[we]ls.
She comes to the pleasance of Dubr-[land],
    To the beauty of Shihlmemat-field.
She [comes] upon Baal
    Fal[len] on the ground:
    She puts on (*sackcloth*) and loincloth.
Then weeps she her fill of weeping;
    Deep she drinks tears, like wine.
Loudly she calls
    Unto the Gods' Torch Shapsh.
"Lift Puissant Baal, I pray,
    Onto me."
Hearkening, Gods' Torch Shapsh
    Picks up Puissant Baal,
    Sets him on Anath's shoulder.
Up to Zaphon's *Fastness* she brings him,
    Bewails him and buries him too,
    Lays him in the hollows of the earth-ghosts
She slaughters seventy buffaloes.

ANATH DEFEATS MOT AND RESURRECTS BAAL; LIFE RETURNS
TO THE EARTH

She seizes the Godly Mot —
    With sword she doth cleave him.
With fan she doth winnow him —
    With fire she doth burn him.
With hand-mill she grinds him —
    In the field she doth sow him.

Birds eat his *remnants*,
  Consuming his *portions*,
  Flitting from remnant to remnant.
[That Puissant Baal had died],
  That the Prince [Lord of Earth] had perished.
And behold, alive is [Puissant Baal]!
  And behold, existent the Prince, Lo[rd of Earth]!
In a dream, O Kindly El Benign,
  In a vision, Creator of Creatures,
The heavens fat did rain,
  The wadies flow with honey.
So I knew
That alive was Puissant Baal!
  Existent the Prince, Lord of Earth!
The heavens fat did rain,
  The wadies flow with honey!" —
The Kindly One El Benign's glad.
  His feet on the footstool he sets,
  And parts his *jaws* and laughs.
He lifts up his voice and cries:
  "Now will I sit and rest
  And my soul be at ease in my breast.
For alive is Puissant Baal,
  Existent the Prince, Lord of Earth!"

2. The Warrior Messiah of Israel[6]

Rejoice, rejoice, daughter of Zion,
shout aloud, daughter of Jerusalem;
for see, your king is coming to you,
his cause won, his victory gained,
humble and mounted on an ass,
on a foal, the young of a she-ass.
He shall banish chariots from Ephraim
  and war-horses from Jerusalem;
the warrior's bow shall be banished.
He shall speak peaceably to every nation,
and his rule shall extend from sea to sea,
from the River to the ends of the earth.

A day is coming for the Lord to act, and the plunder taken from you shall be shared out while you stand by. I will gather all the peoples to fight against Jerusalem; the city shall be taken, the houses plundered and the women raped. Half the city shall go into exile, but the rest of the nation in the city shall not be wiped out. The Lord will come out and fight against those peoples, as in the days of his prowess on the field of battle. On that day his feet will stand on the Mount of Olives, which is opposite Jerusalem to the east, and the mountain shall be cleft in two by an immense valley running east and west; half the mountain shall move northwards and half southwards. The valley between the hills shall be blocked, for the new valley between them will reach as far as Asal. Blocked it shall be as it was blocked by the earthquake in the time of Uzziah king of Judah, and the Lord my God will appear with all the holy ones.

On that day there shall be neither heat nor cold nor frost. It shall be all one day, whose coming is known only to the Lord, without distinction of day or night, and at evening-time there shall be light.

On that day living water shall issue from Jerusalem, half flowing to the eastern sea and half to the western, in summer and winter alike. Then the Lord shall become king over all the earth; on that day the Lord shall be one Lord and his name the one name. The whole land shall be levelled, flat as the Arabah from Geba to Rimmon southwards; but Jerusalem shall stand high in her place, and shall be full of people from the Benjamin Gate [to the point where the former gate stood,] to the Corner Gate, and from the Tower of Hananel to the king's winevats. Men shall live in Jerusalem, and never again shall a solemn ban be laid upon her; men shall live there in peace. The Lord will strike down all the nations who warred against Jerusalem, and the plague shall be this: their flesh shall rot while they stand on their feet, their eyes shall rot in their sockets, and their tongues shall rot in their mouths.

On that day a great panic, sent by the Lord, shall fall on them. At the very moment when a man would encourage his comrade his hand shall be raised to strike him down. Judah too shall join in the fray in Jerusalem, and the wealth of the surrounding nations will be swept away — gold and silver and apparel in great abundance. And slaughter shall be the fate of horse and mule, camel and ass, the fate of every beast in those armies.

All who survive of the nations which attacked Jerusalem shall come up year by year to worship the King, the Lord of Hosts, and to keep the pilgrim-feast of Tabernacles. If any of the families of the earth do not go up to Jerusalem to worship the King, the Lord of Hosts, no rain shall fall upon them. If any family of Egypt does not go up and enter the city, then the same disaster shall overtake it as that which the Lord will inflict on any nation which does not go up to keep the feast. This shall be the punishment of Egypt and of any nation which does not go up to keep the feast of Tabernacles.

3. The Warrior Christ of the Last Judgment[7]

Then I saw heaven wide open, and there before me a white horse; and its rider's name was Faithful and True, for he is just in judgment and just in war. His eyes flamed like fire, and on his head were many diadems. Written upon him was a name known to none but himself, and he was robed in a garment drenched in blood. He was called the Word of God, and the armies of heaven followed him on white horses, clothed in fine linen, clean and shining. From his mouth there went a sharp sword with which to smite the nations; for he it is who shall rule them with an iron rod, and tread the winepress of the wrath and retribution of God the sovereign Lord. And on his robe and on his thigh there was written the name: "King of kings and Lord of lords."

Then I saw an angel standing in the sun, and he cried aloud to all the birds flying in mid-heaven: "Come and gather for God's great supper, to eat the flesh of kings and commanders and fighting men, the flesh of horses and their riders, the flesh of all men, slave and free, great and small!" Then I saw the beast and the kings of the earth and their armies mustered to do battle with the Rider and his army. The beast was taken prisoner, and so was the false prophet who had worked miracles in its presence and deluded those that had received the mark of the beast and worshipped its image. The two of them were thrown alive into the lake of fire with its sulphurous flames. The rest were killed by the sword which went out of the Rider's mouth; and all the birds gorged themselves on their flesh.

Then I saw an angel coming down from heaven with the key of the abyss and a great chain in his hands. He seized the dragon, that serpent of old, the Devil or Satan, and chained him up for a thousand years; he threw him into the abyss, shutting and sealing it over him, so that he might seduce the nations no more till the thousand years were over. After that he must be let loose for a short while.

4. Kenosis Christology: Christ as Servant[8]

Jesus was journeying towards Jerusalem, and on the way he took the Twelve aside, and said to them, "We are now going to Jerusalem, and the Son of Man will be given up to the chief priests and the doctors of the law; they will condemn him to death and hand him over to the foreign power, to be mocked and flogged and crucified, and on the third day he will be raised to life again."

The mother of Zebedee's sons then came before him, with her sons. She bowed low and begged a favour. "What is it you wish?" asked Jesus. "I want you," she said, "to give orders that in your kingdom my two sons here may sit next to you, one at your right, and the other at your left." Jesus turned to the brothers and said, "You do not understand what you are asking. Can you drink the cup that I am to drink?" "We can," they replied. Then he said to them, "You shall indeed share my cup; but to sit at my right or left is not for me to grant; it is for those to whom it has already been assigned by my Father."

When the other ten heard this, they were indignant with the two brothers. So Jesus called them to him and said, "You know that in the world, rulers lord it over their subjects, and their great men make them feel the weight of authority; but it shall not be so with you. Among you, whoever wants to be great must be your servant, and whoever wants to be first must be the willing slave of all — like the Son of Man; he did not come to be served, but to serve, and to give up his life as a ransom for many."

FOLLOWING CHRIST IS TO SERVE ONE ANOTHER

Jesus then addressed the people and his disciples in these words: "The doctors of the law and the Pharisees sit in the chair of Moses; therefore do what they tell you; pay attention to their words. But do not follow their practice; for they say one thing and do another. They make up heavy packs and pile them on men's shoulders, but will not raise a finger to lift the load themselves. Whatever they do is done for show. They go about with broad phylacteries and with large tassels on their robes; they like to have places of honour at feasts and the chief seats in synagogues, to be greeted respectfully in the street, and to be addressd as 'rabbi.'

"But you must not be called 'rabbi'; for you have one Rabbi, and you are all brothers. Do not call any man on earth 'father'; for you have one Father, and he is in heaven. Nor must you be called 'teacher'; you have one Teacher, the Messiah. The greatest among you must be your servant. For whoever exalts himself will be humbled; and whoever humbles himself will be exalted."

PAUL REFLECTS ON THE THEOLOGY OF GOD'S SERVANTHOOD IN THE INCARNATION OF CHRIST

For the divine nature was his from the first; yet he did not think to snatch at equality with God, but made himself nothing, assuming the nature of a slave. Bearing the human likeness, revealed in human shape, he humbled himself, and in obedience accepted even death — death on a cross. Therefore God raised him to the heights and bestowed on him the name above all names, that at the name of Jesus every knee should bow — in heaven, on earth, and in the depths — and every tongue confess, "Jesus Christ is Lord," to the glory of God the Father.

5. *Logos Christology: Christ as Cosmic Lord*[9]

When all things began, the Word already was. The Word dwelt with God, and what God was, the Word was. The Word, then, was with God at the beginning, and through him all things came to be; no single thing was created without him. All that came to be was alive with his life, and that life was the light of men. The light shines on in the dark, and the darkness has never mastered it.

He was in the world, but the world, though it owed its being to him, did not recognize him. He entered his own realm, and his own would not receive him. But to all who did receive him, to those who have yielded him their allegiance, he gave the right to become children of God, not born of any human stock, or by the fleshly desire of a human father, but the offspring of God himself. So the Word became flesh; he came to dwell among us, and we saw his glory, such glory as befits the Father's only Son, full of grace and truth.

He rescued us from the domain of darkness and brought us away into the kingdom of his dear Son, in whom our release is secured and our sins forgiven. He is the image of the invisible God; his is the primacy over all created things. In him everything in heaven and on earth was created, not only things visible but also the invisible orders of thrones, sovereignties, authorities, and powers: the whole universe has been created through him and for him. And he exists before everything, and all things are held together in him. He is, moreover, the head of the body, the church. He is its origin, the first to return from the dead, to be in all things alone supreme. For in him the complete being of God, by God's own choice, came to dwell. Through him God chose to reconcile the whole universe to himself, making peace through the shedding of his blood upon the cross — to reconcile all things, whether on earth or in heaven, through him alone.

6. The Androgynous Christ and Redeemed Humanity of Gnosticism[10]

THE GOSPEL OF THE EGYPTIANS

They say that the Savior himself said, "I came to destroy the works of the female," meaning by "female" desire, and by "works" birth and corruption.

Salome says: "Until when shall men die?" The Lord gave a cautious answer — "As long as women bear children," that is, as long as the desires are active. "Therefore, as through one man sin entered the world, and through sin death came to all men, in that all sinned, and death reigned from Adam to Moses" [Rom. 5:12, 14], says the apostle. By natural necessity in the divine plan death follows birth, and the coming together of soul and body is followed by their dissolution. If birth exists for the sake of learning and knowledge, dissolution leads to the final restoration. As woman is regarded as the cause of death because she brings birth, so also for the same reason she may be called the originator of life.

THE GOSPEL OF PHILIP

The Sophia whom they call barren is the mother of the angels. And the consort [of Christ] is Mary Magdalene. [The Lord loved Mary] more than [all] the disciples, and kissed her on her mouth often. The other too. . . . they said to him, "Why do you love her more than all of us?" The Saviour answered and said to them, "Why do I not love you like her?"

    If the woman had not separated from the man, she would not die with the man. His separation became the beginning of death. Because of this Christ came, in order that he might remove the separation which was from the beginning, and again unite the two; and that he might give life to those who died in the separation, and unite them. But the woman is united to her husband in the bridal chamber. But those who have united in the bridal chamber will no longer be separated. Because of this Eve separated from Adam, because she was not united with him in the bridal chamber.

THE GOSPEL OF THOMAS

Simon Peter said to them:
    Let Mariham go away from us.
    For women are not worthy of life.
Jesus said:
    Lo, I will draw her
    so that I will make her a man
    so that she too may become a living spirit
    which is like you men;
    for every woman who makes herself a man
    will enter into the kingdom of heaven.

7. Christ as Mother: The Vision of a Woman Mystic[11]

And thus, in our making, God almighty is our kindly Father; and God all-wisdom is our kindly Mother, with the love and goodness of the Holy Ghost; which is all one God, one Lord. And in the knitting and the oneing he is our very true Spouse, and we his loved wife and his fair maiden. With which wife he was never displeased; for he says: "I love thee, and thou lovest me, and our love shall never be parted in two."

I beheld the working of all the blessed Trinity. In which beholding I saw and understood these three properties: the property of the Fatherhood, and the property of the Motherhood, and the property of the Lordship — in one God. In our Father almighty we have our keeping and our bliss, in respect of the substance of our kind, which is applied to us by our creation, from without-beginning. And in the second Person (i.e., of the Trinity) in understanding the wisdom, we have our keeping in respect of our sensuality, our restoring and our saving. For he is our Mother, Brother and Saviour. And in our good Lord the Holy Ghost we have our rewarding and our enrichment for our living and our travail; which, of his high, plenteous grace, and in his marvellous courtesy, endlessly surpasses all that we desire.

And furthermore, I saw that the second Person, who is our Mother substantially — the same very dear Person is now become our Mother sensually. For of God's making we are double: that is to say, substantial and sensual. Our substance is that higher part which we have in our Father, God almighty. And the second Person of the Trinity is our Mother in kind, in our substantial making — in whom we are grounded and rooted; and he is our Mother of mercy in taking our sensuality. And thus "our Mother" means for us different manners of his working, in whom our parts are kept unseparated. For in our Mother Christ, we have profit and increase; and in mercy he re-forms and restores us: and by the power of his passion, his death and his uprising, oned us to our substance. Thus our Mother in mercy works to all his beloved children who are docile and obedient to him.

Thus Jesus Christ, who does good against evil, is our very Mother. We have our being of him, there, where the ground of Motherhood begins; with all the sweet keeping of love that endlessly follows. As truly as God is our Father, so truly is God our Mother.

8. Jesus and Mary as Co-Redeemers in Catholic Piety[12]

And, St. Bonaventure addresses her thus: Blessed are those who know thee, oh mother of God! for to know thee is the path to immortal life, and to publish thy virtues is the way to eternal salvation.

In the Franciscan chronicles it is related of brother Leo, that he once saw a red ladder, upon which Jesus Christ was standing, and a white one, upon which stood his holy mother. He saw persons attempting to ascend the red ladder; they ascended a few steps and then fell; they ascended again, and again fell. Then they were exhorted to ascend the white ladder, and on that he saw them succeed, for the blessed Virgin offered them her hand, and they arrived in that manner safe in paradise. St. Denis the Carthusian asks: Who will ever be saved? Who will ever reign in heaven? They are saved, and will certainly reign, he himself answers, for whom this queen of mercy offers her prayers. And this Mary herself affirms: By me kings reign: "Per me reges regnant." Through my intercession souls reign first in the mortal life on this earth, by governing their passions, and then they go to reign eternally in heaven, where, as St. Augustine declares, all are kings: "Quot cives, tot reges." Mary, in a word, as Richard of St. Laurence says, is the mistress of paradise, since there she commands according to her pleasure, and introduces into it whom she will. Therefore, applying to her the words of Ecclesiasticus, he adds: "My power is in Jerusalem:" I command what I will, and introduce whom I will. And as she is the mother of the Lord of paradise, she is with reason, also, says Rupert, the Lady of paradise. She possesses, by right, the whole kingdom of her Son.

This divine mother, with her powerful prayers and assistance, has obtained for us paradise, if we place no obstacle to our entrance there. Wherefore those who are servants of Mary, and for whom Mary intercedes, are as secure of paradise as if they were already there. To serve Mary and to belong to her court, adds St. John of Damascus, is the greatest honor we can attain; for to serve the queen of heaven is to reign already in heaven, and to live in obedience to her commands is more than to reign.

9. Woman Worship in Nineteenth-Century Romanticism[13]

Feudalism introduced for the first time the worship of Woman. But in this it met with little support from Catholicism, and was in many respects thwarted by it. The habits of Christianity were in themselves adverse to real tenderness of heart; they only strengthened it indirectly, by promoting one of the indispensable conditions of true affection, purity of life. In all other respects Chivalry was constantly opposed by the Catholic system; which was so austere and anti-social, that it could not sanction marriage except as an infirmity which it was necessary to tolerate, but which was hazardous to personal salvation.

It was reserved for the more comprehensive system of Positivism, in which sound practice is always supported by sound theory, to give full expression to the feeling of veneration for women. In the new religion, tenderness of heart is looked upon as the first of Woman's attributes.

Positivism then, as the whole tendency of this chapter indicates, encourages, on intellectual as well as on moral grounds, full and systematic expression of the feeling of veneration for Women, in public as well as in private life, collectively as well as individually. Born to love and to be loved, relieved from the burdens of practical life, free in the sacred retirement of their homes, the women of the West will receive from Positivists the tribute of deep and sincere admiration which their life inspires. They will feel no scruple in accepting their position as spontaneous priestesses of Humanity; they will fear no longer the rivalry of a vindictive Deity. From childhood each of us will be taught to regard their sex as the principal source of human happiness and improvement, whether in public life or in private.

The treasures of affection which our ancestors wasted upon mystical objects, and which these revolutionary times ignore, will then be carefully preserved and directed to their proper purpose. The enervating influence of chimerical beliefs will have passed away; and men in all the vigour of their energies, feeling themselves the masters of the known world, will feel it their highest happiness to submit with gratitude to the beneficent power of womanly sympathy. In a word, Man will in those days kneel to Woman, and to Woman alone.

The source from which these reverential feelings for the sympathetic sex proceed, is a clear appreciation in the other sex of benefits received, and a spirit of deep thankfulness for them. The Positivist will never forget that moral perfection, the primary condition of public and private happiness, is principally due to the influence of Woman over Man, first as mother, then as wife. Such a conviction cannot fail to arouse feelings of loving veneration for those with whom, from their position in society, he is in no danger of rivalry in the affairs of life. When the mission of woman is better understood, and is carried out more fully, she will be regarded by Man as the most perfect impersonation of Humanity.

10. The Female Messiah in Shaker Theology[14]

The first or natural creation is a similitude of the spiritual, *"the first man Adam of the earth a figure"* of the second man, or last Adam, *"the Lord from heaven."*

As, then, the first Adam was not complete, in the order of natural generation, without Eve, the first mother of the human race and children of this world; so neither could the second Adam be complete in the order of spiritual regeneration, without the second Eve, who of course would be manifested in the "first begotten of the dead," in the line of the female, and become the first mother of the redeemed, the children of the kingdom of promise.

It is written, "As in Adam all die, even so in (not out of) Christ shall all be made alive." How, *even so in* Christ shall all be made alive? Was it not through the disobedience of the first woman *Eve*, that in the first Adam we all die? Certainly it was. Even so, then, through the obedience of the first woman in the work of redemption in *Christ*, the second Adam, shall all be made alive.

For, as the first Adam and Eve, and the line of their progeny were *one flesh*, and "they that live after the flesh shall die;" even so Christ, the second Adam and the second Eve, are *one Spirit*, and they who, through that Spirit, mortify the deeds of the flesh, shall live; and living they shall never die, because they are born of the Spirit, through a spiritual Parentage, a spiritual Father and a spiritual Mother.

The woman was the first in the transgression, but the man was equally in fault, if not more so, he being the stronger vessel; and, it would be inconsistent with all the attributes of Eternal Wisdom, that the daughter of earth, a being made in her own image, and after her likeness, and designed to be on earth, the glory and perfection of all the works of God, should by one act of disobedience plunge herself and all her posterity into sin and misery;

And yet, that, she in her own line and order, should for this *one act* be forsaken and forgotten of her Lord and Creator, and thus be prevented having any agency in the work of restoration and redemption. We say, that, should such be the case, it would be entirely inconsistent with all the attributes of the Eternal Father and his Holy Wisdom.

But such is not the case: God promised, that, in the *restitution of all things*, a woman should stand in her proper lot and order, as the first Mother in the new creation, as Bride of the Redeemer, and co-worker with him in the work of man's redemption, and thus, according to the promise of God, she now really stands.

It is but true, however, that proud and fallen man with vain and fleshly applause, and for no other than his own sinful purposes, worships and adores the woman, and extols her even above himself; and yet, that he has excluded her from having any lot or agency in the work of his redemption. So inconsistent is lost man.

And to this purpose he has been taught and supported, by false religion, to misapply and pervert the inspired and prophetic writings, which peculiarly and emphatically relate to the woman, and to her lot and standing in the new creation, in the Zion of God's likeness in the latter days. This they do, by indiscriminately applying those prophecies to a personal Christ in the male order! or, as indiscriminately to a mixed, impure and compound body of males and females, called "the Church," or to something to which the spirit of the Prophets had no kind of allusion.

The first promise God made for the restoration of man from the effects of the fall, was made to be accomplished through the woman: *That "she and her seed should crush the serpent's head."* Yet, plain and distinct as his promise is, "blind guides" have perverted both the words and their meaning, by applying the promise to "Christ" as being the *seed of the woman.*

How can Christ be the "seed of the woman"? Of what woman was He the seed? Was Christ the seed of Mary, the Mother of Jesus? That is impossible. But Jesus was created of the nature of fallen man, the seed of Abraham, through his preternatural Mother, Mary, in order that, through the power of Christ manifested in him, he might crucify and put the serpentine nature to death, by nailing it to the cross! And thus did he open the way of redemption from *"sin and death"* and from the *"curse of the law."*

And the Lord said to the serpent: "I will put enmities between thee and the woman, and thy seed and her seed: She [and her seed] shall crush thy head and thou shall lie in wait for her heel.

However, the ages of the world may pass away before all the promises of God shall be fulfilled: yet his faithfulness can never fail. Four thousand years had passed away before the Messiah appeared — still he did appear as predicted of him, and finished the work which the Father had given him for the time being.

And in like manner, thousands of years had passed away, since the promise was made in the garden of Eden, concerning the *woman;* and the promised Saviour had come, and gone again from mortal view, when by the revelation of Jesus Christ to his beloved John, there was shown in vision, the particular and peculiar character of the *"woman and her seed,"* unto whom the promise was made.

Here was seen, "A woman clothed with the sun, and the moon under her feet, and upon her head a crown of twelve stars; and she being with child cried, travailing in birth, and pained to be delivered." This vision represented Holy Wisdom, the Eternal Mother, who brought forth the "man-child," the Christ, who first appeared in the male order; and which the Dragon sought to devour.

The Dragon here represented the *spirit of persecution,* which began in Herod's seeking to destroy *the child,* and continued to operate in various stages with increased violence, until the primitive Church was cast down to the earth. Then this Christ Spirit was caught up from the apostate Church *to God and his throne,* out of the reach of the serpent, ready (in due season) to appear the second time, in and with his Bride.

And after the war of Michael and his angels, by which the Dragon and his angels were cast out of heaven, that is from the regions where Christ had established his kingdom, in the world of spirits; then the Eternal Mother brought forth her own likeness and representative, the Mother Spirit of Christ, in the woman, to whom "was given the two wings of a great eagle, that she might fly to her place, from the face of the serpent."

This is the woman, the *Daughter,* in the likeness of the Eternal Mother, even as the Son was in the likeness of the Eternal Father. And when this *Daughter,* who had now become the Mother of the new creation, had escaped from the serpent's power, she was *nourished* in her place in the wilderness, until the time of her manifestation.

"In the day that God created man, in the image and likeness of God made he him; male and female created he them; and called their name Adam." What can be plainer than this, to show that the *male and female* are *one.* That they are *one in nature and essence,* in the *likeness* of their Creator? What can be plainer than this, to show that man could not, and consequently did not exist without the woman?

As therefore the first Adam was a figure of Christ, the second Adam, how could it be otherwise than that Christ, the second Adam, should also be made manifest in the order of male and female? He likewise being in the likeness, and "after the image of Him that created him."

If it could be consistently shown how Adam could have both *begotten* and brought forth children, and peopled the earth *without Eve*, or before the time that the woman should stand in her own proper lot and order, as the *"mother of all living"*; then it might be consistently shown, how Christ the second Adam, *without the woman*, could both *beget* and *bring forth* a spiritual offspring, to people the *"new heavens and the new earth,"* by the *"second birth."* But this can never be shown.

[Mother Ann Lee is the Female Christ foretold in Scripture . . .]

"Hearken, O Daughter, and consider, and incline thine ear; forget also thine own people, and thy father's house; so shall the King greatly desire thy beauty; for he is thy Lord; and worship thou him. . . . The King's Daughter is all glorious within; her clothing is of wrought gold. She shall be brought unto the King in raiment of needle work; the virgins her companions that follow her, shall be brought unto the King. With gladness and rejoicing shall they be brought: they shall enter into the King's palace. Instead of thy father's, shall be thy children, whom thou mayest make princes in all the earth."

These are the words of the Divine Spirit of prophecy, in relation to that peculiar personage whom we call "Mother." And in her, and in her spiritual offspring of the present day, they were and are fulfilled, and are still being fulfilled. In obedience to the revelation and will of God, and in love to the Lord her Redeemer, whom she worshipped and served, she did forsake her own people and her father's house. She left also the land of oppression, and fled to this wilderness, the land of freedom, as the Lord directed her.

In this particular, God fulfilled through her, the promise made to his Church and people of the latter days: *"Behold I will allure her, and bring her into the wilderness, and speak comfortably unto her. And I will give her her vineyards from thence, and the valley of Achor,"* [the confession of sins,] *"for a door of hope; and she shall sing there as in the days of her youth."*

By her faithfulness and her toils; by her cross-bearing and self-denying life; by the persecutions, and deprivations, and imprisonments, she endured for the testimony of Christ against the hidden works and abominations of fallen man; and by her sorrows and sufferings of soul; her incessant tears and cries to God; she became a sanctified and *"chosen vessel unto the Lord;"* to *"do his work, his strange work; and bring to pass his act, his strange act:"* and that in her, the word of God, by the Prophet Jeremiah might be fulfilled, which says, *"The Lord hath created a new thing in the earth, A woman shall compass a man."*

Through the valley of humiliation and sufferings she was brought; in the furnace of affliction she was tried, until her soul became cleansed and purified; and being thus prepared, she became the fit tabernacle and the abode of the *"only begotten"* Daughter of the Most High, the *faithful witness;* and the true *"representative of the Eternal Mother."*

Hence she was filled with the power and gifts of God; with charity and love; with the gifts of visions, of songs, of tongues, of revelation, and of prophecy; with the gift of wisdom, and the fear of the Lord; with the gift of discerning spirits, and the moral state and condition of man; as also, with the gift of of repentance, and of the knowledge of the mind and will of God.

11. I Scream for Johanna, My Eternal Mother[15]

Johanna
on the other side
of locked door
my mother   unavailable
you have my chart
written by a male
by order of heavenly doctors,
eternally prescribing
when I can be born.

They threw me
into this white cell
naked
under sterile cloths

I scream for
Johanna,
my eternal mother

Eternal Mother,
I can't wait in uterine darkness,
terrorized,
rattling steel knobs
furiously
to be born

I scream again,
Johanna!

When she comes
I can only see her eyes
each one framed
in hexagons of chicken wire
pressed wide between glass window

"Johanna,
Who is my eternal mother?
Go find her
Get the key!"

Johanna kneels
as if to pray
but only whispers through the lock
    "Eternal Mother?
    She has only eyes
    no body
    no body
    Nobody
    in this androcentric world
    of bastioned doors
    with phallic keys
    to bastard Kingdoms."

12. *Unless a WomanChrist Comes, We Will All Die*[16]

We're sitting in the path of the bomb
nuclear nuttiness
waiting
knitting furiously to cover
warheads with yarn snares

feeding our babies
mother milk

fighting against the mushroom menace

watching

looking to the hills

Our special agony
is
we know we will die
unless
a WomanChrist pops up
(like a rabbit out of a hat)
between breasted mountains

and gently
oh so   very   tenderly
strokes those bound warheads

loving them exquisitely
until red anger packed within
slowly turns toward
green earth's gaping mouth
and spills its seed
into the healing ground.

Serene and grace-filled, she arises from the waters of birth and rebirth, assisted by ministering women.

The Birth of Aphrodite. Greek marble relief, fifth century B.C., Museo Nazionale delle Terme, Rome.

7

Repentance, Conversion, Transformation

DOCUMENTS

1. *Jonah and the Repentance of Nineveh*
2. *"Repent, the Kingdom Is at Hand": John the Baptist and the Baptism of Jesus*
3. *Dying and Rising in Christ in Pauline Theology*
4. *Reawakening to One's Transcendent Identity in Gnostic Theology*
5. *Divine Grace to Overcome Concupiscence: Augustine's Conversion*
6. *The Spiritual Marriage: The Seventh Mansion in Teresa of Avila's* **Interior Castle**
7. *Terror, Glory, and the Gift of Reading in a Black American Evangelist*
8. *"You Are Enough!" A Woman Seminarian's Story*

The definition of repentance and conversion is, by nature, relative. What conversion means is relative to how one has defined what is wrong with humanity. The goal of conversion will be an ideal correction of this definition of what is wrong. Concepts of conversion will also be shaped by whether one thinks humans have the ability to choose the good in opposition to their present evil state and by how some divinely given standard of rightness or agent of salvation relates to their present state. For much of Christian history, domination by sexual feelings was thought to be the sign of the fallenness of the soul into alien material world, and conversion took the form of overcoming sexual desires. Today alienation from our sexuality is more likely to be seen as what is wrong, and so we develop various forms of therapies to help people "convert" to a wholistic integration of self and sexuality.

Likewise, through most of Christian history the subordination of women was thought to be God's will. And so the conversion of women demanded their overcoming of feelings of rebelliousness and a docile acceptance of their subordination to the authorities of the family, Church, and society. Today feminism sees this subordination of women as itself a sin against the humanity of women. So there are feminist conversion experiences that take the form of rejection of male domination.

The concept of conversion has always been an ambivalent one for women. Although women have been taught to internalize the demand for obedience to patriarchal authority as the expression of their obedience to God, for many women conversion experiences actually functioned to free them from repressive social authority by transferring their exclusive obedience to God or Christ. Most classical conversion stories of women contain an odd mixture of these two opposite tendencies.

This chapter provides a range of conversion texts from the Old and New Testaments to contemporary feminism to provide something of the sweep of these different options for understanding conversion. The chapter opens with a brief text from the Book of Jonah that provides one perspective on Jewish views of conversion. Jonah is sent to the great city of Nineveh, capital of the Assyrian empire, a city that symbolized all manner of evil for traditional Jews. Jonah is told to tell the inhabitants of Nineveh that unless they repent of their sins they will be overthrown by God. Jonah tries to run away from his mission because he doesn't want Nineveh to be saved. But, after various adventures, he is forced to carry out his mission. To his great chagrin, all the inhabitants of Nineveh repent, from the highest to the lowest. They proclaim a public fast, put on sackcloth, and sit in ashes. When God sees this repentance of Neneveh, he repents of his plans and spares the city.

What message is derived from this text? The story of the repentance of Nineveh is told as a joke on Jewish particularists who believed that God wills the salvation only of the Jews. This is why the conversion of Nineveh is told in an amazing way. The author wants to make the point that God's concern extends to all peoples. All are equally under the hand of his wrath or mercy. But second, we may note several assumptions of the writer. Sin is understood as public and collective. Although sins may include various kinds of licentiousness, this too is thought of as public and collective. Nineveh is an evil city because in it reign conditions of all types of corruption, both injustice and debauchery. There is no division of private, personal sins (sexual) and public sins (injustice).

Repentance likewise is public and collective. The whole city, from the king right down to the animals (!), make a public scene of their intention to change their lifestyle. Punishment for sin also is seen as public and historical. Divine wrath against sin takes the form of some great historical misfortune (defeat in war, plague, drought) that destroys the city. This historical misfortune is understood as divine punishment. But human repentance can make God "change his mind," that is, repent of his intention to punish a city for its sins. It is assumed that humans are capable of such a choice of change of life that is adequate to appease God and turn away divine wrath. All of these assumptions are quite different from those which have come to be taken for granted in Christianity.

The second text, from Matthew, is important because it contains what appears to have been the basic formula of the preaching of both John the Baptist and Jesus: "Repent, the Kingdom of God is at hand." The context of such a message of repentance is apocalyptic. It is assumed that the present world system is in its last days. God is about to intervene to judge the righteous and the unrighteous, and so the prophet offers people a last chance to change their lifestyle before this great separation of the wheat from the tares. However, the text is replete with contradictions that have come about through the imposition of later Christian assumptions on this earlier Jewish apocalyptic context.

John the Baptist represented a Jewish apocalyptic sectarianism that believed that all Jews, even the observant of temple and synagogue, had fallen away and were counted among the gentiles. Thus the proselyte baptism, which the Pharisees would offer only to gentiles, is offered to Jews as a sign of their conversion.[1] But the Pharisees did not believe in such a baptism of Jews, so it makes no sense to say that they had come out to receive it.[2] Moreover, they are then polemicized against by the Baptist because they think they are already children of Abraham on the basis of birth and so don't need such a conversion to become members of the community of God's Elect. The Baptist (and Christianity), however, believes in a spiritual community of the Elect (the messianic Israel) that one enters through baptism and conversion.

The Messiah whom the Baptist announced as the one to come after him is the apocalyptic Messiah of the last judgment.[3] But the Christian community have overlaid on this their own assumption that the Baptist was announcing Jesus as the Messiah. Jesus is portrayed as coming out and receiving baptism from John. This could have happened only if Jesus accepted John's sectarian assumptions, including the assumption that, as a Jew, he was nevertheless a gentilized sinner and needed such a baptism to enter the Elect Community. But the community of Matthew believes Jesus was the Messiah and was sinless. So they create a meaningless dialogue between John and Jesus in which John says the baptism is unnecessary and Jesus asks for it anyway "for old time's sake."

Finally, the Jewish sectarian community would have believed that conversion means a change of lifestyle to strict moral living, through some notion of rigorous observance of the Torah. But the Christian community believes one cannot appease God by observance of the Law but only by "belief" in Jesus as the Messiah. So exactly what it means to repent is also unclear. Thus while the passage provides the key text for John and Jesus' mission to Israel, its contradictions also reveal a transition from one set of assumptions of Jewish apocalyptic sects to another set of assumptions, which we see in the text from Paul's epistle to the Romans.

The passage from Paul's letter summarizes the classic Pauline theology of baptism. Baptism is understood as a spiritual participation in the crucifixion and resurrection of Christ by which we throw off the "old nature" that we inherited from Adam and take on a new nature that derives from the eschatological "New Being" of the Risen Christ. Such a theology of conversion has broken in significant ways with Judaism. First, it believes that the "shift of the aeons" from the old fallen, historical age of sin to a new messianic world of eternal life has already taken place on a cosmic spiritual plane, although this shift is not yet manifest on the bodily, historical level. Such a split between a spiritual advent of messianic being, apart from outward historical change, was unthinkable in Judaism. If the worldly systems of oppressive power have not been defeated historically, the messianic age has not come. Thus this Christian split of an inward messianic advent, apart from outward historical change, allows Christianity to spiritualize conversion in a way severed from historical change in public ethics.

Second, Paul believes that one cannot make a fundamental change in one's moral lifestyle adequate to make one acceptable to God on the basis of one's human nature as derived from Adam. One needs to die to this Adamic nature and be imbued with a new eschatological nature, which derives from the being of the resurrected Christ, in order to be acceptable to God. This new nature is not earned by acts of free will, but rather it is given by divine grace. Only when one is reborn into this new, eschatological nature can there then flow good deeds fitting salvation.

Paul still demands the good deeds of conventional morality. But these now are expressions of one's reborn nature and not one's Adamic humanity. For Paul, Torah symbolizes not the way of righteousness that we are enjoined to follow but a revelation of sin, since it commands good deeds that we are incapable of doing appropriately on the basis of our fallen nature. These assumptions break from Judaism, which believed that Torah was the revealed way of salvation and one was able to follow it on the basis of one's present created nature.

Gnostics also shared with Paul the radical split between one's eschatological and one's material historical nature. But they made this split more consistent by also denying that one's present bodily nature derived from God. For the Gnostics, the "spirit" was the transcendent or divine part of the soul that comes from the heavenly world. The material world was not created by true deity but came about through a fall in which an antidivine chaos was organized into an evil cosmos through false gods. The spirit in the soul is a spark of the divine world above, which has fallen into this world of darkness and forgotten its true nature and heavenly home. It is awakened to begin the journey of fleeing from earth to heaven. In the "Hymn of the Pearl," excerpted here, we have an allegorical rendering of this gnostic perspective on the drama of the fall of the spirit (the Pearl) into self-forgetfulness and material existence and its reawakening and escape through a revelation from its heavenly Parents.[4]

Augustine is the great Latin Church Father of the fifth century A.D. who translated the Pauline theology of the Old and New Adam into psychological terms. It is through Augustine that Pauline anthropology becomes normative for the Western Christian understanding of grace and conversion. Augustine worked out this theology on the basis of his own biographical journey, as recounted in his *Confessions*. For Augustine the fallen nature of Adam dismembered the original rational control of the mind over the senses. This fallen nature is transmitted through the sexual act, which, in fallen humanity, cannot take place without sinful lust. This fallen nature holds us in bondage to pride and concupiscence. We are unable to break this bondage by our own free will but require an act of redeeming grace to break the bondage of the will and to transform our nature from self-love to love of God.

In Augustine's own biographical journey to faith, the renunciation of sexual activity and the adoption of a life of chastity expressed his conversion from concupiscence. He believed that he was unable to break this bondage by his own free will and could do so only by a transcendent gift of grace. This gift of grace expressed itself in his life in a process of transformation that culminated in his conversion experience. Such grace, for Augustine, cannot be merited by any human effort. It is the manifestation of an a priori act of divine election by which God chooses among the damned of humanity to bestow such redeeming grace on a few, Augustine among them.

In this passage from his *Confessions* we see Augustine struggling in the last climactic moments to shake off his attraction to sexual pleasure and then the transformative experience of grace that breaks his bondage to self-will and gives him the power to choose God and chastity. Augustine believes that the sexual relationship is animalistic and precludes the possibility of friendship between men and women. Aside from his relationship with his mother, he is incapable of nonsexual friendship with women. So, in practice, the renunciation of sex coincides with a renunciation of relationship with women for relationship with God.

Teresa of Avila's *Interior Castle* represents a classical expression of the Catholic mystical journey from various stages of purgation of the senses and intellect to final union with Christ. Teresa of Avila (1515–1582) lived at the height of Spanish imperial and cultural power. An intelligent, vital girl, she plunged herself into the religious life at the age of twenty and experienced almost twenty years of neurotic illness that very likely expressed her own struggle against this repression of her healthy impulses.[5] At age forty she had a conversion experience that enabled her increasingly to assert herself as an independent person, defy her superiors, and become a leader and reformer of the Carmelite order in her own right. This conversion experience took the form of the establishment of a spiritual, erotic relationship with Christ as her lover who also gave her permission to defy the authorities of her Church and society.

In her book *Interior Castle*, she maps this journey to union with Christ for the community of her sisters for whom she now acts as both prioress and spiritual guide. The nuptial imagery of union with Christ allowed Teresa both to find a focus for her own intellectual and erotic energies in this relationship and also to receive back from this relationship an ego empowered to act with authority. Although she images Christ as a male lover, she also does not hesitate to use other, maternal images, such as breasts overflowing with milk that nurtures the whole community who journey toward this union with Christ. Through her mystical journey Teresa was able to win the sanction to use her own intelligence and vital energies autonomously and also to become an esteemed "daughter of the Church" who would be canonized as a saint and accorded the rank of Doctor of Mystical Theology.

The appropriation of the conversion experience as an empowerment of the self, enabling the female increasingly to free herself from patriarchal authority and limitations, also becomes evident in the life story of the Black mystic, evangelist, and Shaker Elderess Rebecca Jackson (1795–1871). In the passage excerpted here, we see her conversion in 1830, with which she opens her diary of her mystical visions. This conversion experience transformed her from feelings of terror of a punishing God and her own self-abnegation to an increasingly assertive woman whose obedience to the guidance of her inner spirit gave her permission to defy the authority of her brother (a Church Elder), the clergy of the African Methodist Episcopal Church who opposed her preaching career, and, finally, the Elderess of the Shaker community which she eventually entered in her journey toward a female-identified community, centered in a female deity (see chapter I, reading 6).

Jackson's stories of her visions are always stories of her personal empowerment and growth toward autonomy against the restrictions of her society. One striking example of such a visionary empowerment is her story of an experience in which God literally gave her the ability to read and thereby escape from the illiteracy which bound her to a shameful dependence on male authorities, especially her brother, upon whom she had previously had to rely for such small favors as writing her letters. Empowered by God with literacy, she could, above all, take up the text of the Bible and become an interpreter of it in her own right. Jackson thereafter embarked on her own preaching itinerancy. Another battle with authority, this time with white female authority, ensued when she entered the Shakers. But Jackson was able to emerge triumphant from these struggles as well, being authorized by the Shaker community at Watervliet, New York, to form her own Black female Shaker community in Philadelphia.

The final text of the chapter comes from Nancy Ore, a seminarian at Garrett-Evangelical Theological Seminary. Here we see, in terse language, a forty-year life of repressive domination by patriarchal family and Church figures. Her conversion takes the form of a death and resurrection experience: a total physical-psychological-spiritual collapse and waiting for death and then an equally dramatic gift of new life. In her risen life she does not marry Christ but becomes Christ as one who rises on the third day and "flies away" from the structures of repression that had previously formed her identity.

Reflection

In reading these selections you might try to list what seems to be the "evil" from which one is to be converted in the successive accounts.

What are the content and nature of the evil? What is your own view of the evil from which one should be converted? If you don't believe in such a concept of conversion, what is your own view of human development?

Assuming some process of change or development from a lesser to a better state, how is the self held in bondage to these negative forces? Where is the "seat of power" of these negative forces? In the self? In society?

What are the processes that make conversion and transformation possible? Is an outside agent from God or the intervention of a power transcendent to the (present state of) the self necessary for the change to occur? Why?

What is the new state toward which one wants to be converted and transformed? What characteristics does it have? How does it resolve the previous problems or save one from the previous negative state?

How do you see such a conversion process related to male development of identity in the context of patriarchal religion and society? How might a conversion experience be related to female development of identity in relation to (or over against) patriarchal religion and society?

1. Jonah and the Repentance of Nineveh[6]

Then the word of the Lord came to Jonah the second time, saying, "Arise, go to Nineveh, that great city, and proclaim to it the message that I tell you." So Jonah arose and went to Nineveh, according to the word of the Lord. Now Nineveh was an exceedingly great city, three days' journey in breadth. Jonah began to go into the city, going a day's journey. And he cried, "Yet forty days, and Nineveh shall be overthrown!" And the people of Nineveh believed God; they proclaimed a fast, and put on sackcloth, from the greatest of them to the least of them.

Then tidings reached the king of Nineveh, and he arose from his throne, removed his robe, and covered himself with sackcloth, and sat in ashes. And he made proclamation and published through Nineveh, "By the decree of the king and his nobles: Let neither man nor beast, herd nor flock, taste anything; let them not feed, or drink water, but let man and beast be covered with sackcloth, and let them cry mightily to God; yea, let everyone turn from his evil way and from the violence which is in his hands. Who knows, God may yet repent and turn from his fierce anger, so that we perish not?''

When God saw what they did, how they turned from their evil way, God repented of the evil which he had said he would do to them; and he did not do it.

2. "Repent, the Kingdom Is at Hand": John the Baptist and the Baptism of Jesus[7]

In those days came John the Baptist, preaching in the wilderness of Judea, "Repent, for the kingdom of heaven is at hand." For this is he who was spoken of by the prophet Isaiah when he said,

"The voice of one crying in the wilderness:
Prepare the way of the Lord,
make his paths straight."

Now John wore a garment of camel's hair, and a leather girdle around his waist; and his food was locusts and wild honey. Then went out to him Jerusalem and all Judea and all the region about the Jordan, and they were baptized by him in the river Jordan, confessing their sins.

But when he saw many of the Pharisees and Sadducees coming for baptism, he said to them, "You brood of vipers! Who warned you to flee from the wrath to come? Bear fruit that befits repentance, and do not presume to say to yourselves, 'We have Abraham as our father'; for I tell you, God is able from these stones to raise up children to Abraham. Even now the ax is laid to the root of the trees; every tree therefore that does not bear good fruit is cut down and thrown into the fire.

"I baptize you with water for repentance, but he who is coming after me is mightier than I, whose sandals I am not worthy to carry; he will baptize you with the Holy Spirit and with fire. His winnowing fork is in his hand, and he will clear his threshing floor and gather his wheat into the granary, but the chaff he will burn with unquenchable fire."

Then Jesus came from Galilee to the Jordan to John, to be baptized by him. John would have prevented him, saying, "I need to be baptized by you, and do you come to me?"

But Jesus answered him, "Let it be so now; for thus it is fitting for us to fulfil all righteousness." Then he consented. And when Jesus was baptized, he went up immediately from the water, and behold, the heavens were opened and he saw the Spirit of God descending like a dove, and alighting on him; and lo, a voice from heaven, saying, "This is my beloved Son, with whom I am well pleased."

3. Dying and Rising in Christ in Pauline Theology[8]

Do you not know that all of us who have been baptized into Christ Jesus were baptized into his death? We were buried therefore with him by baptism into death, so that as Christ was raised from the dead by the glory of the Father, we too might walk in newness of life.

For if we have been united with him in a death like his, we shall certainly be united with him in a resurrection like his. We know that our old self was crucified with him so that the sinful body might be destroyed, and we might no longer be enslaved to sin. For he who has died is freed from sin. But if we have died with Christ, we believe that we shall also live with him. For we know that Christ being raised from the dead will never die again; death no longer has dominion over him. The death he died he died to sin, once for all, but the life he lives he lives to God. So you also must consider yourselves dead to sin and alive to God in Christ Jesus.

Let not sin therefore reign in your mortal bodies, to make you obey their passions. Do not yield your members to sin as instruments of wickedness, but yield yourselves to God as men who have been brought from death to life, and your members to God as instruments of righteousness. For sin will have no dominion over you, since you are not under law but under grace.

What then? Are we to sin because we are not under law but under grace? By no means! Do you not know that if you yield yourselves to any one as obedient slaves, you are slaves of the one whom you obey, either of sin, which leads to death, or of obedience, which leads to righteousness? But thanks be to God, that you who were once slaves of sin have become obedient from the heart to the standard of teaching to which you were committed, and, having been set free from sin, have become slaves of righteousness. I am speaking in human terms, because of your natural limitations. For just as you once yielded your

members to impurity and to greater and greater iniquity, so now
yield your members to righteousness for sanctification.

When you were slaves of sin, you were free in regard to
righteousness. But then what return did you get from the things
of which you are now ashamed? The end of those things is death.
But now that you have been set free from sin and have become
slaves of God, the return you get is sanctification and its end,
eternal life. For the wages of sin is death, but the free gift of God
is eternal life in Christ Jesus our Lord.

4. Reawakening to One's Transcendent Identity in Gnostic Theology[9]

I [he?] warned him [me?] against the Egyptians and the contact
with the unclean ones. Yet I clothed myself in their garments, lest
they suspect me as one coming from without to take the Pearl and
arouse the serpent against me. But through some cause they
marked that I was not their countryman, and they ingratiated
themselves with me, and mixed me [drink] with their cunning,
and gave me to taste of their meat; and I forgot that I was a
king's son and served their king. I forgot the Pearl for which my
parents had sent me. Through the heaviness of their nourishment
I sank into deep slumber.

All this that befell me, my parents marked, and they were
grieved for me. It was proclaimed in our kingdom that all should
come to our gates. And the kings and grandees of Parthia and all
the nobles of the East wove a plan that I must not be left in
Egypt. And they wrote a letter to me, and each of the great ones
signed it with his name.

From thy father the King of Kings, and from thy mother,
mistress of the East, and from thy brother, our next in rank, unto
thee, our son in Egypt, greeting. Awake and rise up out of thy
sleep, and perceive the words of our letter. Remember that thou
art a king's son: behold whom thou hast served in bondage. Be
mindful of the Pearl, for whose sake thou hast departed into
Egypt. Remember thy robe of glory, recall thy splendid mantle,
that thou mayest put them on and deck thyself with them and thy
name be read in the book of the heroes and thou become with thy
brother, our deputy, heir in our kingdom.

Like a messenger was the letter that the King had sealed with
his hand against the evil ones, the children of Babel and the
rebellious demons of Sarbûg. It rose up in the form of an eagle,

the king of all winged fowl, and flew until it alighted beside me and became wholly speech. At its voice and sound I awoke and arose from my sleep, took it up, kissed it, broke its seal, and read. Just as was written on my heart were the words of my letter to read. I remembered that I was a son of kings, and that my freeborn soul desired its own kind. I remembered the Pearl for which I had been sent down to Egypt, and I began to enchant the terrible and snorting serpent. I charmed it to sleep by naming over it my Father's name, the name of our next in rank, and that of my mother, the queen of the East. I seized the Pearl, and turned to repair home to my Father. Their filthy and impure garment I put off, and left it behind in their land, and directed my way that I might come to the light of our homeland, the East.

My letter which had awakened me I found before me on my way; and as it had awakened me with its voice, so it guided me with its light that shone before me, and with its voice it encouraged my fear, and with its love it drew me on. I went forth. . . . My robe of glory which I had put off and my mantle which went over it, my parents . . . sent to meet me by their treasurers who were entrusted therewith. Its splendor I had forgotten, having left it as a child in my Father's house. As I now beheld the robe, it seemed to me suddenly to become a mirror-image of myself: myself entire I saw in it, and it entire I saw in myself, that we were two in separateness, and yet again one in the sameness of our forms. . . . And the image of the King of kings was depicted all over it. . . . I saw also quiver all over it the movements of the gnosis. I saw that it was about to speak, and perceived the sound of its songs which it murmured on its way down: "I am that acted in the acts of him for whom I was brought up in my Father's house, and I perceived in myself how my stature grew in accordance with his labors." And with its regal movements it pours itself wholly out to me, and from the hands of its bringers hastens that I may take it; and me too my love urged on to run towards it and to receive it. And I stretched towards it and took it and decked myself with the beauty of its colors. And I cast the royal mantle about my entire self. Clothed therein, I ascended to the gate of salutation and adoration. I bowed my head and adored the splendor of my Father who had sent it to me, whose commands I had fulfilled as he too had done what he promised. . . . He received me joyfully, and I was with him in his kingdom.

5. *Divine Grace to Overcome Concupiscence: Augustine's Conversion*[10]

Thus soul-sick was I, and tormented, accusing myself much more severely than my wont, rolling and turning me in my chain, till that were wholly broken, whereby I now was but just, but still was, held. And Thou, O Lord, pressedst upon me in my inward parts by a severe mercy, redoubling the lashes of fear and shame, lest I should again give way, and not bursting that same slight remaining tie, it should recover strength, and bind me the faster. For I said within myself, "Be it done now, be it done now." And as I spake, I all but enacted it; I all but did it, and did it not: yet sunk not back to my former state, but kept my stand hard by, and took breath. And I essayed again, and wanted somewhat less of it, and somewhat less, and all but touched, and laid hold of it; and yet came not at it, nor touched nor laid hold of it; hesitating to die to death and to live to life: and the worse whereto I was inured, prevailed more with me than the better whereto I was unused: and the very moment wherein I was to become other than I was, the nearer it approached me, the greater horror did it strike into me; yet did it not strike me back, nor turned me away, but held me in suspense.

The very toys of toys, and vanities of vanities, my ancient mistresses, still held me; they plucked my fleshly garment, and whispered softly, "Dost thou cast us off? and from that moment shall we no more be with thee for ever? and from that moment shall not this or that be lawful for thee for ever?" And what was it which they suggested in that I said, "this or that," what did they suggest, O my God? Let Thy mercy turn it away from the soul of Thy servant. What defilements did they suggest! what shame! And now I much less than half heard them, and not openly showing themselves and contradicting me, but muttering as it were behind by back, and privily plucking me, as I was departing, but to look back on them. Yet they did retard me, so that I hesitated to burst and shake myself free from them, and to spring over whither I was called; a violent habit saying to me, "Thinkest thou, thou canst live without them?"

But now it spake very faintly. For on that side whither I had set my face, and whither I trembled to go, there appeared unto me the chaste dignity of Continency, serene, yet not relaxedly, gay, honestly alluring me to come and doubt not; and stretching forth to receive and embrace me, her holy hands full of multitudes of good examples: there were so many young men and maidens here, a multitude of youth and every age, grave widows and aged virgins; and Continence herself in all, not barren, but a fruitful mother of children of joys, by Thee her Husband, O Lord. And she smiled on me with a persuasive mockery, as would she say, "Canst not thou what these youths, what these maidens can? or can they either in themselves, and not rather in the Lord their God? The Lord their God gave me unto them. Why standest thou in thyself, and so standest not? cast thyself upon Him, fear not He will not withdraw Himself that thou shouldest fall; cast thyself fearlessly upon Him, He will receive, and will heal thee." And I blushed exceedingly, for that I yet heard the muttering of those toys, and hung in suspense. And she again seemed to say, "Stop thine ears against those thy unclean members on the earth, that they may be mortified. They tell thee of delights, but not as doth the law of the Lord thy God." This controversy in my heart was self against self only. But Alypius sitting close by my side, in silence waited the issue of my unwonted emotion.

But when a deep consideration had from the secret bottom of my soul drawn together and heaped up all my misery in the sight of my heart; there arose a mighty storm, bringing a mighty shower of tears. Which that I might pour forth wholly, in its natural expressions, I rose from Alypius: solitude was suggested to me as fitter for the business of weeping; so I retired so far that even his presence could not be a burden to me. Thus was it then with me, and he perceived something of it; for something I suppose I had spoken, wherein the tones of my voice appeared choked with weeping, and so had risen up. He then remained where we were sitting, most extremely astonished. I cast myself down I know not how, under a certain figtree, giving full vent to my tears; and the floods of mine eyes gushed out an acceptable sacrifice to Thee. And, not indeed in these words, yet to this purpose, spake I much unto Thee: and Thou, O Lord, how long? how long, Lord, wilt Thou be angry for ever? Remember not our former iniquities, for I felt that I was held by them. I sent up these sorrowful words: How long, how long, "to-morrow, and to-morrow?" Why not now? why not is there this hour an end to my uncleanness?

So was I speaking and weeping in the most bitter contrition of my heart, when, lo! I heard from a neighbouring house a voice, as of boy or girl, I know not, chanting, and oft repeating, "Take up and read; Take up and read." Instantly, my countenance altered, I began to think most intently whether children were wont in any kind of play to sing such words: nor could I remember ever to have heard the like. So checking the torrent of my tears, I arose; interpreting it to be no other than a command from God to open the book, and read the first chapter I should find. For I had heard of Antony,[11] that coming in during the reading of the Gospel, he received the admonition, as if what was being read was spoken to him: Go, sell all that thou hast, and give to the poor, and thou shalt have treasure in heaven, and come and follow me: and by such oracle he was forthwith converted unto Thee. Eagerly then I returned to the place where Alypius was sitting; for there had I laid the volume of the Apostle when I arose thence. I seized, opened, and in silence read that section on which my eyes first fell: Not in rioting and drunkenness, not in chambering and wantonness, not in strife and envying; but put ye on the Lord Jesus Christ, and make not provision for the flesh, in concupiscence. No further would I read; nor needed I: for instantly at the end of this sentence, by a light as it were of serenity infused into my heart, all the darkness of doubt vanished away.

6. The Spiritual Marriage: The Seventh Mansion in Teresa of Avila's **Interior Castle**[12]

I am hopeful, sisters, that, not for my sake but for your sakes, He will grant me this favour, so that you may understand how important it is that no fault of yours should hinder the celebration of His Spiritual Marriage with your souls, which, as you will see, brings with it so many blessings. . . .

When Our Lord is pleased to have pity upon this soul, which suffers and has suffered so much out of desire for Him, and which He has now taken spiritually to be His bride, He brings her into this Mansion of His, which is the seventh, before consummating the Spiritual Marriage. For He must needs have an abiding-place in the soul, just as He has one in Heaven, where His Majesty alone dwells: so let us call this a second Heaven. It is very important, sisters, that we should not think of the soul as of something dark. It must seem dark to most of us, as we cannot see it, for we forget that there is not only a light which we can see, but also an interior light, and so we think that within our soul there is some kind of darkness. . . .

This secret union takes place in the deepest centre of the soul, which must be where God Himself dwells, and I do not think there is any need of a door by which to enter it. I say there is no need of a door because all that has so far been described seems to have come through the medium of the senses and faculties and this appearance of the Humanity of the Lord must do so too. But what passes in the union of the Spiritual Marriage is very different. The Lord appears in the centre of the soul, not through an imaginary, but through an intellectual vision. . . .

This instantaneous communication of God to the soul is so great a secret and so sublime a favour, and such delight is felt by the soul, that I do not know with what to compare it, beyond saying that the Lord is pleased to manifest to the soul at that moment the glory that is in Heaven, in a sublimer manner than is possible through any vision or spiritual consolation. It is impossible to say more than that, as far as one can understand, the soul (I mean the spirit of this soul) is made one with God, Who, being likewise a Spirit, has been pleased to reveal the love that He has for us by showing to certain persons the extent of that love, so that we may praise His greatness. For He has been pleased to unite Himself with His creature in such a way that they have become like two who cannot be separated from one another: even so He will not separate Himself from her.

Perhaps when St. Paul says: "He who is joined to God becomes one spirit with Him," he is referring to this sovereign Marriage, which presupposes the entrance of His Majesty into the soul by union. And he also says: *Mihi vivere Christus est, mori lucrum.* This, I think, the soul may say here, for it is here that the little butterfly to which we have referred dies, and with the greatest joy, because Christ is now its life.

This, with the passage of time, becomes more evident through its effects; for the soul clearly understands, by certain secret aspirations, that it is endowed with life by God. Very often these aspirations are so vehement that what they teach cannot possibly be doubted: though they cannot be described, the soul experiences them very forcibly. . . .

For from those Divine breasts, where it seems that God is ever sustaining the soul, flow streams of milk, which solace all who dwell in the Castle.

7. Terror, Glory, and the Gift of Reading in a Black American Evangelist[13]

In the year 1830, July, I was wakened by thunder and lightning at the break of day. . . . I rose up and walked the floor back and forth wringing my hands and crying under great fear. I heard it said to me, "This day thy soul is required of thee," and all my sins from my childhood rushed into my mind like an over swelling tide, and I expected every clap of thunder to launch my soul at the bar of God with all my sins that I had ever done. I have no language to describe my feelings. . . . I then thought to attempt to pray to God to forgive me all my sins just as I was agoing to die — I thought it would be an insult to such a merciful God. And all this time it was athundering and lightning as if the heavens and earth were acoming together — so it seemed to me at that time. And I felt it was just that I should be damned for sinning against a just and holy God. I then felt a love mingled with sorrow toward an insulted God, whom I had sinned against all my days. While these thoughts with many more rolled against my troubled breast, they covered me with shame, fear, and confusion to think of living all my days in sin and then dying and being driven from the presence of a merciful and holy God. It was more than I could bear.

I then thought, "I might as well go to Hell off my knees acrying for mercy as anywhere else." So I kneeled at the head of the garret stairs, which was the first impression, and down I kneeled and I cried and prayed to God with all my might and strength. The more I prayed, the worse I felt. My sins like a mountain reached to the skies, black as sack cloth of hair and the heavens was as brass against my prayers and everything above my head was of one solid blackness. And the fearful foreboding of my sudden destruction caused me to cry out in the bitterness of my soul, "Lord, I never will rise from my knees till thou for Christ's sake has mercy on my poor sinking soul or sends me to Hell." For I felt as though my soul had come into the chamber of death.

And in this moment of despair the cloud bursted, the heavens was clear, and the mountain was gone. My spirit was light, my heart was filled with love for God and all mankind. And the lightning, which was a moment ago the messenger of death, was now the messenger of peace, joy, and consolation. And I rose from my knees, ran down stairs, opened the door to let the lightning in the house, for it was like sheets of glory to my soul.

My brother came downstairs. I said, "Oh, I have found the Lord." "Has thee?" he said. "Oh, yes, yes, I have. Come and help me praise Him." "Oh, yes, sister, I will. I am glad thee has found the Lord again." And at every clap of thunder I leaped from the floor praising the God of my salvation. I opened all the

windows in the house to let the lightning in for it was like
streams of bright glory to my soul and in this happy state I
praised the Lord for about an hour without ceasing. My brother
then said, "Sister, let us now return the Lord thanks for what He
has done for us." "Oh, yes, yes, my brother, we will." And
down we kneeled. My brother made a feeling prayer. When he
closed, I lifted up my voice in prayer, in thanks to Almighty God
who had heard my prayer for Christ's sake.

After I received the blessing of God, I had a great desire to
read the Bible. I am the only child of my mother that had not
learning. And now, having the charge of my brother and his six
children to see to, and my husband, and taking in sewing for a
living, I saw no way that I could now get learning without my
brother would give me one hour's lesson at night after supper or
before he went to bed. . . . And my brother so tired when he
would come home that he had not power so to do, and it would
grieve me. Then I would pray to God to give me power over my
feelings that I might not think hard of my brother. Then I would
be comforted. . . . I felt hurt, when he refused me these little
things. And at this time. I could not keep from crying. And these
words were spoken in my heart, "Be faithful, and the time shall
come when you can write." These words were spoken in my
heart as though a tender father spoke them. My tears were gone
in a moment.

One day I was sitting finishing a dress in haste and in prayer.
This word was spoken in my mind, "Who learned the first man
on earth?" "Why, God." "He is unchangeable, and if He learned
the first man to read, He can learn you." I laid down my dress,
picked up my Bible, ran upstairs, opened it, and kneeled down
with it pressed to my breast, prayed earnestly to Almighty God if
it was consisting to His holy will, to learn me to read His holy
word. And when I looked on the word, I began to read. And
when I found I was reading, I was frightened— then I could not
read one word. I closed my eyes again in prayer and then opened
my eyes, began to read. So I done, until I read the chapter. I
came down. "Samuel, I can read the Bible." "Woman, you are
agoing crazy!" "Praise the God of heaven and of earth, I can read
His holy word!" Down I sat and read through. . . .

So I tried, took my Bible daily and praying and read until I
could read anywhere. The first chapter that I read I never could
know it after that day. I only knowed it was in James, but what
chapter I never can tell.

Oh how thankful I feel for this unspeakable gift of Almighty God to me! Oh may I make a good use of it all the days of my life!

8. *"You Are Enough!" A Woman Seminarian's Story*[14]

It is not enough
said her father
that you
> get all A's each quarter
> play Mozart for your kinfolk
> win starred-firsts in contest
you must
come home on your wedding night.

It is not enough
said her mother
that you
> smile at Auntie Lockwood
> take cookies to the neighbors
> keep quiet while I'm napping
you must
cure my asthma.

It is not enough
said her husband
that you
> write letters to my parents
> fix pumpkin pie and pastry
> forget your name was Bauer
you must
always
you must
never.

It is not enough
said her children
that you
> make us female brownies
> tend our friends and puppies
> buy us Nike tennies

you must
let us kill you.

It is not enough
said her pastor
that you
    teach the second graders
    change the cloths and candles
    kneel prostrate at the altar
as long as there are starving children in the world
you must
not eat
without guilt.

It is not enough
said her counselor
that you
    struggle with the demons
    integrate your childhood
    leave when time is over
you must
stop crying
clarify your poetic symbols
and
not feel
that you are
not enough.

I give up
she said
I am not enough
and laid down
into the deep blue pocket
of night
to wait
for death.

She waited . . .

and
finally
her heart exploded
her breathing stopped

They came with stretcher
took her clothes off
covered her with linen
then went away
and left her locked
in deep blue pocket tomb

The voice said
   YOU ARE ENOUGH

       naked
       crying
       bleeding
       nameless
       starving
       sinful
   YOU ARE ENOUGH

And the third day
she sat up
   asked for milk and crackers
   took ritual bath with angels
   dressed herself with wings
and flew away.

Mother Church shelters her children under her protective arms and cloak. Does such a Mother Church only smother us or can she help us to become WomanChurch?

Madonna of Mercy. Painting by Giovanni di Paolo, 1437, Chiesa dei Servi, Siena.

8

Redemptive Community

DOCUMENTS

1. The Ecclesia of Israel as a Male Exodus Community
2. Israel as God's Wayward Wife
3. Mary as Liberated Israel, Representative of the Oppressed
4. The Church as Model Patriarchal Family
5. The Church as Eschatological Bride of Christ, Model of Wifely Submission
6. The Church as Virginal Mother, Womb of Rebirth to Immortal Life
7. Spiritual Community in Gnosticism and the Defense of Women's Apostolic Authority
8. WomanChurch as a Feminist Exodus Community

The word *Ecclesia* means a citizen assembly gathered to do the business of the community. This was the word adopted for the Church in the New Testament. In the Greek Septuagint this term was also used for the assembly of Israel. It thus took on the connotation of a religious assembly gathered before God. In the Exodus narrative this assembly of Israel is established as a people whom God had liberated from slavery and led into the desert to be consecrated exclusively to his service and to receive the commandments from Mount Sinai. In reading this Exodus account of the assembly of the people before God at Sinai, we realize that the author assumes this to be an all-male gathering. As part of their consecration to God to make themselves holy to receive the commandments, the male community is told not to go near a woman.

Here we have the key contradiction in the concept of the assembly of Israel as an exodus community. An exodus community is a community defined by its liberation from slavery and oppression. God functions as liberator who leads the people out of the land of slavery to the land of Promise. In their revolt against their former slave masters, the male community become tightly bonded with one another. Yet this definition of liberation from bondage does not include the bondage of women under patriarchy. The liberated fraternity define themselves through the exclusion of women. Women are, again and again, betrayed by male exodus communities, whether those be the assembly of ancient Israel at Sinai, the eighteenth-century French and American Revolutions, or Black and Latin American liberation theology today.[1] They work enthusiastically for the liberation of "their people," only to discover, when the liberated community assembles its new institutions, that they are not included as active members but are relegated again to dependency. The laws of the new male state are rewritten to sanctify patriarchy and to make male heads of families the representatives of the community before God and the representatives of the word of God to women, children, and servants.

This patriarchal community that excludes women from leadership also symbolizes itself collectively as female, as a Bride or Wife of God and Mother of God's People. Why? This bridal-maternal imagery stands within the basic symbol system of patriarchy. If God is like a great Patriarch and the assembly of males like his "sons" or "servants," then the community collectively can be imaged as like a wife of God whom God elects. Such symbolism of the covenant of Israel as like a patriarchal sacred marriage reverses the sacred marriage imagery of Sumerian, Babylonian, and Canaanite religion. Here the Goddess was the dominant divine figure, and the bridegroom represented the king, the representative of the human community.

In the second text, from Hosea, we see this Hebrew appropriation of the Sacred Marriage motif as a struggle to displace the earlier Canaanite sacred marriage. Israel is pictured as a wayward or harlot wife. Why? Because Israel encompasses a people and a land conquered by Hebrew desert patriarchy who had originally seen themselves collectively in the light of Anath's marriage of Baal. They are nostalgic for this earlier love relationship and continue to believe that the earlier religious rites were more efficacious in agricultural blessings, bringing rains in season and fertility to the land. They suspect the desert patriarch is not as good at agricultural blessings.

But the Hebrew God, who now claims Israel as his people and Canaan as his promised land, also claims to be the true Lord of agricultural blessings. In good patriarchal fashion, he will punish his bride and threaten to throw her out in the desert in summary divorce if she does not give up her straying after her former husband, Baal. But he also hopes to win her over to exclusive attachment to him. He will woo her into the desert, speak tenderly to her, and get her to identify herself with the exodus community whom he led out of Egypt and betrothed at Sinai, so that she will accept her new relationship to her jealous patriarchal Lord.

In the New Testament this imagery of the sacred marriage of Israel and God is applied to the relationship of the Church to God or to Christ. In the New Testament there are different possible meanings for this female symbol of the Church. In the Luke text of the Magnificat, Mary represents the Messianic Israel. This hymn, based on the hymn of Hannah, Samuel's mother (1 Sam. 2:1-10), describes Mary as exulting in her liberation by God from social oppression. Through God's liberating power, the mighty have been put down from their thrones, and she, representative of the humble, has been lifted up.

Luke, particularly among the gospel writers, uses women to represent the marginated and oppressed people to whom Christ brings the good news of God's favor, over against the powerful of religion and society who refuse to hear this liberating word. One enters this community of liberation by renouncing privilege and status and identifying with the despised of the society. The Scribes and the Pharisees will go into the Kingdom of God behind the prostitutes and tax collectors (Matt. 21:31). The wealthy and mighty will be overthrown and sent empty away, or, like Zacchaeus (Luke 19:1-10), will be included in the Messianic Israel by identifying with the poor and giving fourfold amendment fo their former oppression. Thus the Magnificat at least opens up the possibility of a Christian interpretation of redemptive community as a community of liberation for all, starting with women of the poorest and most despised classes.[2]

However, this potential vision of a more radical and inclusive exodus community has been betrayed by a new triumph of patriarchy in the post-Pauline tradition of the New Testament. Here the Church is portrayed as making its peace not with only patriarchy but with the authorities of the Roman Empire as well. The Church will settle into a quiet and respectable life as an established religion that prays for divine blessings on kings and all in authority. The leaders of the Church — bishops and deacons — are to be modeled after ideal paterfamilias who have proven their authority by keeping their children submissive and respectful. Women are still acknowledged as deaconesses, but they are probably being relegated to lesser roles as ministers to women in certain private functions, rather than equal to deacons as public ministers of the Church, as in Paul (Rom. 16:1).[3] Women are especially enjoined to keep silent, a command that inadvertently reveals that women were not presumed to be silent in some Christian churches at this time. Some churches still clung to the early Christian vision of the Church as a community that liberated women and slaves and enabled them to prophesy and teach. Thus the text reveals the struggle of patriarchal Christianity to suppress this earlier, more inclusive vision.[4]

In the New Testament the idea of the Church as God's messianic people is also translated into the vision of the eschatological Israel, the New Jerusalem (Rev. 21:2), that appears from heaven to be presented to Christ as his bride. Unlike the old Israel, the wayward bride still prone to harlotry (infidelity to God), this new Israel will be a chaste or virginal bride "without spot." The Church is seen as a sinless community of saints who anticipate the eschatological community of saints of the Messianic era.

In the Epistle to the Ephesians this concept of the Church as a sinless community of saints, a "spotless" bride of Christ, is oddly identified with the submissive wife of patriarchal marriage. Patriarchalizing Christianity reiterates its demands that "wives obey your husbands; slaves obey your masters; children obey your parents" in an effort to suppress the earlier vision of the Church as a community of revolutionized social relations.[5] It does this by trying to get the subjugated groups in the patriarchal family to internalize their submission to their husband, father, or master by seeing this submission as an expression of their submission and obedience to Christ. Christ becomes the sanction of patriarchal dominance rather than the liberator. Ephesians 5 represents this internalized patriarchalism in which male heads are told to exercise their authority in a kindly and loving manner while wives, children, and slaves are exhorted to accept their obedience to men as expressions of their submission to Christ.

However, this effort to bring together the concepts of patriarchal marriage and of the Church as eschatological bride of Christ was challenged in early Christianity by a different interpretation of this bridal symbol. In ascetic Christianity, redeemed Christians manifest their eschatological life in Christ by renouncing marriage and anticipating that heavenly community "where there is no more marriage or giving in marriage" (Matt. 22:30). The virginal motherhood of the Church is not simply that she is presented to her Lord as a chaste and sinless bride. She also represents baptized Christians reborn in her virginal womb from the "filth" of sexual reproduction to virginal chastity. The Church as bride of Christ is seen as the womb of baptismal waters, impregnated by the passion of Christ, through which Christians reject the sinful birth from which they will die as mortal beings and be reborn to the virginal state of immortal life.

Here the bridal and maternal symbolism of the Church, identified with virginal Christians, becomes hostile to sexual women who bear children. These now become the lowest-class citizens in the Church, one step removed from outright prostitutes beyond the pale of redemption. In the words of St. Jerome (fourth century A.D.),[6] mothers can be redeemed and allowed a humble place in the Church by bearing children who can be won to remain virgins and exemplars of redeemed life.

Gnostic Christians in the second and third centuries A.D. also accepted this identification of redemption with chastity. But, unlike patriarchal ascetic Christians, they retained the early Christian vision of the Church as an exodus community that overcame patriarchy. They envisioned the Church as a spiritual community of equals in which men and women who had renounced sexual roles and functions also shared in spiritual authority. In the fragment of the gnostic Gospel of Mary, we see this affirmation of the Church as an egalitarian spiritual community over against that patriarchal Church which identified its episcopal hierarchical authority with an apostolic descent from the Prince of the Apostles, Peter.[7]

In the Gospel of Mary (as well as several other similar pericopes in other gnostic gospels),[8] Peter becomes the representative of patriarchal hostility toward women's equality in ministry. Mary Magdalene exemplifies the apostolic authority of women. She is seen as the beloved disciple of Christ. She is especially adept at understanding the Christian gnosis and so is called upon to communicate it to the frightened disciples once the risen Lord has departed from their midst. A dispute then ensues among the male disciples in which her authority is challenged by Peter but defended by Levi. The rest of the disciples affirm Levi's view. Thus fortified by the power of the Spirit communicated through Mary, the disciples go out to preach the gospel, adhering to the last words of Christ "not to lay down any other rule or law other than that which the savior gave to them," a reference to the gnostic Christians' rejection of the creeds, rules, and hierarchical Church structures being developed by the Petrine Church.[9]

The last text in this chapter is a portion of a sermon I gave at the WomanChurch Speaks conference in Chicago in November 1983. This sermon represented the new vision of Church being generated through the union of Christianity and feminism. For the first time the vision of the Church as an exodus community from patriarchy is being developed by feminist Christians. The ancient vision of Church as an exodus community is reworked here, not only to include women but to name patriarchy as the key symbol of the system of "rape, genocide, and war" that oppresses women, children, and the earth. Men too are called upon to identify with this exodus community and to flee from the idol of patriarchy.

Reflection

What is the root of the male need to exclude women from leadership in religion? Why do male exodus communities ignore or exclude women from their defintion of liberation from oppression? Give historical and contemporary examples of this.

Why is holiness before God identified in Exodus with not "touching a woman"? How is this translated in Christianity into the idea of holiness (purity) as virginity? Discuss the implied identification of birth with mortality and of rejection of sex and procreation with conquering mortality, that is, with immortal life? How is sex associated with fear of death in male? Is this different in females?

Discuss the differences of four models of Church: (1) the Church as model patriarchal family, (2) the Church as male exodus community, (3) the Church as eschatological Bride of Christ, mother of the Redeemed, (4) WomanChurch as a feminist exodus community.

Gather in small groups and design a model of a community of liberation from patriarchy. What would be the leadership pattern of such a community? What would be its understandings of the function and relationship of ministry and community? How would it understand worship? What would be its key symbols and sacraments? What would be its social praxis?

1. The Ecclesia of Israel as a Male Exodus Community[10]

On the third new moon after the people of Israel had gone forth out of the land of Egypt, on that day they came into the wilderness of Sinai, and there Israel encamped before the mountain. And Moses went up to God, and the Lord called him out of the mountain, saying, "Thus you shall say to the house of Jacob, and tell the people of Israel: You have seen what I did to the Egyptians, and how I bore you on eagles' wings and brought

you to myself. Now therefore, if you will obey my voice and keep
my covenant, you shall be my own possession among all peoples;
for all the earth is mine, and you shall be to me a kingdom of
priests and a holy nation. These are the words which you shall
speak to the children of Israel.''

So Moses came and called the elders of the people, and set
before them all these words which the Lord had commanded him.
And all the people answered together and said, ''All that the Lord
has spoken we will do.'' And Moses reported the words of the
people to the Lord. And the Lord said to Moses, ''Lo, I am
coming to you in a thick cloud, that the people may hear when I
speak with you, and may also believe you for ever.''

Then Moses told the words of the people to the Lord. And the
Lord said to Moses, ''Go to the people and consecrate them today
and tomorrow, and let them wash their garments, and be ready
by the third day; for on the third day the Lord will come down
upon Mount Sinai in the sight of all the people. When the
trumpet sounds a long blast, they shall come up to the
mountain.'' So Moses went down from the mountain to the
people, and consecrated the people; and they washed their
garments.

And he said to the people, ''Be ready by the third day; do not
go near a woman.''

On the morning of the third day there were thunders and
lightnings, and a thick cloud upon the mountain, and a very loud
trumpet blast, so that all the people who were in the camp
trembled. Then Moses brought the people out of the camp to
meet God; and they took their stand at the foot of the mountain.

And Mount Sinai was wrapped in smoke, because the Lord
descended upon it in fire;

And God spoke all these words, saying,

''I am the Lord your God, who brought you out of the land of
Egypt, out of the house of bondage.

''You shall have no other gods before me.''

2. Israel as God's Wayward Wife[11]

''Plead with you mother, plead —
  for she is not my wife,
  and I am not her husband —

that she put away her harlotry from her face,
    and her adultery from between her breasts;
lest I strip her naked
    and make her as in the day she was born,
and make her like a wilderness,
    and set her like a parched land,
    and slay her with thirst.
Upon her children also I will have no pity,
    because they are children of harlotry.
For their mother has played the harlot;
    she that conceived them has acted shamefully.
For she said, 'I will go after my lovers,
    who give me my bread and my water,
    my wool and my flax, my oil and my drink.'
Therefore I will hedge up her way with thorns;
    and I will build a wall against her,
    so that she cannot find her paths.
She shall pursue her lovers,
    but not overtake them;
and she shall seek them,
    but shall not find them.
Then she shall say, 'I will go
    and return to my first husband,
    for it was better with me then than now.'
And she did not know
    that it was I who gave her
    the grain, the wine, and the oil,
and who lavished upon her silver
    and gold which they used for Ba'al.
Therefore I will take back
    my grain in its time,
    and my wine in its season;
and I will take away my wool and my flax,
    which were to cover her nakedness.
Now I will uncover her lewdness
    in the sight of her lovers,
    and no one shall rescue her out of my hand.
And I will put an end to all her mirth,
    her feasts, her new moons, her sabbaths,
    and all her appointed feasts.
And I will lay waste her vines and her fig trees,
    of which she said,

'These are my hire,
   which my lovers have given me.'
I will make them a forest,
   and the beasts of the field shall devour them.
And I will punish her for the feast days of the Ba'als
   when she burned incense to them
and decked herself with her ring and jewelry,
   and went after her lovers,
   and forgot me, says the Lord.

"Therefore, behold, I will allure her,
   and bring her into the wilderness,
   and speak tenderly to her.
And there I will give her her vineyards,
   and make the valley of Achor a door of hope.
And there she shall answer as in the days of her youth,
   as at the time when she came out of the land of Egypt.

"And in that day, says the Lord, you will call me, 'My
husband,' and no longer will you call me, 'My Ba'al.' For I will
remove the names of the Ba'als from her mouth, and they shall be
mentioned by name no more. And I will make for you a covenant
on that day with the beasts of the field, the birds of the air, and
the creeping things of the ground; and I will abolish the bow, the
sword, and war from the land; and I will make you lie down in
safety. And I will betroth you to me for ever; I will betroth you to
me in righteousness and in justice, in steadfast love, and in
mercy. I will betroth you to me in faithfulness; and you shall
know the Lord."

3. Mary as Liberated Israel, Representative of the Oppressed[12]

And when Elizabeth heard Mary's greeting, the baby stirred in
her womb. Then Elizabeth was filled with the Holy Spirit and
cried aloud, "God's blessing is on you above all women, and his
blessing is on the fruit of your womb. Who am I, that the mother
of my Lord should visit me? I tell you, when your greeting
sounded in my ears, the baby in my womb leapt for joy. How
happy is she who has had faith that the Lord's promise would
be fulfilled!"

And Mary said:

"Tell out, my soul, the greatness of the Lord,
rejoice, rejoice, my spirit, in God my saviour;
so tenderly has he looked upon his servant,
    humble as she is.
For, from this day forth,
all generations will count me blessed,
so wonderfully has he dealt with me,
    the Lord, the Mighty One.
    His name is Holy;
his mercy sure from generation to generation
    toward those who fear him;
the deeds his own right arm has done
    disclose his might:
the arrogant of heart and mind he has put to rout,
he has brought down monarchs from their thrones,
    but the humble have been lifted high.
The hungry he has satisfied with good things,
    the rich sent empty away.
He has ranged himself at the side of Israel his servant;
    firm in his promise to our forefathers,
he has not forgotten to show mercy to Abraham
    and his children's children, for ever."

Mary stayed with her about three months and then returned home.

4. The Church as Model Patriarchal Family[13]

First of all, then, I urge that supplications, prayers, intercessions, and thanksgivings be made for all men, for kings and all who are in high positions, that we may lead a quiet and peaceable life, godly and respectful in everyway. This is good, and it is acceptable in the sight of God our Savior, who desires all men to be saved and to come to the knowledge of the truth. For there is one God, and there is one mediator between God and men, the man Christ Jesus, who gave himself as a ransom for all.

I desire then that in every place the men should pray, lifting holy hands without anger or quarreling.

Let a woman learn in silence with all submissiveness. I permit no woman to teach or to have authority over men; she is to keep silent.

The saying is sure: If anyone aspires to the office of bishop, he desires a noble task. Now a bishop must be above reproach, married only once, temperate, sensible, dignified, hospitable, an apt teacher, no drunkard, not violent but gentle, not quarrelsome, and no lover of money. He must manage his own household well, keeping his children submissive and respectful in every way; for if a man does not know how to manage his own household, how can he care for God's church?

Deacons likewise must be serious, not double-tongued, not addicted to much wine, not greedy for gain; they must hold the mystery of the faith with a clear conscience. And let them also be tested first; then if they prove themselves blameless let them serve as deacons. The women likewise must be serious, no slanderers, but temperate, faithful in all things.

Let deacons be married only once, and let them manage their children and their households well; for those who serve well as deacons gain a good standing for themselves and also great confidence in the faith which is in Christ Jesus.

5. The Church as Eschatological Bride of Christ, Model of Wifely Submission[14]

Therefore be imitators of God, as beloved children. And walk in love, as Christ loved us and gave himself up for us, a fragrant offering and sacrifice to God.

But immorality and all impurity or covetousness must not even be named among you, as is fitting among saints. . . .

But be filled with the Spirit, addressing one another in psalms and hymns and spiritual songs, singing and making melody to the Lord with all your heart, always and for everything giving thanks in the name of our Lord Jesus Christ to God the Father.

Be subject to one another out of reverence for Christ. Wives, be subject to your husbands, as to the Lord. For the husband is the head of the wife as Christ is the head of the church, his body, and is himself its Savior. As the church is subject to Christ, so let wives also be subject in everything to their husbands. Husbands, love your wives, as Christ loved the church and gave himself up for her, that he might sanctify her, having cleansed her by the washing of water with the word, that the church might be presented before him in splendor, without spot or wrinkle or any such thing, that she might be holy and without blemish. Even so husbands should love their wives as their own bodies. He who loves his wife loves himself. For no man ever hates his own flesh, but nourishes and cherishes it, as Christ does the church, because we are members of his body. "For this reason a man shall leave his father and mother and be joined to his wife, and the two shall become one." This is a great mystery, and I take it to mean Christ and the church; however, let each one of you love his wife as himself, and let the wife see that she respects her husband.

6. The Church as Virginal Mother, Womb of Rebirth to Immortal Life

CYPRIAN[15]

Our discourse is now to virgins, for whom, as their glory is the more exalted, our solicitude is also greater. They are the flower of the Church burgeoning forth, the fair adornment of spiritual grace, a charming disposition, a work perfect and pure of glorious praise, the image of God reflecting the holiness of the Lord, the peerless part of Christ's flock. Through them *Mother Church* rejoices in her glorious fruitfulness, and in them it flowers in adundance; and the more an abounding virginity adds to its numbers, the greater is the *Mother's* joy. . .

There is only one head and only one source, only one *Mother* abounding in the issue of her fruitfulness. *By her bearing are we born, by her milk are we nourished, by her are we animated.*

She, the *Bride of Christ,* cannot be adulterous; she is untainted and chaste. She knows only one home, the sanctity of one bedchamber she guards with chaste modesty. She it is that keeps us unharmed for God, she appoints *the sons she has begotten* to His kingdom. Whosoever separates himself from the Church and attaches himself to an adulteress, separates himself from the promises of the Church, nor will he who leaves the Church, attain to the rewards of Christ. He is a stranger, he is unholy, he is an enemy. *He cannot have God for father, who has not the Church for mother.*

METHODIUS[16]

Thus did the Apostolic very accurately refer the circumstances of Adam to Christ. For thus can there be perfect harmony in saying

that out of His bones and flesh the Church was born; that indeed
for her sake the Logos left His Father in heaven and came down,
to cleave to His Wife; and that He slept in the ecstasy of His
passion, choosing to die for her "that He Himself might cleanse
her in the bath and present her to Himself a Church glorious and
without blemish," prepared to receive the spiritual and blessed
seed which He Himself sows, implanting it with whisperings in
the depths of the mind. And the Church after the manner of a
woman conceives and forms it, so as to give birth to and rear up
virtue. Thus, too, is the command, "Increase and multiply,"
meetly fulfilled, the Church increasing with each succeeding day
in greatness and beauty and multitude through the embrace of the
Logos and her intercourse with Him, who even now comes down
to us and goes into ecstasy in the memorial of His passion.
Otherwise the Church could not conceive the faithful and give
them new birth by the bath of rebirth, if Christ did not for their
sake too empty Himself, that He might be received in the
recapitulation of His passion, as I stated, and die again, having
come down from heaven; and if He did not unite Himself to His
Wife, the Church, and thus provide for a certain power to be
taken from His own side, so that all who are built up in Him,
who are born by the bath, may grow up, taking of His bones and
His flesh, that is to say, of His holiness and His glory. For he
who says that the bones and flesh of wisdom are understanding
and virtue, speaks most correctly, and that the side is the spirit of
truth, the Paraclete: taking from Him, the enlightened
(= baptized) are fitly reborn to immortality.

7. Spiritual Community in Gnosticism and the Defense of Women's Apostolic Authority[17]

The Savior said, "All natures, all formations, all creatures exist in
and with one another, and they will be resolved again into their
own roots. For the nature of matter is resolved into (the roots of)
its nature alone. He who has ears to hear, let him hear."

Peter said to him, "Since you have explained everything to
us, tell us this also: What is the sin of the world?" The Savior
said, "There is no sin, but it is you who make sin when you do
the things that are like the nature of adultery, which is called
'sin.' That is why the Good came into your midst, to the essence
of every nature, in order to restore it to its root." Then he

continued and said, "That is why you [become sick] and die, for
[. . .] of the one who [. . . He who] understands, let him
understand. [Matter gave birth to] a passion that has no equal,
which proceeded from (something) contrary to nature. Then there
arises a disturbance in the whole body. That is why I said to you,
'Be of good courage,' and if you are discouraged (be) encouraged
in the presence of the different forms of nature. He who has ears
to hear, let him hear."

When the blessed one had said this, he greeted them all,
saying, "Peace be with you. Receive my peace to yourselves.
Beware that no one lead you astray, saying, 'Lo here!' or 'Lo
there!' For the Son of Man is within you. Follow after him! Those
who seek him will find him. Go then and preach the gospel of the
kingdom. Do not lay down any rules beyond what I appointed for
you, and do not give a law like the lawgiver lest you be
constrained by it." When he had said this, he departed.

But they were grieved. They wept greatly, saying, "How shall
we go to the Gentiles and preach the gospel of the kingdom of
the Son of Man? If they did not spare him, how will they spare
us?" Then Mary stood up, greeted them all, and said to her
brethren, "Do not weep and do not grieve nor be irresolute, for
his grace will be entirely with you and will protect you. But rather
let us praise his greatness, for he has prepared us (and) made us
into men." When Mary said this, she turned their hearts to the
Good, and they began to discuss the words of the [Savior].

Peter said to Mary, "Sister, We know that the Savior loved
you more than the rest of women. Tell us the words of the Savior
which you remember — which you know (but) we do not nor
have we heard them." Mary answered and said, "What is hidden
from you I will proclaim to you." And she began to speak to
them these words: "I," she said, "I saw the Lord in a vision and
I said to him, 'Lord, I saw you today in a vision.' He answered
and said to me, 'Blessed are you, that you did not waver at the
sight of me. For where the mind is, there is the treasure.' I said to
him, 'Lord, now does he who sees the vision see it [through] the
soul [or] through the spirit?' The Savior answered and said, 'He
does not see through the soul nor through the spirit, but the mind
which [is] between the two — that is [what] sees the vision and it
is [. . .].'

"And desire said, 'I did not see you descending, but now I
see you ascending. Why do you lie, since you belong to me?' The
soul answered and said, 'I saw you. You did not see me nor

recognize me. I served you as a garment, and you did not know me.' When it had said this, it went away rejoicing greatly.

"Again it came to the third power, which is called ignorance. [It (the power)] questioned the soul, saying, 'Where are you going? In wickedness are you bound. But you are bound; do not judge!' And the soul said, 'Why do you judge me, although I have not judged? I was bound, though I have not bound. I was not recognized. But I have recognized that the All is being dissolved, both the earthly (things) and the heavenly.'

"When the soul had overcome the third power, it went upwards and saw the fourth power, (which) took seven forms. The first form is darkness, the second desire, the third ignorance, the fourth is the excitement of death, the fifth is the kingdom of the flesh, the sixth is the foolish wisdom of flesh, the seventh is the wrathful wisdom. These are the seven [powers] of wrath. They ask the soul, 'Whence do you come, slayer of men, or where are you going, conqueror of space?' The soul answered and said, 'What binds me has been slain, and what turns me about has been overcome, and my desire has been ended, and ignorance has died. In a [world] I was released from a world, [and] in a type from a heavenly type, and (from) the fetter of oblivion which is transient. From this time on will I attain to the rest of the time, of the season, of the aeon, in silence.' "

When Mary said this, she fell silent, since it was to this point that the Savior had spoken with her. But Andrew answered and said to the brethren, "Say what you (wish to) say about what she has said. I at least do not believe that the Savior said this. For certainly these teachings are strange ideas." Peter answered and spoke concerning these same things. He questioned them about the Savior: "Did he really speak privately with a woman (and) not openly to us? Are we to turn about and all listen to her? Did he prefer her to us?"

Then Mary wept and said to Peter, "My brother Peter, what do you think? Do you think that I thought this up myself in my heart, or that I am lying about the Savior?" Levi answered and said to Peter, "Peter, you have always been hot-tempered. Now I see you contending against the woman like the adversaries. But if the Savior made her worthy, who are you indeed to reject her? Surely the Savior knows her very well. That is why he loved her more than us. Rather let us be ashamed and put on the perfect man, and separate as he commanded us and preach the gospel, not laying down any other rule or other law beyond what the

Savior said." When [. . .] and they began to go forth [to] proclaim
and to preach.

8. WomanChurch as a Feminist Exodus Community[18]

As Woman-Church we repudiate the idol of patriarchy. We
repudiate it and denounce it in the name of God, in the name of
Christ, in the name of Church, in the name of humanity, in the
name of earth. Our God and Goddess, who is mother and father,
friend, lover and helper, did not create this idol and is not
represented by this idol. Our brother Jesus did not come to this
earth to manufacture this idol, and he is not represented by this
idol. The message and mission of Jesus, the child of Mary, which
is to put down the mighty from their thrones and uplift the lowly,
is not served by this idol. Rather, this idol blasphemes by
claiming to speak in the name of Jesus and to carry out his
redemptive mission, while crushing and turning to its opposite all
that he came to teach. . . . The Powers and Principalities of rape,
genocide and war achieve their greatest daring by claiming to be
Christ, to represent Christ's mission. The Roman Empire clothes
itself in the mantle of the Crucified and sits itself anew upon its
imperial throne.

As Woman-Church we cry out: horror, blasphemy, deceit, foul
deed! This is not the voice of our God, the face of our redeemer,
the mission of our Church. Our humanity is not, cannot be
represented, but is excluded in this dream, this nightmare of
salvation. As Woman-Church we claim the authentic mission of
Christ, the true mission of Church, the real agenda of our Mother-
Father God who comes to restore and not to destroy our
humanity, who comes to ransom the captives and to reclaim the
earth as our Promised Land. We are not in exile but the Church is
in exodus with us. God's Shekinah, Holy Wisdom, the Mother-
face of God has fled from the high thrones of patriarchy and has
gone into exodus with us. She is with us as we flee from the
smoking altars where women's bodies are sacrificed, as we cover
our ears to blot out the inhuman voice that comes forth from the
idol of patriarchy.

As Woman-Church we are not left to starve for the words of
Wisdom; we are not left without the bread of life. Ministry too
goes with us into exodus. We learn all over again what it means
to minister; not to lord over, but to minister to and with each

other, to teach each other to speak the words of life. Eucharist comes with us into exodus. The waters of baptism spring up in our midst as the waters of life, and the tree of life grows in our midst with fruits and flowers. We pluck grain and make bread, harvest grapes and make wine, and we pass them around as the body and blood of our new life, the life of the new humanity which has been purchased by the bloody struggles of our martyrs, of the bloody struggle of our brother Jesus, and Perpetua and Felicitas, and all the women who were burned and beaten and raped, and Jean Donovan and Maura Clarke and Ita Ford and Dorothy Kazel, and the women of Guatemala, Honduras, El Salvador and Nicaragua who stuggle against the Leviathan of patriarchy and imperialism. This new humanity has been purchased by their blood, by their lives, and we dare to share the fruits of their victory together in hope and faith that they did not die in vain, but they have risen, they are rising from the dead. They are present with us as we share this sacrament of the new humanity, as we build together this new earth freed from the yoke of patriarchy.

We are Woman-Church, not in exile, but in exodus. We flee the thundering armies of Pharoah. We are not waiting for a call to return to the land of slavery to serve as altar girls in the temples of patriarchy. No! We call our brothers also to flee from the temples of patriarchy; . . . to flee with us from the idol with flashing eyes and smoking nostrils who is about to consume the earth. We call our brothers to join us in exodus from the land of patriarchy, to join us in our common quest for that Promised Land where there will be no more war, no more burning children, no more violated women, no more discarded elderly, no more rape of the earth. Together let us break up that great idol and grind it into powder; dismantle the great Leviathan of violence and misery who threatens to destroy the earth, plow it into the soil, and transform it back into the means of peace and plenty, so that all the children of earth can sit down together at the banquet of life.

Mary Magdalene preaching the good news of the resurrection to the frightened male apostles. She represents woman's apostolic authority, first recognized and then repressed by Christianity. In reclaiming her as our foremother, can we reclaim the Christian gospel?

Albani Psalter, Hildesheim, twelfth century.

9

Foremothers of WomanChurch

DOCUMENTS

1. *Miriam, Priest and Prophet*
2. *Deborah the Judge*
3. *Huldah the Prophet*
4. *Mary Magdalene, Apostle to the Apostles*
5. *Thecla, Apostle Sent by Paul*
6. *Perpetua and Felicitas, Martyrs*
7. *Maximilla and Priscilla, Prophets of the Last Days*

In this chapter we lift up the names of women leaders in Israel and early Christianity. We could easily extend this list down through the centuries as we increasingly recover our history as WomanChurch and discover the many women mystics, prophets, ministers, healers, church founders, and apostles who have carried out their vision of redemptive community inclusive of women, often against their brother religious leaders. Rather than to make the story endless, we restrict the texts to a few classical exemplars for the foundational periods of the Jewish and Christian communities. Although these women can be called by such titles as priest, judge, apostle, martyr, and mystic, the primary category for women's leadership in Biblical religion is prophet(ess).

Women were restricted from established institutional roles. Nevertheless, the communities of biblical faith never denied that God's Spirit might empower whoever it wills and that this might include women. Prophecy represents the power of freedom and newness of life in which God's word breaks in to speak in judgment on established modes of life and to open up new possibilities. It is significant, therefore, that the power of authentic prophecy was the one ministry never denied in theory to women, although any particular woman claiming this power might be vilified and rejected.

Of all the women in Hebrew Scripture, Miriam is the most important. She is named as the sister of Moses and Aaron (Num. 26:59; 1 Chron. 6:2), identified in rabbinic commentary with the sister who saved Moses by watching guard over him in the bullrushes and giving him to the daughter of Pharoah to raise.[1] This may be a later tradition that is intended to cover up the earlier view of Miriam as an independent leader, along with Moses and Aaron, in the exodus community.[2] Moses, Aaron, and Miriam are continually cited in the tradition as the three leaders in Israel's liberation from Egypt (Micah 6:3-4). It is likely that Miriam was seen, like Aaron, as exercising priestly leadership. She is described as standing before the tent of meeting with Aaron. She is called as a prophet who leads the women of Israel in a song of rejoicing after crossing the Reed Sea.

In Numbers 12 we see the threat posed for the patriarchal tradition by this memory of a powerful female priest and prophet in the foundation of Israel and the need to demote her by telling a story of God's judgment against her. In this story both Miriam and Aaron challenge Moses' leadership by rebuking him for marrying a Cushite woman. But only Miriam is punished. When called forth before the tent of meeting, the cloud of God's presence descends over her and she is turned into a leper. She is then exiled from the camp for seven days. God's punishment is compared to a father's spitting in his daughter's face. Healed of this expression of God's wrath, Miriam is then brought back into the camp, noting that the people did not set out on their march until she returned. Clearly, Miriam was seen as the formidable rival of Moses' leadership who must be put in her place!

The figure of Deborah also indicates the important leadership roles played by women in early Israelite society (twelfth century B.C.). Deborah is called a judge, the highest leadership position in the period before the establishment of the kingship by Saul and David. As judge, she functioned as a magistrate, dispensing justice and deciding disputed cases that were brought to her by the community. She is also described as leading and inspiring the army of Israel to win the victory against their enemy. She saves the community, along with Jael, who invited the enemy, General Sisera, into her tent, and struck him dead with a tent peg. Deborah and the Israelite general Barak then sing a song of thanksgiving for this victory.

Huldah was the third woman to whom Hebrew Scripture gives the title of prophet (*nebiah*). Huldah lived during the reign of the re-

formist Yahwist king Josiah in the latter part of the seventh century
B.C. Josiah was engaged in reforms of the Solomonic temple that sought
to drive out the priestesses and the worship of the Goddess that had
been functioning there.[3] Josiah received a copy of the Book of the Law
(an early version of the Book of Deuteronomy), which had been discovered in the temple. He was upset because its prescriptions were
not being followed. He then sought a guiding word from Yahweh by
sending his chief men to Huldah, the prophet, who was said to be
dwelling in the city of Jerusalem. Huldah supported his reform by pre-
dicting divine wrath against the idolators who were worshipping other
deities but the blessings of God upon Josiah for his reform. It is significant that Josiah, in his effort to purge the temple by driving out the
Goddess and her priestesses, felt the need to turn to a woman prophet to sanction this reform.

In the Christian tradition, Mary Magdalene occupies a position similar to that of Miriam in the exodus community. Mary is continually
mentioned in the gospels as the leading woman disciple in Jesus' company. The gnostic tradition continued this high estimate of her role
by making her the exemplar of women's apostolic authority and the
disciple closest to Jesus. Gnostics even speak of Jesus' affection for her,
"kissing her many times on the mouth" (see chapter VI, reading 6).
In all the gospels, Mary Magdalene plays the part of the leader of that
company of women disciples who remain faithful to Jesus at the cross
when the male disciples have run away. She then leads the women
disciples to the tomb on Easter morning where she and the other
women become the first witnesses of the resurrection, commissioned
by the risen Lord to carry this message back to the male disciples who
huddle in the upper room.

The Gospel of John emphasizes this close relationship of Jesus and
Mary Magdalene by developing a special scene in which he appears
to her. She recognizes him and tries to embrace him. He warns her
not to hold him, an admonishment that has been misinterpreted in
the Christian tradition to indicate Jesus' abhorrence of woman's touch.
In fact, Mary's spontaneous move to embrace on this occasion points
to John's assumption that Jesus and Mary were accustomed to do so.
But Jesus' risen body is in a special state of *mana* (dangerous spiritual
power) so he warns her not to touch him at this time. He then com-
missions her to go and tell the good news of his resurrection to the
other disciples.

Like the role of Miriam in Hebrew Scripture, this powerful role
of Mary Magdalene, as beloved disciple and apostle to the apostles
of the Lord's resurrection, threatened to sanction leadership for women

in a later patriarchal Christianity. So Mary Magdalene is demoted in the tradition by being made into a converted prostitute, thereby fixing her image as a weeping sinner at Jesus' feet, wiping his feet with her hair. However, this concept has not yet appeared in the New Testament. Although Mary is said to have been healed by Jesus of "seven demons," this kind of healing always refers in the New Testament to some kind of violent illness (epilepsy) and not to sins such as prostitution.

The misinterpretation of Mary as a converted prostitute is created by conflation of the texts about an unknown woman who signs Jesus' impending death by breaking a jar of funerary ointment on his head (Mark 14:3-9) (a prophetic gesture, not an expression of penitence for sin) with Luke's rewriting of this incident as the story of an unnamed woman sinner who breaks the ointment on Jesus' feet as a sign of penitence (Luke 7:36-50) and a third version of the text that identifies the prophet (not the sinner) version of the story with Mary of Bethany (John 12:1–8). By combining these texts, the Church paints a picture of Mary Magdalene as weeping sinner, thereby displacing her from her original high status as the leader of the faithful remnant of Jesus' apostles who founds the Church's kerygma of the resurrection.

After Mary Magdalene, the woman who represents the foremost sanction for woman's ministry in early Christianity is Thecla, a disciple of Paul. The story of Thecla belongs to a popular ascetic Christianity that began as early as the first century of the Church. This ascetic Christianity should not be confused with gnosticism. Although gnosticism carried some of its tendencies into dualistic cosmological theologies, popular asceticism remained recognized as orthodox by the mainstream church. Its heroes and martyrs continued to be honored as saints, even while the patriarchal Church carefully discouraged other Christians from following their example literally. Such popular asceticism understood the Church as a community where women became men's spiritual equals by being freed through chastity from sex roles in the family.

In the popular *Acts of Paul and Thecla*, Thecla is described as adopting this life of chastity as a result of her conversion by Paul. She is then represented as persecuted by the representatives of patriarchal authority of family and state. Thrown to the lions twice, she miraculously escapes, baptizing herself on the second occasion. The female perspective of the narrative is revealed by the fact that all the male authorities, other than Paul, are seen as Thecla's enemies while the females, including the queen and even the female animals in the arena, espouse her cause. Her mother, who identifies with patriarchal claims of the family against Thecla's chosen freedom, is the one exception. But at the end of the narrative Thecla is sent back to Iconium to convert her mother. As a final imprimatur on her authority, Paul is shown commissioning her as an apostle, with the words "go and teach the Word of God."

Recent studies have shown that such popular narratives represented a female-identified early Christianity. They were either written by or associated with the communities of widows, virgins, and deaconesses whose ministry to women included catechetics, baptism, and bringing the Eucharist to women. Women seem to have constructed such popular stories, perhaps in the process of teaching other women, to celebrate their new freedom as women in Christ, which they identified with rejection of marriage.[4] Very likely this story of Thecla was already current in oral form at the end of the first century A.D. The patriarchalizing Epistles of Timothy, which make Paul the authority for the rejection of women's right to preach and teach, were written to repress this rival Pauline tradition that made Paul the one who mandated women evangelists.[5]

Becoming a martyr might not seem like a liberating leadership role for women. Martyrdom has come to be associated with a long-suffering endurance of women's suppression by patriarchy. But in early Christianity the woman martyr was seen quite differently. Martyrdom among the more radical groups of early Christians was seen as both the highest act of resistance against the evil power of the state that represented the Kingdom of Evil and also the closest possible identification with Christ. The martyr literally was seen as becoming another Christ in the act of suffering for Christ. Thus, the "Acts of the Martyrs of Lyons and Vienne" has no hesitation in describing the woman martyr Blandina as becoming Christ "in the form of our sister."[6]

Resistance to the state also sanctioned the right of Christian women to reject the claims of the patriarchal family. The high-born Roman woman Perpetua spurns the claims of her father, as well as the appeal to her recent motherhood, to brave the conflict. In her dream of her coming struggle in the arena, she is seen as transformed into a male where she bests the devil. This reflects a typical early Christian motif in which the woman saint and ascetic overcomes the limits of her female role and becomes "virile and manly." Thecla, one might note, also cuts her hair and dresses as a male in her adventures. Martyrdom overcomes social division, so Perpetua and her slave woman, Felicitas, also a recent mother, become sisters in the struggle. The emphasis on their maternity is intended to make all the more wondrous their triumph over female "weakness" in their empowerment by Christ.

By the second and third centuries these kinds of women apostles, prophets, and martyrs were becoming increasingly unacceptable to the new patriarchal leadership class of the Church, headed by bishops. Prophets came to be seen as representing both a radical Christianity that kept up the conflict of Church and state and also a rival seat of charismatic authority that Christians looked to rather than to bishops for teaching, healing, and forgiveness of sins.[7] The Didache, the second-century Church order, even regards prophets as the normal ones to preside at the Eucharist, with presbyters as a second choice, to be allowed only if a community lacks an authentic prophet.[8]

When a new prophetic movement arose in Phrygia (Syria) seeking to revive this earlier charismatic Christianity, episcopal authority moved to crush it by condemning it as heretical. The fact that two of its three leaders were women, Maximilla and Priscilla, only further accelerated the efforts of patriarchalizing Christianity to discredit female leadership. In the tiny fragments from the utterances of the Montanist women prophets that survive in the diatribes of their episcopal enemies, we are startled to see that Maximilla claims to be the final prophet of the Spirit before the consummation of the world. Also, she does not hesitate to envision the risen Christ in female form. Such female prophets carry on the earliest Christian view that the risen Lord poured forth the prophetic power of the new creation on men and women alike.[9] The community itself, as an ecstatic fellowship, continues the presence of Christ. In its exemplary members, the prophets and martyrs, one can encounter Christ "in the form of our sister."

Reflection

Name as many women as you can remember whom you see as foremothers of WomanChurch. Who were they and what was their story? What kinds of ministries did they embody — were they mystics? apostles? healers? church founders? prophets? teachers? Construct a litany of the saints to celebrate the memory of these women.

List the males whom you think of as liberators of oppressed people. Do you know whether they also included the liberation of women in their agenda? List males you know or remember from history who advocated women's rights. Does there seem to be little correlation between great male liberators of their "people" and the liberation of women? Why?

Develop a liturgical drama or a play around several women liberators of women, speaking in their voice and dramatizing their work.

1. *Miriam, Priest and Prophet*[10]

Then Miriam, the prophetess, the sister of Aaron, took a timbrel in her hand; and all the women went out after her with timbrels and dancing.

And Miriam sang to them:
"Sing to the Lord, for he has triumphed gloriously;
the horse and his rider he has thrown into the sea."

THE CONFLICT OF MIRIAM AND MOSES[11]

Miriam and Aaron spoke against Moses because of the Cushite woman whom he had married, for he had married a Cushite woman; and they said, "Has the Lord indeed spoken only through Moses? Has he not spoken through us also?" And the Lord heard it. Now the man Moses was very meek, more than all men that were on the face of the earth. And suddenly the Lord said to Moses and to Aaron and Miriam, "Come out, you three, to the tent of meeting." And the three of them came out. And the Lord came down in a pillar of cloud, and stood at the door of the tent, and called Aaron and Miriam; and they both came forward. And he said, "Hear my words: If there is a prophet among you, I the Lord make myself known to him in a vision, I speak with him in a dream. Not so with my servant Moses; he is entrusted with all my house. With him I speak mouth to mouth, clearly, and not in dark speech; and he beholds the form of the Lord. Why then were you not afraid to speak against my servant Moses?"

And the anger of the Lord was kindled against them, and he departed; and when the cloud removed from over the tent, behold, Miriam was leprous, as white as snow. And Aaron turned towards Miriam, and behold, she was leprous. And Aaron said to Moses, "Oh, my lord, do not punish us because we have done foolishly and have sinned. Let her not be as one dead, of whom the flesh is half consumed when he comes out of his mother's womb." And Moses cried to the Lord, "Heal her, O God, I beseech thee." But the Lord said to Moses, "If her father had but spit in her face, should she not be shamed seven days? Let her be shut up outside the camp seven days, and after that she may be brought in again." So Miriam was shut up outside the camp seven days; and the people did not set out on the march till Miriam was brought in again. After that the people set out from Hazeroth, and encamped in the wilderness of Paran.

2. *Deborah the Judge*[12]

Now Deborah, a prophetess, the wife of Lappidoth, was judging
Israel at that time. She used to sit under the palm of Deborah
between Ramah and Bethel in the hill country of Ephraim; and
the people of Israel came up to her for judgment. She sent and
summoned Barak the son of Abino-am from Kedesh in Naphtali,
and said to him, "Does not the Lord, the God of Israel, command
you, 'Go, gather your men at Mount Tabor, taking ten thousand
from the tribe of Naphtali and the tribe of Zebulun? And I will
draw out Sisera, the general of Jabin's army, to meet you by the
river Kishon with his chariots and his troops; and I will give him
into your hand.' " Barak said to her, "If you will go with me, I
will go; but if you will not go with me, I will not go." And she
said, "I will surely go with you; nevertheless, the road on which
you are going will not lead to your glory, for the Lord will sell
Sisera into the hand of a woman." Then Deborah arose, and went
with Barak to Kedesh. And Barak summoned Zebulun and
Naphtali to Kedesh; and ten thousand men went up at his heels;
and Deborah went up with him.
. . . Sisera called out all his chariots, nine hundred chariots of
iron, and all the men who were with him, from Harosheth-ha-
goiim to the river Kishon. And Deborah said to Barak, "Up! For
this is the day in which the Lord has given Sisera into your hand.
Does not the Lord go out before you?" So Barak went down from
Mount Tabor with ten thousand men following him. And the Lord
routed Sisera and all his chariots and all his army before Barak at
the edge of the sword; and Sisera alighted from his chariot and
fled away on foot. . . .
But Sisera fled away on foot to the tent of Jael, the wife of
Heber the Kenite; . . . And Jael came out to meet Sisera, and said
to him, "Turn aside, my lord, turn aside to me; have no fear." So
he turned aside to her into the tent, and she covered him with a
rug. And he said to her, "Pray, give me a little water to drink; for
I am thirsty." So she opened a skin of milk and gave him a drink
and covered him. And he said to her, "Stand at the door of the
tent, and if any man comes and asks you, 'Is any one here?' say,
No." But Jael the wife of Heber took a tent peg, and took a
hammer in her hand and went softly to him and drove the peg
into his temple, till it went down into the ground, as he was lying
fast asleep from weariness. So he died.

THE SONG OF DEBORAH[13]

Then sang Deborah and Barak
the son of Abino-am on that day:
"Hear, O kings; give ear, O princes;
 to the Lord I will sing,
 I will make melody to the Lord,
  the God of Israel.
"In the days of Shamgar, son of Anath,
 in the days of Jael, caravans ceased
 and travelers kept to the byways.
The peasantry ceased in Israel, they ceased
 until you arose, Deborah,
 arose as a mother in Israel.
"Awake, awake, Deborah!
 Awake, awake, utter a song!
Arise, Barak, lead away your captives,
 O son of Abino-am.
Then down marched the remnant of the noble;
 the people of the Lord marched
 down for him against the mighty.
From Ephraim they set out thither into the valley,
 following you, Benjamin, with your kinsmen;
from Machir marched down the commanders,
 and from Zebulun those who bear the marshal's staff;
the princes of Issachar came with Deborah,
 and Issachar faithful to Barak;
 into the valley they rushed forth at his heels.
"Most blessed of women be Jael,
 the wife of Heber the Kenite,
 of tent-dwelling women most blessed.
He asked water and she gave him milk,
 she brought him curds in a lordly bowl.
She put her hand to the tent peg
 and her right hand to the workmen's mallet;
she struck Sisera a blow,
 she crushed his head,
 she shattered and pierced his temple.
He sank, he fell,
 he lay still at her feet;
at her feet he sank, he fell;

where he sank, there he fell dead.
"So perish all thine enemies,
   O Lord!
But thy friends be like the sun
   as he rises in his might."

3. Huldah the Prophet[14]

And when the king heard the words of the book of the law, he
rent his clothes. And the king commanded Hilkiah the priest, and
Ahikam the son of Shaphan, and Achbor the son of Micaiah, and
Shaphan the secretary, and Asaiah the king's servant, saying,
"Go, inquire of the Lord for me, and for the people, and for all
Judah, concerning the words of this book that has been found; for
great is the wrath of the Lord that is kindled against us, because
our fathers have not obeyed the words of this book, to do
according to all that is written concerning us."

So Hilkiah the priest, and Ahikam, and Achbor, and Shaphan,
and Asaiah went to Huldah the prophetess, the wife of Shallum
the son of Tikvah, son of Harhas, keeper of the wardrobe (now
she dwelt in Jerusalem in the Second Quarter); and they talked
with her. And she said to them, "Thus says the Lord, the God of
Israel: 'Tell the man who sent you to me, Thus says the Lord,
Behold, I will bring evil upon this place and upon its inhabitants,
all the words of the book which the king of Judah has read.
Because they have forsaken me and have burned incense to other
gods, that they might provoke me to anger with all the work of
their hands, therefore my wrath will be kindled against this place,
and it will not be quenched.

"But as to the king of Judah, who sent you to inquire of the
Lord, thus shall you say to him, Thus says the Lord, the God of
Israel: Regarding the words which you have heard, "because your
heart was penitent, and you humbled yourself before the Lord,
when you heard how I spoke against this place, and against its
inhabitants, that they should become a desolation and a curse,
and you have rent your clothes and wept before me. I also have
heard you, says the Lord. Therefore, behold, I will gather you to
your fathers, and you shall be gathered to your grave in peace,
and your eyes shall not see all the evil which I will bring upon
this place.' " And they brought back word to the king.

4. Mary Magdalene, Apostle to the Apostles[15]

Now on the first day of the week Mary Magdalene came to the
tomb early, while it was still dark, and saw that the stone had
been taken away from the tomb. So she ran, and went to Simon
Peter and the other disciple, the one whom Jesus loved, and said
to them, "They have taken the Lord out of the tomb, and we do
not know where they have laid him." Peter then came out with
the other disciple, and they went toward the tomb. They both
ran, but the other disciple outran Peter and reached the tomb
first; and stooping to look in, he saw the linen cloths lying there,
but he did not go in. Then Simon Peter came, following him, and
he went into the tomb; he saw the linen cloths lying, and the
napkin, which had been on his head, not lying with the linen
cloths but rolled up in a place by itself. Then the other disciple,
who reached the tomb first, also went in, and he saw and
believed; for as yet they did not know the scripture, that he must
rise from the dead. Then the disciples went back to their homes.

But Mary stood weeping outside the tomb, and as she wept
she stooped to look into the tomb; and she saw two angels in
white, sitting where the body of Jesus had lain, one at the head
and one at the feet. They said to her, "Woman, why are you
weeping?" She said to them, "Because they have taken away my
Lord, and I do not know where they have laid him." Saying this,
she turned round and saw Jesus standing, but she did not know
that it was Jesus. Jesus said to her, "Woman, why are you
weeping? Whom do you seek?" Supposing him to be the
gardener, she said to him, "Sir, if you have carried him away, tell
me where you have laid him, and I will take him away." Jesus
said to her, "Mary." She turned and said to him in Hebrew,
"Rab-boni!" (which means Teacher). Jesus said to her, "Do not
hold me, for I have not yet ascended to the Father; but go to my
brethren and say to them, I am ascending to my Father and your
Father, to my God and your God."

Mary Magdalene went and said to the disciples, "I have seen
the Lord"; and she told them that he had said these things to her.

5. Thecla, Apostle Sent by Paul[16]

And while Paul was thus speaking in the midst of the church in
the house of Onesiphorus, a certain virgin Thecla, the daughter of

Theocleia, betrothed to a man *named* Thamyris, sitting at the
window close by, listened night and day to the discourse of
virginity and prayer, and did not look away from the window, but
paid earnest heed to the faith, rejoicing exceedingly. And when
she still saw many women going in beside Paul, she also had an
eager desire to be deemed worthy to stand in the presence of
Paul, and to hear the word of Christ; for never had she seen his
figure, but heard his word only.

And Thamyris going near, and kissing her, but at the same
time also being afraid of her overpowering emotion, said: Thecla,
my betrothed, why dost thou sit thus? . . . Thecla did not turn
round, but kept attending earnestly to the word of Paul.

And Thamyris starting up, went forth into the street, and kept
watching those going in to him and coming out. And he saw two
men bitterly contending with each other; and he said: Men, tell
me who this is among you, leading astray the souls of young
men, and deceiving virgins, so that they do not marry, but remain
as they are. . . . For I am no little distressed about Thecla, because
she thus loves the stranger, and I am prevented from marrying.
. . .

And Thamyris, hearing these things, being filled with anger
and rage, rising up early, went to the house of Onesiphorus with
archons and public officers, and a great crowd with batons,
saying: Thou hast corrupted the city of the Iconians, and her that
was betrothed to me, so that she will not have me: let us go to
the governor Castelios. And all the multitude said: Away with the
magician; for he has corrupted all our wives, and the multitudes
have been persuaded *to change their opinions.*
. . . And the proconsul having heard, ordered Paul to be
bound, and sent to prison, until, said he, I, being at leisure, shall
hear him more attentively.

And Thecla by night having taken off her bracelets, gave them
to the gatekeeper; and the door having been opened to her, she
went into the prison; and having given the jailor a silver mirror,
she went in beside Paul, and, sitting at his feet, she heard the
great things of God. And Paul was afraid of nothing, but ordered
his life in the confidence of God. And her faith also was increased,
and she kissed his bonds.
. . . But the proconsul gladly heard Paul upon the holy works
of Christ. And having called a council, he summoned Thecla, and
said to her: Why dost thou not obey Thamyris, according to the

law of the Iconians? But she stood looking earnestly at Paul. And
when she gave no answer, her mother cried out, saying: Burn the
wicked *wretch;* burn in the midst of the theatre her that will not
marry, in order that all the women that have been taught by this
man may be afraid.

And the governor was greatly moved; and having scourged
Paul, he cast him out of the city, and condemned Thecla to be
burned. And immediately the governor went away to the theatre,
and all the crowd went forth to the spectacle of Thecla. But as a
lamb in the wilderness looks round for the shepherd, so she kept
searching for Paul. And having looked upon the crowd, she saw
the Lord sitting in the likeness of Paul, and said: As I am unable
to endure my lot, Paul has come to see me. And she gazed upon
him with great earnestness, and he went up into heaven. But the
maid-servants and virgins brought the faggots, in order that
Thecla might be burned. And when she came in naked, the
governor wept, and wondered at the power that was in her. And
the public executioners arranged the faggots for her to go up on
the pile. And she, having made the sign of the cross, went up on
the faggots; and they lighted them. And though a great fire was
blazing, it did not touch her; for God, having compassion upon
her, made an underground rumbling, and a cloud overshadowed
them from above, full of water and hail; and all that was in the
cavity of it was poured out, so that many were in danger of
death. And the fire was put out, and Thecla saved.

And they had five loaves, and herbs, and water; and they
rejoiced in the holy works of Christ. And Thecla said to Paul: I
shall cut my hair, and follow thee whithersoever thou mayst go.
And he said: It is a shameless age, and thou are beautiful. I am
afraid lest another temptation come upon thee worse than the
first, and that thou withstand it not, but be cowardly. And Thecla
said: Only give me the seal in Christ, and temptation shall not
touch me. And Paul said: Thecla, wait with patience, and thou
shalt receive the water.

And Paul sent away Onesiphorus and all his house to
Iconium; and thus, having taken Thecla, he went into Antioch.
And as they were going in, a certain Syriarch, Alexander by
name, seeing Thecla, became enamoured of her, and tried to gain
over Paul by gifts and presents. And taking hold of Alexander,
she tore his cloak, and pulled off his crown, and made him a
laughing-stock. And he, at the same time loving her, and at the

same time ashamed of what had happened, led her before the
governor; and when she had confessed that she had done these
things, he condemned her to the wild beasts. And the women
were struck with astonishment, and cried out beside the tribunal:
Evil judgment! impious judgment! And she asked the governor,
that, said she, I may remain pure until I shall fight with the wild
beasts. And a certain Tryphaena, whose daughter was dead, took
her into keeping, and had her for a consolation.

And when the beasts were exhibited, they bound her to a
fierce lioness; and Tryphaena accompanied her. But the lioness,
with Thecla sitting upon her, licked her feet; and all the multitude
was astonished. And the charge on her inscription was:
Sacrilegious. And the women cried out from above: An impious
sentence has been passed in this city! And after the exhibition,
Tryphaena again receives her. For her daughter Falconilla had
died, and said to her in a dream: Mother, thou shalt have this
stranger Thecla in my place, in order that she may pray
concerning me, and that I may be transferred to the place of the
just. . . .

Then a tumult arose, and a cry of the people, and the women
sitting together, the one saying: Away with the sacrilegious
person! the others saying: Let the city be raised against this
wickedness. Take off all of us, O proconsul! Cruel sight! evil
sentence!

And Thecla, having been taken out of the hand of Tryphaena,
was stripped, and received a girdle, and was thrown into the
arena, and lions and bears and a fierce lioness were let loose upon
her; and the lioness having run up to her feet, lay down; and the
multitude of the women cried aloud. And a bear ran upon her;
but the lioness, meeting the bear, tore her to pieces. And again a
lion that had been trained against men, which belonged to
Alexander, ran upon her; and she, *the lioness*, encountering the
lion, was killed along with him. And the women made great
lamentation, since also the lioness, her protector, was dead.

Then they sent in many wild beasts, she standing and
stretching forth her hands, and praying. And when she had
finished her prayer, she turned and saw a ditch full of water, and
said: Now it is time to wash myself. And she threw herself in,
saying: In the name of Jesus Christ I am baptized on my last day.
And the women seeing, and the multitude, wept, saying: Do not
throw thyself into the water; so that also the governor shed tears,

because the seals were going to devour such beauty. She then threw herself *in* in the name of Jesus Christ; but the seals having seen the glare of the fire of lightning, floated about dead. And there was round her, as she was naked, a cloud of fire; so that neither could the wild beasts touch her, nor could she be seen naked. . . . But Tryphaena fainted standing beside the arena, so that the crowd said: Queen Tryphaena is dead. And the governor put a stop to the games, and the city was in dismay. And Alexander entreated the governor, saying: Have mercy both on me and the city, and release this woman. For if Caesar hear of these things, he will speedily destroy the city also along with us, because his kinswoman Queen Tryphaena has died beside the ABACI.

And the governor having heard this, ordered her garments to be brought, and to be put on. And Thecla said: He that clothed me naked among the wild beasts, will in the day of judgment clothe thee with salvation. And taking the garments, she put them on. The governor therefore immediately issued an edict, saying: I release to you the God-fearing Thecla, the servant of God. And the women shouted aloud, and with one mouth returned thanks to God, saying: There is one God, *the God* of Thecla; so that the foundations of the theatre were shaken by their voice. And Tryphaena having received the good news, went to meet the holy Thecla, and said: Now I believe that the dead are raised; now I believe that my child lives. Come within, and I shall assign to thee all that is mine. She therefore went in along with her, and rested eight days, having instructed her in the word of God, so that most even of the maid-servants believed. And there was great joy in the house.

And Thecla kept seeking Paul; and it was told her that he was in Myra of Lycia. And taking young men and maidens, she girded herself; and having sewed the tunic so as to make a man's cloak, she came to Myra, and found Paul speaking the word of God. And Paul was astonished at seeing her, and the crowd with her, thinking that some new trial was coming upon her. And when she saw him, she said: I have received the baptism, Paul; for He that wrought along with thee for the Gospel has wrought in me also for baptism. And Paul, taking her, led her to the house of Hermaeus, and hears everything from her, so that those that heard greatly wondered, and were comforted, and prayed over Tryphaena. And she rose up, and said: I am going to Iconium. And Paul said: Go, and teach the word of God.

6. *Perpetua and Felicitas, Martyrs*[17]

The young catechumens, Revocatus and his fellow-servant
Felicitas, Saturninus and Secundulus, were apprehended. And
among them also was Vivia Perpetua, respectably born, liberally
educated, a married matron, having a father and mother and two
brothers, one of whom, like herself, was a catechumen, and a son
an infant at the breast. She herself was about twenty-two years of
age. From this point onward she shall herself narrate the whole
course of her martyrdom, as she left it described by her own hand
and with her own mind.

. . . "After a few days there prevailed a report that we should
be heard. And then my father came to me from the city, worn out
with anxiety. He came up to me, that he might cast me down,
saying, 'Have pity my daughter, on my grey hairs. Have pity on
your father, if I am worthy to be called a father by you. If with
these hands I have brought you up to this flower of your age, if I
have preferred you to all your brothers, do not deliver me up to
the scorn of men. Have regard to your brothers, have regard to
your mother and your aunt, have regard to your son, who will
not be able to live after you. Lay aside your courage, and do not
bring us all to destruction; for none of us will speak in freedom if
you should suffer anything.' These things said my father in his
affection, kissing my hands, and throwing himself at my feet; and
with tears he called me not Daughter, but Lady. And I grieved
over the grey hairs of my father, that he alone of all my family
would not rejoice over my passion. And I comforted him, saying,
'On that scaffold whatever God wills shall happen. For know that
we are not placed in our own power, but in that of God.' And he
departed from me in sorrow. . . . Then, because my child had
been used to receive suck from me, and to stay with me in the
prison, I sent Pomponius the deacon to my father to ask for the
infant, but my father would not give it him. And even as God
willed it, the child no longer desired the breast, nor did my breast
cause me uneasiness, lest I should be tormented by care for my
babe and by the pain of my breasts at once. . . .

"The day before that on which we were to fight, I saw in a
vision that Pomponius the deacon came hither to the gate of the
prison, and knocked vehemently. I went out to him, and opened
the gate for him; and he was clothed in a richly ornamented white
robe, and he had on manifold calliculae. And he said to me,
'Perpetua, we are waiting for you; come!' And he held his hand

to me, and we began to go through rough and winding places.
Scarcely at length had we arrived breathless at the amphitheatre,
when he led me into the middle of the arena, and said to me, 'Do
not fear, I am here with you, and I am labouring with you;' and
he departed. And I gazed upon an immense assembly in
astonishment. And because I knew that I was given to the wild
beasts, I marvelled that the wild beasts were not let loose upon
me. Then there came forth against me a certain Egyptian, horrible
in appearance, with his backers, to fight with me. And there came
to me, as my helpers and encouragers, handsome youths; and I
was stripped, and became a man. Then my helpers began to rub
me with oil, as is the custom for contest; and I beheld that
Egyptian on the other hand rolling in the dust. And a certain
man came forth, of wondrous height, so that he even overtopped
the top of the amphitheatre; and he wore a loose tunic and a
purple robe between two bands over the middle of the breast; and
he had on *calliculae* of varied form, made of gold and silver; and
he carried a rod, as if he were a trainer of gladiators, and a green
branch upon which were apples of gold. And he called for silence,
and said, 'This Egyptian, if he should overcome this woman, shall
kill her with the sword; and if she shall conquer him, she shall
receive this branch.' Then he departed. And we drew near to one
another, and began to deal out blows. He sought to lay hold of
my feet, while I struck at his face with my heels; and I was lifted
up in the air, and began thus to thrust at him as if spurning the
earth. But when I saw that there was some delay I joined my
hands so as to twine my fingers with one another; and I took
hold upon his head, and he fell on his face, and I trod upon his
head. And the people began to shout, and my backers to exult.
And I drew near to the trainer and took the branch; and he kissed
me, and said to me, 'Daughter, peace be with you:' and I began
to go gloriously to the Sanavivarian gate. Then I awoke, and
perceived that I was not to fight with beasts, but against the devil.
Still I knew that the victory was awaiting me.''

But respecting Felicitas (for to her also the Lord's favour
approached in the same way), when she had already gone eight
months with child (for she had been pregnant when she was
apprehended), as the day of the exhibition was drawing near, she
was in great grief lest on account of her pregnancy she should be
delayed, — because pregnant women are not allowed to be
publicly punished. — . . . they poured forth their prayer to the
Lord three days before the exhibition. Immediately after their

prayer her pains came upon her, and when with the difficulty natural to an eight months' delivery, in the labour of bringing forth she was sorrowing, some one of the servants of the *Cataractarii* said to her, "You who are in such suffering now, what will you do when you are thrown to the beasts, which you despised when you refused to sacrifice?" And she replied, "Now it is I that suffer what I suffer; but then there will be another in me, who will suffer for me, because I also am about to suffer for Him." Thus she brought forth a little girl, which a certain sister brought up as her daughter.

The day of their victory shone forth, and they proceeded from the prison into the amphitheatre, as if to an assembly, joyous and of brilliant countenances; if perchance shrinking, it was with joy, and not with fear. Perpetua followed with placid look, and with step and gait as a matron of Christ, beloved of God; casting down the luster of her eyes from the gaze of all. Moreover, Felicitas, rejoicing that she had safely brought forth, so that she might fight with the wild beasts; from the blood and from the midwife to the gladiator, to wash after childbirth with a second baptism.

Moreover, for the young women the devil prepared a very fierce cow, provided especially for that purpose contrary to custom, rivalling their sex also in that of the beasts. And so stripped and clothed with nets, they were led forth. The populace shuddered as they saw one young woman of delicate frame, and another with breasts still dropping from her recent childbirth. So, being recalled, they are unbound. Perpetua is first led in. She was tossed, and fell on her loins; and when she saw her tunic torn from her side, she drew it over her as a veil for her middle, rather mindful of her modesty than her suffering. Then she was called for again, and bound up her dishevelled hair; for it was not becoming for a martyr to suffer wth dishevelled hair, lest she should appear to be mourning in her glory. So she rose up; and when she saw Felicitas crushed, she approached and gave her her hand, and lifted her up. And both of them stood together; and the brutality of the populace being appeased, they were recalled to the Sanavivarian gate. Then Perpetua was received by a certain one who was still a catechumen, Rusticus by name, who kept close to her; and she, as if aroused from sleep, so deeply had she been in the Spirit and in an ecstasy, began to look round her, and to say to the amazement of all, "I cannot tell when we are to be led out to that cow." And when she had heard what had already happened, she did not believe it until she had perceived certain signs of injury in her body and in her dress, and had recognized the catechumen. Afterwards causing that catechumen and the brother to approach, she addressed them, saying, "Stand fast in the faith, and love one another, all of you, and be not offended at my sufferings."

And when the populace called for them into the midst, that as the sword penetrated into their body they might make their eyes partners in the murder, they rose up of their own accord, and transferred themselves whither the people wished; but they first kissed one another, that they might consummate their martyrdom with the kiss of peace. The rest indeed, immoveable and in silence, received the sword-thrust; much more Saturus, who also had first ascended the ladder, and first gave up his spirit, for he also was waiting for Perpetua. But Perpetua, that she might taste some pain, being pierced between the ribs, cried out loudly, and she herself placed the wavering right hand of the youthful gladiator to her throat. Possibly such a woman could not have been slain unless she herself had willed it, because she was feared by the impure spirit.

7. Maximilla and Priscilla, Prophets of the Last Day[18]

Hear not me, but hear Christ. (Maximilla.)

The Lord sent me to be the party-leader, informer, interpreter of this task, profession, and covenant, constrained, whether he will or nill, to learn the knowledge of God. (Maximilla.)

I am driven as a wolf from the sheep. I am not a wolf. I am word and *spirit and power*. (Maximilla.)

After me shall be no prophetess any more, but the consummation. . . . (Maximilla.)

Christ came to me in the likeness of a woman, clad in a bright robe, and planted wisdom in me and revealed that this place (Pepuza) is holy, and that here Jerusalem comes down from heaven. (Priscilla.)

Women of all races bond together to reclaim the earth for children, animals, and all living things.

Drawing by Meinrad Craighead for *Reclaim the Earth* (London: Woman's Press, 1983).

10

The New Earth: Visions of Redeemed Society and Nature

DOCUMENTS

1. *The Biblical Vision*
   The Laws of Jubilee
   Isaiah's Vision of the Messianic Age
   Jesus Proclaims His Mission: Good News to the Poor
2. *The Liberal Vision: The Perfectibility of Humanity*
3. *A Religious Scientist's Vision: Cosmic Noogenesis*
4. *The Socialist Vision: The Withering Away of the State*
5. *An Eco-Anarchist Vision: Harmony of Humanity and Nature*
6. *A Romantic Feminist Vision: The Return of the Goddess*

Hopes for redemption in Western religion have moved on several different planes. There are the hopes for a reconciled self that believes in its acceptance of God and hence is able to be both confident and realistic about itself. Much of contemporary theology operates on this personal level, which is paralleled by psychology. Our chapter on conversion addressed some of this personal dimension. There are also the hopes for the redeemed society, which establishes a new age of peace and justice. Finally, there are the eschatological hopes for transcendence of mortality, both on the personal and the cosmic level. We will reflect on these in the final chapter. In this chapter, we focus on the hopes for a new social order.

The hopes for a new age of peace and justice constituted the meaning of redemption most central to prophetic Judaism. In Hebrew Scripture, these hopes are not generally thought of "eschatologically," that is, as a fulfillment in an eternal time beyond history, but historically, as a redemption that takes place in a future time within the limits of creaturely mortality. One of the most striking expressions of this struggle for a just society is the laws of Jubilee in Leviticus 25. Such laws mandate a periodic social revolution. The normative social order commanded by God is seen as that of an egalitarian society of free small landholders. Ideally, no one should be enslaved to another. No one should have to sell her or his self or property for debt and pass into a serf status.

However, the laws recognize that there is a continual drift toward alienation of society and land. Some get rich and others poor, and so people lose their land and their freedom. Thus, periodically, every fifty years (a great Sabbath, i.e., after every seven times seven or forty-nine years), there should be a restoration of society to the ideal norm. Those who have been enslaved will be released. Those who have lost their land will be able to redeem it. Land should lie fallow for a season and animals also should be allowed to rest. This is a very important idea because it recognizes that redemption (a term based on ransoming a slave) is not simply spiritual or eschatological, nor does it refer simply to some total new age at the end of history. Rather, it is a continuous process that needs to be done over and over again *within* history.

In the collection of well-known passages from Isaiah we see all the Hebrew hopes for redemption summed up in an ideal vision. All the nations of the earth will be converted to one unifying faith in God. Peace will be established between nations. The instruments of war will be converted into the peaceful tools of agriculture. Even the enmity of nature will be overcome. Redeemed life is seen not as immortal life but rather as the fulfillment of human life within its proper finite limits. All will fill out their days (ideally, to a hundred years) without disease or premature death. No one will have land stolen by enemies or till the soil only to have the produce taken away. This vision of a blessed existence as prosperous, peaceful, and just within finite, human limits is the basic messianic vision.

It is likely that Jesus' own announcement of messianic hope belonged to this same prophetic tradition. According to Luke, in Jesus' announcement of his mission in his hometown synagogue in Nazareth, he chose the text from Isaiah 61:1–2, a text that also hearkens back to the Jubilee tradition. The Kingdom of God, the acceptable year of the Lord, is understood to mean that great release of the slaves and captives of society. Jesus' reliance on this understanding of the Kingdom is also underscored in the Lord's Prayer, a text that most likely goes back to his actual words. Here the Kingdom of God means that time in history when God's will is done on earth, that is, not an escape from earth to an eternal heavenly world. This is further defined in terms of fulfillment of basic human needs: daily bread, release from debt, avoidance of temptation and evil.[1]

These this-worldly hopes were put aside in the Christian tradition for an interpretation of redemption that concentrated on personal reconciliation with God and life after death. So it is only in modern times, as Western civilization threw off the tutelage of the Church, that social movements arose reiterating in new ways these ancient hopes for a good society that would come about through some redemptive process within history. In this chapter we have assembled five different expressions of this modern hope for social redemption: (1) a liberal, progressive vision; (2) a vision of a religious scientist of biological evolution; (3) a socialist vision; (4) an ecological vision; and (5) a feminist vision.

Although each writer believes he or she is speaking about human possibilities within history, we note in each an ecstatic quality that rivals the ancient messianic language. In their hopes for the future, the ideal takes over and carries them to heights of expectations where they can imagine a new age delivered from all evil once for all. There is a a leap to a new option so qualitatively better than the old that it can be seen as conversion from evil to good. There is an effort to show that this better future is in line with the "laws of history."

Condorcet's *Sketch . . . of the Progress of the Human Mind* was written in 1793, ironically enough while he was in hiding from the radicals who had taken over the French Revolution. In 1794, he ventured forth from hiding, was arrested, and died in prison. Of all the great thinkers of the French Enlightenment, Condorcet was the most consistent in extending his vision of emancipation to all people — to women, to all social classes, and to the colonized nations of the globe. His sketch of human progress is a work of self-consolation for the negative turn taken by the revolution that he himself had promoted. In it he dares to believe that, nevertheless, the very laws of nature make progress inevitable. The expansion of science and its communication through general education will assure a process of equalization both between social classes and among nations as well as continual conquest of the ancient human enemies of ignorance, want, and disease. Finally, death itself will be, for all practical purposes, conquered.

This optimistic vision was promoted for the eighteenth and nineteenth centuries particularly by what appeared to be continual progress in scientific knowledge, which, in turn, assured continual expansion of human control over nature through technology. Such optimistic hopes based on science were furthered by the development of the science of biological evolution, which appeared to show that progress from lesser to better was the very law of the universe itself, based on the unfolding stages of biological forms. No scientist developed the visionary possibilities of the science of evolution to more ecstatic heights than the Jesuit scientist and philosopher Pierre Teilhard de Chardin. In his various books, which were published only after his death because of his censure by the Church (he died in 1951), we see a union of the biological doctrine of evolution and the Christian vision of cosmic redemption.

Teilhard saw his own work as bringing together these two hopes, the religious hope for redemption of the soul and the modern secular hope for worldly redemption, showing their unity and compatibility with each other. Teilhard believed that biological evolution showed a continual movement through successive stages of life, leading the cosmos from the most primitive level of primal matter through plant and animal life to human life, culminating in consciousness. Human consciousness is now expanding through systems of communication, leading to a cosmic noogenesis or the development of the unitary cosmic Mind that approximates, on the creaturely level, the divine Mind, bringing the whole process to a final point of unity of creation and Creator.

However, already by the mid-nineteenth century, many Western thinkers believed that hopes for social betterment could not be guaranteed simply by the expansion of scientific knowledge, education, and technological conquest of material needs. Expanding power and wealth would not automatically lead to its sharing among all people. Rather, there must be a social revolution that would seize the means of production that had been built by the Industrial Revolution from its present powerholders, the capitalist class, and reorganize the ownership of the means of production in the hands of the social base of society, the workers. Only then could expanding wealth also become expanding well-being for all members of society.

This viewpoint distinguishes socialists from liberal progressives. In a classic statement in his pamphlet *Socialism, Utopian and Scientific* (1882), Friedrich Engels lays out his vision of this revolution in the social organization of the means of production. He believes that this revolution will cause the state itself, as a repressive apparatus designed by the ruling class to subjugate the working classes, to wither away. One will still have structures for the administration of the exchange of goods, but no longer a state in its traditional police and military functions because class antagonism will have disappeared. Once the ownership of the means of production has been appropriated by the class that represents the vast majority of society, then the expansive powers of science and technology can take off to an infinite betterment of all, no longer hindered by class antagonisms, which presently cause expanding wealth to be used for war and luxurious waste by the wealthy.

By the 1960s, however, these optimistic hopes of socialism began to sound as naive and misguided as the previous hopes of liberal progressives. Socialist revolutions had taken place in many countries, but the state showed no signs of withering away under these regimes. On the contrary, it grew ever more repressive as a system of collective state ownership of the entire apparatus of society. Moreover, it appeared as though Western scientific technology had greatly misjudged the ability of nature itself to sustain infinite progress, defined as expanding technological production. This seemed to be creating a rapid denouement of the whole Western industrial enterprise in proliferating pollution, poisoning the air, water, and soil that support human life. Industrialism is rapidly eating up the nonrenewable fossil fuels and chemicals on which this industrial revolution is based. Competing industrialized empires, capitalist and socialist, scrambling for scarce resources, threaten to end the planet itself in nuclear holocaust.

Murray Bookshin's writings represent the response of a New Left radical to the failures of socialism and scientific technology. Bookshin calls for the recovery of the anarchist-communitarian (or utopian) tradition that has been spurned by Marxists like Engels, who saw themselves as "scientific socialists." Bookshin thinks that the mistake of Marxism has been the reliance on the repressive apparatus of the nation state to create the revolution. A socialist revolution made by the state will never reorganize the ownership of the means of production in the hands of the masses of the people. Rather, it will create a new, yet more repressive ruling class, the state bureaucrat, who now will combine control over the economy with control over the police powers of the state.

For Bookshin, the socialist revolution must be anarchist. That is, it must take place by a process that dismantles the state. This means that the people, in their communities, factories, and farms, must recommunalize social life at the local level and take back the power to govern themselves. For Bookshin, this anarcho-communitarian dream of self-governing, self-sufficient local communities combines with the new radical science, ecology. Ecology provides the new scientific laws for a sustainable relation between humans and nature within balanced ecosystems. For Bookshin, this also provides a principle of social organization in human communities, defined within ecosystems, that can bring together liberated social life and the renewal of nature. The social redemption and the redemption of nature have become one and the same.

The romantic movement that arose in the nineteenth century also represents a reaction against scientism and the failures of modern technological society. Romanticism saw the emphasis on scientific rationality and an increasingly artificial environment as indicating the alienation of humanity from nature. Far from creating a new world of freedom, romanticism saw such "progress" heading toward the nightmare of totalitarian bondage of humanity to its machines. Romanticism sought to reclaim the repressed underside of rationalist culture — the feminine, intuitive and poetic modes of knowledge, nature unspoiled by human technology. It idealized the subjugated peoples of white, male domination — women, Indians, peasants, and South Sea islanders — and saw them as representing an original paradise of harmony of humanity and nature.

Radical feminism, from the late nineteenth century until the present, continues to draw inspiration from the romantic perspective. Drawing on anthropological theories of a primitive matriarchal society before the rise of patriarchy,[2] radical feminists theorized that the ancient time of mother-rule and goddess worship represented an unalienated stage of human culture when humanity lived in harmony with nature and each other and peace reigned on the earth. Masculine culture represents the destruction of this Eden and the substitution of a culture based on narrow functional rationality, materialism, strife, and war. The only hope for human planetary survival lies in the overthrow of alienated male civilization and the "return of the Goddess" or the restoration of matriarchal values. The excerpt from Elizabeth Gould Davis's The First Sex represents a recent restatement of this perspective.

One should not conclude from the above that feminism has identified only with the romantic perspective. Indeed, all of the various modern movements of social hope have had exponents who applied these hopes to the emancipation of women. Although most of the men of the Enlightenment ignored women in their doctrine of "universal rights of man" (and excluded them when the possibility of including them in this doctrine was raised),[3] there were male liberals, such as Condorcet[4] and John Stuart Mill,[5] who argued that such a defense of human rights must also include women in the rights of citizenship. Feminism arose in the late eighteenth and early nineteenth centuries, primarily in the context of liberalism. Feminists, such as Mary Wollstonecraft, the Grimké sisters, Susan B. Anthony, and Elizabeth Cady Stanton, fought for the inclusion of women in civil rights, equal education, access to professions, property holding, and the franchise.[6]

Socialists also have believed that the emancipation of the worker would free women from bondage. Engels himself argued (see chapter V, reading 9) that socialism would free women by restoring them to economic independence. They would then be able to contract marriages freely, purely for love and companionship, and not in order to sell their sexuality and domestic labor for economic maintenance. Contemporary Marxists go beyond the traditional socialist emphasis on the paid labor of working women and analyze the unpaid domestic labor of women in the home as the chief source of women's continued subjugation.[7]

Finally, ecological communitarian radicals have also seen women's emancipation coming about through the reclaiming of organic society that reintegrates family and production, field and factory. Feminist utopian writers have typically favored this kind of vision of a familial communitarian society over the Marxist faith in science and technology.[8]

Reflection

Discuss your vision of what a good society would be like. What would be its family and social organization? What would be its political system? Its organization of work and economic relations? What would be its technological apparatus? How would it relate human to nonhuman ecology? How would it relate local, regional, national, continental, and global community? What are the negative forces today that threaten freedom, justice, and human and planetary survival? How central is the emancipation of women to your social vision? Write about a utopia, describing your best visions for a good society and including the ways such a society would correct itself against the drift toward new forms of domination.

Do you think such a society is possible? If not, why not? What is the alternative? What do you see as the human prospect for the next hundred years? Is this prospect catastrophic or hopeful? What are the most important things to be done in the light of the present situation and its likely future?

1. The Biblical Vision

THE LAWS OF JUBILEE[9]

"And you shall hallow the fiftieth year, and proclaim liberty throughout the land to all its inhabitants; it shall be a jubilee for you, when each of you shall return to his property and each of you shall return to his family. A jubilee shall that fiftieth year be to you; in it you shall neither sow, nor reap what grows of itself, nor gather the grapes from the undressed vines. For it is a jubilee; it shall be holy to you; you shall eat what it yields out of the field.

"In this year of jubilee each of you shall return to his property. And if you sell to your neighbor or buy from your neighbor, . . . You shall not wrong one another, but you shall fear your God; for I am the Lord your God. . . . The land shall not be sold in perpetuity, for the land is mine; for you are strangers and sojourners with me. And in all the country you possess, you shall grant a redemption of the land.

"If your brother becomes poor, and sells part of his property, then his next of kin shall come and redeem what his brother has sold. If a man has no one to redeem it, and then himself becomes prosperous and finds sufficient means to redeem it, let him reckon the years since he sold it and pay back the overpayment to the man to whom he sold it; and he shall return to his property. But if he has not sufficient means to get it back for himself, then what he sold shall remain in the hand of him who bought it until the year of jubilee; in the jubilee it shall be released, and he shall return to his property.

"And if your brother becomes poor beside you, and sells himself to you, you shall not make him serve as a slave: he shall be with you as a hired servant and as a sojourner. He shall serve with you until the year of the jubilee; then he shall go out from you, he and his children with him, and go back to his own family, and return to the possession of his fathers. For they are my servants, whom I brought forth out of the land of Egypt; they shall not be sold as slaves."

ISAIAH'S VISION OF THE MESSIANIC AGE[10]

It shall come to pass in the latter days
   that the mountain of the house of the Lord

shall be established as the highest of the mountains,
    and shall be raised above the hills;
and all the nations shall flow to it,
    and many peoples shall come, and say:
"Come, let us go up to the mountain of the Lord,
    to the house of the God of Jacob;
that he may teach us his ways
    and that we may walk in his paths."
For out of Zion shall go forth the law,
    and the word of the Lord from Jerusalem.
He shall judge between the nations,
    and shall decide for many peoples;
and they shall beat their swords into plowshares,
    and their spears into pruning hooks;
nation shall not lift up sword against nation,
    neither shall they learn war any more.

The wolf shall dwell with the lamb,
    and the leopard shall lie down with the kid,
and the calf and the lion and the fatling together,
    and a little child shall lead them.
The cow and the bear shall feed;
    their young shall lie down together;
    and the lion shall eat straw like the ox.
The sucking child shall play over the hole of the asp,
    and the weaned child shall put his hand on the adder's den.
They shall not hurt or destroy
    in all my holy mountain;
for the earth shall be full of the knowledge of the Lord
    as the waters cover the sea.

A voice cries:
"In the wilderness prepare the way of the Lord,
    make straight in the desert a highway for our God.
Every valley shall be lifted up,
    and every mountain and hill be made low;
the uneven ground shall become level,
    and the rough places a plain.
And the glory of the Lord shall be revealed,
    and all flesh shall see it together,
    for the mouth of the Lord has spoken."

"For behold, I create new heavens

and a new earth;
and the former things shall not be remembered
    or come into mind.
But be glad and rejoice for ever
    in that which I create;
for behold, I create Jerusalem a rejoicing,
    and her people a joy.
I will rejoice in Jerusalem,
    and be glad in my people;
no more shall be heard in it the sound of weeping
    and the cry of distress.
No more shall there be in it
    an infant that lives but a few days,
    or an old man who does not fill out his days,
They shall build houses and inhabit them;
    they shall plant vineyards and eat their fruit.
They shall not build and another inhabit;
    they shall not plant and another eat;
for like the days of a tree shall the days of my people be,
    and my chosen shall long enjoy the work of their hands.
They shall not labor in vain,
    or bear children for calamity;
for they shall be the offspring of the blessed of the Lord,
    and their children with them.
Before they call I will answer,
    while they are yet speaking I will hear.
The wolf and the lamb shall feed together,
    the lion shall eat straw like the ox;
    and dust shall be the serpent's food.
They shall not hurt or destroy
    in all my holy mountain,
        says the Lord.''

JESUS PROCLAIMS HIS MISSION: GOOD NEWS TO THE POOR[11]

And Jesus returned in the power of the Spirit into Galilee, and a
report concerning him went out through all the surrounding
country.

And he taught in their synagogues, being glorified by all.

And he came to Nazareth, where he had been brought up;
and he went to the synagogue, as his custom was, on the sabbath

day. And he stood up to read; and there was given to him the
book of the prophet Isaiah. He opened the book and found the
place where it was written,
"The Spirit of the Lord is upon me,
because he has anointed me to preach good news to the poor.
He has sent me to proclaim release to the captives
and recovering of sight to the blind,
to set at liberty those who are oppressed,
to proclaim the acceptable year of the Lord."
    And he closed the book, and gave it back to the attendant,
and sat down; and the eyes of all in the synagogue were fixed on
him. And he began to say to them, "Today this scripture has
been fulfilled in your hearing."

2. The Liberal Vision: The Perfectibility of Humanity[12]

Our hopes for the future condition of the human race can be
subsumed under three important heads: the abolition of inequality
between nations, the progress of equality within each nation, and
the true perfection of mankind. . . .
    Are those differences which have hitherto been seen in every
civilized country in respect of the enlightenment, the resources,
and the wealth enjoyed by the different classes into which it is
divided, is that inequality between men which was aggravated or
perhaps produced by the earliest progress of society, are these
part of civilization itself, or are they due to the present
imperfections of the social art? Will they necessarily decrease and
ultimately make way for a real equality, the final end of the social
art, in which even the effects of the natural differences between
men will be mitigated and the only kind of inequality to persist
will be that which is in the interests of all and which favours the
progress of civilization, of education, and of industry, without
entailing either poverty, humiliation, or dependence? . . .
    In answering these three questions we shall find in the
experience of the past, in the observation of the progress that the
sciences and civilization have already made, in the analysis of the
progress of the human mind and of the development of its
faculties, the strongest reasons for believing that nature has set no
limit to the realization of our hopes. . . .
    The progress of the sciences ensures the progress of the art of
education which in turn advances that of the sciences. This

reciprocal influence, whose activity is ceaselessly renewed, deserves to be seen as one of the most powerful and active causes working for the perfection of mankind. . . .

All the causes that contribute to the perfection of the human race, all the means that ensure it, must by their very nature exercise a perpetual influence and always increase their sphere of action. . . . We may conclude then that the perfectibility of man is indefinite. Meanwhile we have considered him as possessing the natural faculties and organization that he has at present. How much greater would be the certainty, how much vaster the scheme of our hopes, if we could believe that these natural faculties themselves and this organization could also be improved? This is the last question that remains for us to ask ourselves.

Organic perfectibility or deterioration amongst the various strains in the vegetable and animal kingdom can be regarded as one of the general laws of nature. This law also applies to the human race. No one can doubt that, as preventive medicine improves and food and housing become healthier, as a way of life is established that develops our physical powers by exercise without ruining them by excess, as the two most virulent causes of deterioration, misery and excessive wealth, are eliminated, the average length of human life will be increased and a better health and a stronger physical constitution will be ensured. The improvement of medical practice, which will become more efficacious with the progress of reason and of the social order, will mean the end of infectious and hereditary diseases and illnesses brought on by climate, food, or working conditions. It is reasonable to hope that all other diseases may likewise disappear as their distant causes are discovered. Would it be absurd then to suppose that this perfection of the human species might be capable of indefinite progress; that the day will come when death will be due only to extraordinary accidents or to the decay of the vital forces, and that ultimately the average span between birth and decay will have no assignable value? Certainly man will not become immortal, but will not the interval between the first breath that he draws and the time when in the natural course of events, without disease or accident, he expires, increase indefinitely? . . .

But are not our physical faculties and the strength, dexterity and acuteness of our senses, to be numbered among the qualities whose perfection in the individual may be transmitted? . . .

Finally may we not extend such hopes to the intellectual and moral faculties? May not our parents, who transmit to us the benefits or disadvantages of their constitution, and from whom we receive our shape and features, as well as our tendencies to certain physical affections, hand on to us also that part of the physical organization which determines the intellect, the power of the brain, the ardour of the soul or the moral sensibility? Is it not probable that education, in perfecting these qualities, will at the same time influence, modify and perfect the organization itself? Analogy, investigation of the human faculties and the study of certain facts, all seem to give substance to such conjectures which would further push back the boundaries of our hopes.

These are the questions with which we shall conclude this final stage. How consoling for the philosopher who laments the errors, the crimes, the injustices which still pollute the earth and of which he is often the victim is this view of the human race, emancipated from its shackles, released from the empire of fate and from that of the enemies of its progress, advancing with a firm and sure step along the path of truth, virtue and happiness! It is the contemplation of this prospect that rewards him for all his efforts to assist the progress of reason and the defence of liberty. He dares to regard these strivings as part of the eternal chain of human destiny; and in this persuasion he is filled with the true delight of virtue and the pleasure of having done some lasting good which fate can never destroy by a sinister stroke of revenge, by calling back the reign of slavery and prejudice. Such contemplation is for him an asylum, in which the memory of his persecutors cannot pursue him; there he lives in thought with man restored to his natural rights and dignity, forgets man tormented and corrupted by greed, fear or envy; there he lives with his peers in an Elysium created by reason and graced by the purest pleasures known to the love of mankind.

3. A Religious Scientist's Vision: Cosmic Noogenesis[13]

Any two forces, provided both are positive, must *a priori* be capable of growth by merging together. Faith in God and faith in the World: these two springs of energy, each the source of a magnificent spiritual impulse, must certainly be capable of effectively uniting in such a way as to produce a resulting upward movement. But in practical terms where are we to look for the principle and the generative medium which will bring about this most desirable evolutionary step?

I believe that the principle and the medium are to be found in the idea, duly "realised," that there is in progress, within us and around us, a continual heightening of consciousness in the Universe.

Once he has been brought to accept the reality of a Noogenesis, the believer in this World will find himself compelled to allow increasing room, in his vision of the future, for the values of personalisation and transcendency. Of Personalisation, because a Universe in process of psychic concentration is *identical* with a Universe that is acquiring a personality. And of transcendency because the ultimate stage of "cosmic" personalisation, if it is to be supremely coherent and unifying, cannot be conceived otherwise than as emerging at the summit of the elements it super-personalises in uniting them to itself.

On the other hand, the believer in Heaven, accepting this same reality of a cosmic genesis of the Spirit, must perceive that the mystical evolution of which he dreams presupposes and consecrates all the tangible realities and all the arduous conditions of human progress. If it is to be super-spiritualised in God, must not Mankind first be born and grow in conformity with the entire system of what we call "evolution"? Whence, for the Christian in particular, there follows a radical incorporation of terrestrial values in the most fundamental concepts of his Faith, those of Divine Omnipotence, withdrawal and charity. First, Divine Omnipotence: God creates and shapes us through the process of evolution: how can we suppose, or fear, that He will arbitrarily interfere with the very means whereby He fulfills His purpose? Then, withdrawal: God awaits us when the evolutionary process is complete: to rise above the World, therefore, does not mean to despise or reject it, but to pass through it and sublime it. Finally, charity: the love of God expresses and crowns the basic affinity which, from the beginnings of Time and Space, has drawn together and concentrated the spiritualisable elements of the Universe. To love God and our neighbour is therefore not merely an act of worship and compassion superimposed on our other individual preoccupations. For the Christian, if he be truly Christian, it is Life itself, Life in the integrity of its aspirations, its struggles and its conquests, that he must embrace in a spirit of togetherness and personalising unification with all things.

The sense of the earth opening and exploding upwards into God; and the sense of God taking root and finding nourishment downwards into Earth. A personal, transcendent God and an evolving Universe no longer forming two hostile centres of attraction, but entering into hierarchic conjunction to raise the human mass on a single tide. Such is the sublime transformation which we may with justice foresee, and which in fact is beginning to have its effect upon a growing number of minds, free-thinkers as well as believers: the idea of a spiritual evolution of the Universe. The very transformation we have been seeking!

4. The Socialist Vision: The Withering Away of the State[14]

While the capitalist mode of production more and more completely transforms the great majority of the population into proletarians, it creates the power which, under penalty of its own destruction, is forced to accomplish this revolution. While it forces on more and more the transformation of the vast means of production, already socialized, into state property, it shows itself the way to accomplishing this revolution. *The proletariat seizes political power and turns the means of production into state property.*

But, in doing this, it abolishes itself as proletariat, abolishes all class distinctions and class antagonisms, abolishes also the state as state. Society thus far, based upon class antagonisms, had need of the state. . . . As soon as there is no longer any social class to be held in subjection; as soon as class rule, and the individual struggle for existence based upon our present anarchy in production, with the collisions and excesses arising from these, are removed, nothing more remains to be repressed, and a special repressive force, a state, is no longer necessary. The first act by virtue of which the state really constitutes itself the representative of the whole of society — the taking possession of the means of production in the name of society — this is, at the same time, its last independent act as a state. State interference in social relations becomes, in one domain after another, superfluous, and then dies out of itself; the government of persons is replaced by the administration of things, and by the conduct of processes of production. The state is not "abolished." *It dies out.* . . . The expansive force of the means of production bursts the bonds that the capitalist mode of production had imposed upon them. Their deliverance from these bonds is the one precondition for an unbroken, constantly accelerated development of the productive forces, and therewith for a practically unlimited increase of production itself. . . . The possibility of securing for every member of society, by means of socialized production, an existence not only fully sufficient materially, and becoming day by day more full, but an existence guaranteeing to all the free development and exercise of their physical and mental faculties — the possibility is now for the first time here, but *it is here.*

With the seizing of the means of production by society, production of commodities is done away with, and, simultaneously, the mastery of the product over the producer. Anarchy in social production is replaced by systematic, definite organization. The struggle for individual existence disappears. Then for the first time man, in a certain sense, is finally marked off from the rest of the animal kingdom, and emerges from mere animal conditions of existence into really human ones. The whole sphere of the conditions of life which environ man, and which have hitherto ruled man, now comes under the dominion and control of man, who for the first time becomes the real, conscious lord of Nature, because he has now become master of his own social organization. The laws of his own social action, hitherto standing face to face with man as laws of Nature foreign to, and dominating him, will then be used with full understanding, and so mastered by him. Man's own social organization, hitherto confronting him as a necessity imposed by Nature and history, now becomes the result of his own free action. The extraneous objective forces that have hitherto governed history pass under the control of man himself. Only from that time will man himself, more and more consciously, make his own history — only from that time will the social causes set in movement by him have, in the main and in a constantly growing measure, the results intended by him. It is the ascent of man from the kingdom of necessity to the kingdom of freedom.

5. An Eco-Anarchist Vision: Harmony of Humanity and Nature[15]

It cannot be emphasized too strongly that the anarchist concepts of a balanced community, a face-to-face democracy, a humanistic technology and a decentralized society — these rich libertarian concepts — are not only desirable, they are also necessary. They belong not only to the great visions of man's future, they now constitute the preconditions for human survival. The process of social development has carried them out of the ethical, subjective dimension into a practical, objective dimension. What was once regarded as impractical and visionary has become eminently practical. And what was once regarded as practical and objective has become eminently impractical and irrelevant in terms of man's development towards a fuller, unfettered existence. If we conceive of demands for community, face-to-face democracy, a humanistic liberatory technology and decentralization merely as reactions to the prevailing state of affairs — a vigorous "nay" to the "yea" of what exists today — a compelling, objective case can now be made for the practicality of an anarchist society.

What is most significant about ecology is its ability to convert this often nihilistic rejection of the status quo into an emphatic affirmation of life — indeed, into a reconstructive credo for a humanistic society. The essence of ecology's reconstructive message can be summed up in the word "diversity." From an ecological viewpoint, balance and harmony in nature, in society and, by inference, in behavior, are achieved not by mechanical standardization but by its opposite, organic differentiation.

I submit that an anarchist community would approximate a clearly definable ecosystem; it would be diversified, balanced and harmonious. It is arguable whether such an ecosystem would acquire the configuration of an urban entity with a distinct center, such as we find in the Greek *polis* or the medieval commune, or whether, as Gutkind proposes, society would consist of widely dispersed communities without a distinct center. In any case, the ecological scale for any of these communities would be determined by the smallest ecosystem capable of supporting a population of moderate size.

If the ecological community is ever achieved in practice, social life will yield a sensitive development of human and natural diversity, falling together into a well balanced, harmonious whole. Ranging from community through region to entire continents, we will see a colorful differentiation of human groups and ecosystems, each developing its unique potentialities and exposing members of the community to a wide spectrum of economic, cultural and behavioral stimuli. Falling within our purview will be an exciting, often dramatic, variety of communal forms — here marked by architectural and industrial adaptations to semi-arid ecosystems, there to grasslands, elsewhere by adaptation to forested areas. We will witness a creative interplay between individual and group, community and environment, humanity and nature. The cast of mind that today organizes differences among humans and other lifeforms along hierarchical lines, defining the external in terms of its "superiority" or "inferiority," will give way to an outlook that deals with diversity in an ecological manner. Differences among people will be respected, indeed fostered, as elements that enrich the unity of experience and phenomena. The traditional relationship which pits subject against object will be altered qualitatively; the "external," the "different," the "other" will be conceived of as individual parts of a whole all the richer because of its complexity. This sense of unity will reflect the harmonization of interests between individuals and between society and nature. Freed from an oppressive routine, from paralyzing repressions and insecurities, from the burdens of toil and false needs, from the trammels of authority and irrational compulsion, individuals will finally, for the first time in history, be in a position to realize their potentialities as members of the human community and the natural world.

6. A Romantic Feminist Vision: The Return of the Goddess[16]

In original myth, . . . there is an original Great Goddess who creates the universe, the earth, and the heavens, and finally creates the gods and mankind. Eventually she bears, parthenogenetically, a son who later becomes her lover, then her consort, next her surrogate and finally, in patriarchal ages, the usurper of her power. In the measureless eons of her exclusive reign, however, she inaugurates civilization in all its aspects. Under her rule the earth enjoys a long period of peaceful progress during which time cities are built, law and justice are instituted, crops are planted and harvested, cattle are domesticated for their milk and wool, fire is discovered and utilized, the wheel is invented, ships are first constructed, and the arts, from ceramics and weaving to painting and sculpture, are begun.

Then suddenly all is ended. Paradise is lost. A dark age overtakes the world — a dark age brought on by cataclysm accompanied by a patriarchal revolution. Nomads, barbaric and uncivilized, roving bands of ejected, womanless men, destroy the civilized city states, depose the queens, and attempt to rule in their stead. The result is chaos. War and violence make their appearance, justice and law fly out the window, might replaces right, the Great Goddess is replaced by a stern and vengeful God, man becomes carnivorous, property rights become paramount over human rights, woman is degraded and exploited, and civilization starts on the downward path it still pursues.

Such is the theme of all myth — from the Golden Age of the Greeks and Romans to the Garden of Eden of Jew and Christian, and Happy Hunting Ground of the American Indian, and the Avaiki of the Polynesians — all ending in a fall from paradise and in utter failure. . . .

When man first resolved to exalt the peculiarities of his own sex, muscularity and spiritual immaturity, he adopted the policy that reality meant tangibility and that what could not be seen or touched did not exist. . . . By discrediting the mystic power of woman, man cut himself off from the higher things, the "eternal verities" the sense of which had distinguished him from the lower animals. By crushing every manifestation of supersensory or extrasensory truth and worshiping only sensate matter, man made of himself a mere biological organism and denied to himself the divine ray that once upon a time woman had revealed to him. . . .

Her animal body, however, remained a necessary adjunct to the new physical man, and he set about to remold her from his own base material into a mere biological organism like himself — a fit mate, a help "meet" for him — his biological complement. Through the long centuries he succeeded in brainwashing her to the belief that she was indeed made from his rib, that she was formed to be a comfort to him, the receptacle of his seed, and the incubator of *his* heirs, who were the perpetuators of *his* name.

Thus the sacred flame of her primordial and divine authority was banked and dampened and finally smothered almost to extinction. Throughout the Arian and Piscean ages of strife and materialism, man's denser nature held sway while woman's etheric light lay hidden under the bushel of masculine domination.

We are on the threshold of the new Age of Aquarius, whom the Greeks called Hydrochoos, the water-bearer, the renewer, the reviver, the quencher of raging fire and of thirst. . . .

Today, as then, women are in the vanguard of the aborning civilization; and it is to the women that we look for salvation in the healing and restorative waters of Aquarius.

It is to such a new age that we look now with hope as the present age of masculism succeeds in destroying itself, as have all its predecessors in the incredibly long history of civilizations. . . .

The rot of masculist materialism has indeed permeated all spheres of twentieth-century life and now attacks its very core.

The only remedy for the invading and consuming rot is a return to the values of the matriarchates. . . .

The ages of masculism are now drawing to a close. Their dying days are lit up by a final flare of universal violence and despair such as the world has seldom before seen. Men of goodwill turn in every direction seeking cures for their perishing society, but to no avail. Any and all social reforms superimposed upon our sick civilization can be no more effective than a bandage on a gaping and putrefying wound. Only the complete and total demolition of the social body will cure the fatal sickness. Only the overthrow of the three-thousand-year-old beast of masculist materialism will save the race.

In the new science of the twenty-first century, not physical force but spiritual force will lead the way. Mental and spiritual gifts will be more in demand than gifts of a physical nature. Extrasensory perception will take precedence over sensory perception. And in this sphere woman will again predominate. She who was revered and worshiped by early man because of her power to see the unseen will once again be the pivot — not as sex but as divine woman — about whom the next civilization will, as of old, revolve.

In death we return to the arms of our Mother-Matter-Matrix, from which all life came forth in the beginning.

Night. Sculpture by Jacob Epstein, Transport Executive Building, London, 1929.

11

The New Heaven: Personal and Cosmic Eschatology

DOCUMENTS

1. *Inanna's Descent to the Underworld*
2. *The Hermetic Myth of the Fall and Return of the Soul*
3. *The Platonic Myth of the Fall and Return of the Soul*
4. *The Millennium and Eternal Age in the Book of Revelation*
5. *The Resurrected Body in Paul*
6. *The Trimorphic Protennoia and the New Eon in Gnosticism*
7. *The Redemption of the Cosmos in Irenaeus*
8. *The Assumption of Mary in Christian Apocrypha*
9. *Mary's Assumption: Archetype of the Redeemed Cosmos and Church*
10. *His Religion and Hers: A Poem by Charlotte Perkins Gilman*

The religions of ancient Near Eastern culture, Sumerian, Babylonian and Hebrew, did not originally hold out hope for human escape from mortality. They regarded mortality as intrinsic to the human condition and concentrated their religious hopes on the renewal of life forces within the temporal process. The first great resurrection story of antiquity, *Inanna's Descent to the Underworld*, a Sumerian myth composed sometime in the third millennium B.C., shows this trade-off of human mortality for the renewal of seasonal life. Inanna, the Queen of heaven, decides to challenge her sister who reigns over the realm of death. She decks herself in her jewels, symbols of power and authority, and descends to the underworld. But she is stripped of these jewels one by one as she passes through the seven gates of Hades and finally is brought naked and on bended knee before the throne of her sister, the Queen of Hades. Her sister Ereshkigal and the Anunnaki, the seven judges of the underworld, fix her with the eye of death. Inanna is turned into a corpse and hung by a nail on the wall.

For three days and nights Inanna is dead. (In the Akkadian version of the story, *Ishtar's Descent to the Underworld*, the world above loses its fertility. There is no copulation or birth among humans or animals.) Inanna delegated her servant Ninshubur to appeal to the three father Gods if she failed in her mission. After two failures, the third God, Enki, responds and concocts two beings to carry the "food of life" and the "waters of life" to the underworld to sprinkle on the corpse of Inanna. Inanna revives and begins her reascent to the world above, but she must pay a price for her escape from death. She must send a surrogate in her place. Inanna takes her human lover Dumuzi and hands him over to the demons of death as her substitute. Thus the renewal of the seasonal processes of life are assured, but the human community, represented by its king, the consort of Inanna, must pay for it with its own mortality.

However, in the later stages of the various Mediterranean religions of antiquity, this trade-off of human mortality for seasonal renewal became unsatisfactory. Particularly as human hopes for establishing good societies faded, human longing turned to survival of death. The myths of conquest of death typically took the form of eschatological interpretations of the ancient stories of seasonal renewal. The yearly rebirth of the sown seed in the earth became the metaphor for the eschatological rebirth of the soul to eternal life.

In Egyptian culture Osiris' resurrection through the ministrations of Isis (a variant on the Anath-Baal story; see chapter VI, reading 1) became also the myth for the cult of the dead. First the king and then wealthy aristocracy and merchants might hope to escape death by the rites of embalming and the identification with the resurrected Osiris in the underworld. Likewise in Babylonian culture, the cultivation of astronomy led to speculation on the stars and planets as the dwelling place of the Gods.[1] Human souls were also seen as originating there and becoming incarnate through a process in which they descended to earth through the gates of the seven planetary systems, taking on the destiny of each planet as they descended.

The pathway back to heaven lay in a return journey in which the soul doffed these psychic garments taken on through planetary influence until it finally emerged, purified and shining like light, in its starry home. In this story of the descent and reascent of the soul, the earth becomes the "netherworld" of death (mortal life) into which the soul descends like Inanna, only in reverse of her disrobing. In the vision of the reascent of the soul in the Poimandres we see a version of that astral eschatology in which the soul doffs its various astral garments as it passes through the seven planetary systems until finally it enters the realm of eternal life, naked and pure.

Plato in the *Phaedrus* develops a philosophic version of this Chaldean myth of astral eschatology. The souls originate in the realm of the stars where they accompany the Gods on their journeys in the heavens. Thereby the soul is nourished by its contemplation of the eternal truths that lie in a shining intellectual realm beyond the outward circle of the cosmos. But those souls that cannot control the unruly steed of their passions lose their wings, sink to earth, and take on a body. Those souls who have absorbed the most truth in their contemplative preexistence pass into higher human types; those who have seen less truth pass into lower human types. Through reincarnation souls work their way back upward to purer and higher states of consciousness until, after thousands of years, the soul grows its wings again and escapes from the cycle of rebirth. For Plato, birth in the body is an entrapment in a lower existence, and true life happens only through escape from the body to disincarnate life.

Hebrew religion also focused originally on this-worldly hopes, emphasizing the winning of justice and righteousness through exclusive adherence to the commandments of God. It placed the needs for renewal of fertility within these visions of reestablished right relation to God. Drought and blighted harvests were seen as punishment for sin, while return to faithfulness to God was to be expressed in a society of peace and justice blessed by God with abundant rain and good harvests. Seasonal renewal of life processes is still present in Hebrew hopes, but it is placed in the context of divinely mandated social morality.

However, as these hopes were disappointed by expanding imperial systems, Hebrew hope became increasingly apocalyptic. The Good Age to Come would happen through a total cosmic revolution that would overthrow the present cosmic order of evil and institute a new order. The righteous of past ages would be included in this ideal future through bodily resurrection. Originally resurrection was seen as restricted to the unrewarded righteous of the past and also the unpunished evildoers who would "get theirs" in a final judgment. But this introduction of resurrection of the dead of past times broke the essentially historical context of future hope.

Later apocalypses develop this eschatological element, eventually imagining a historical period (millennium) when the just will reign within history and then an eternal new heaven and earth when the cosmos itself will be regenerated and become capable of bearing immortal life. The dead will rise to a new form of life that is eternal and everlasting.

The last chapters of the Christian Book of Revelation display this more developed eschatology. After the plagues of judgment have fallen on the evil world, symbolized by Babylon (Rome), Satan, the power behind imperial rule, is bound. The just, identified with Christian martyrs, rise from the dead and reign for a thousand years with Christ. After the end of the millennium, Satan is again unleashed and there is a final conflict between the forces of good and the forces of evil. Then there is a general resurrection of all the dead of past ages, a judgment, and a final purging of all negative power. Sinners, and even death and Hades, are thrown into the lake of fire. There is no reason to think that this means sinners suffer for eternity, as later Christian eschatology had it. The author may be following the apocalyptic tradition, derived originally from Persian religion,[2] in which all evil is purged and cleansed by fire and ceases to exist.

There is a regeneration of the cosmos; a new eternal heaven and earth is created. An eternal Holy City, Jerusalem, descends "as a bride" to be the consort of God. Paradise is restored with the tree of life and the waters of life. The temple is no longer necessary as a visible symbol of God's dwelling with humans, nor are the planets necessary to give light, because the cosmos itself is now God's temple and the presence of God provides the light by which to walk. This redeemed age is eternal and everlasting.

In Paul's First Epistle to the Corinthians, written some forty years before this Christian apocalypse, we see the apostle grappling with the question of how mortal flesh can become capable of eternal life in the resurrection. Paul does not distinguish between a millennial age of the reign of the just with Christ and an eternal age. Rather, he refers vaguely to a process in which Christ reigns, overcoming all evil powers, until the last enemy, death, is destroyed. Then Christ submits this perfected cosmos to God in a final unification of creator and redeemed creation.

In attempting to explain how a mortal human body could become immortal in the resurrection, Paul draws on the ancient analogy to the birth of vegetation from the sown seed. The seed buried in earth is seen as analogous to the mortal body that returns to the soil and then "rises again" in a new form of life. This new life, however, is now a glorified flesh that has been purged of its mortal and corruptible characteristics and has "put on" immortality.

In the gnostic texts of the Nag Hammadi library, we see one school of interpretation of this dualism between the present perishable age and the future imperishable age. Gnosticism began to develop systems of philosophic theology as early as the beginning of the second century. In various cities in the eastern Mediterranean, such as Alexandria, it was probably the first type of Christianity to arrive, being displaced later by what comes to be identified as orthodox Christianity.[3] Gnosticism interpreted the apocalyptic dualism between God and Satanic powers that presently govern the world system to mean that these are fallen angelic powers who created this cosmos. The material world, in its socioeconomic and cosmic expressions, is the product of these powers alien from true transcendent being. Since all perceptible, and even intellectually knowable, reality is limited by this fallen world system, knowledge of redeeming truth (*gnosis*) must take the form of mysterious communication that affords us a glimpse into this hidden higher world.

The treatise titled *The Trimorphic Protennoia* is such a glimpse into this heavenly world, the mystery of the overcoming of the present evil eon and its replacement by a new eon that reflects the authentic light and life of true divinity. Particularly fascinating in this text is the way in which masculinity is identified with the fallen world system of injustice while a spiritual femaleness is seen as the revealer of the higher heavenly world. The Protennoia figure is seen as androgynous, with a female persona. She speaks like the Sophia (Wisdom) of the Biblical tradition on whom she is modeled. She is the female revealer of the highest transcendency.

Protennoia was manifest first as Father in the earlier revelation but now comes in a female form as Mother to reveal the imminent overthrow of the present alien cosmos and the coming of the new eon of glory. The cosmic powers that rule this present world system are described as going in consternation to the Archigenitor (modeled after Plato's Demiurgos). But this creator of the fallen cosmos is ignorant of the higher transcendent world. This ignorance and impotence are revealed as the end of the present eon approaches. In its place there will come a new eon of changeless eternal life.

This radical interpretation of the apocalyptic dualism between the fallen and the redeemed cosmos threatened both the unity of God as creator and redeemer and the belief in the ultimate goodness of the creation. Irenaeus, writing at the end of the second century, represents one of the major theologians of emerging orthodoxy who battles against this gnostic radical dualism. Although Irenaeus also believes that humanity and creation have fallen into sin and that the redeemed creation will surpass this present mortal creation and become immortal, he attempts to interpret the fall and ultimate transformation of the cosmos in such a way as to preserve the unity of God and the ultimate goodness of creation. To do this, Irenaeus attempts to set forth a sacramental theology of creation in which the divine Logos or Word of God is not only the revelation of the divine life but is the underlying power of creaturely existence itself. The material world is not alien to the spiritual world, but indeed the material world is the visible bodying-forth of the spiritual world.

Sin, for Irenaeus, is not a fall into materiality but a denial by the creature of its true foundations in divine being. It is a spiritual negation of one's true source of being. But the divine Logos does not cease thereby to uphold the created world. Redemption is a process by which God revivifies creation through the power of that same Word and Spirit through which the world was created in the beginning. This process culminates in the coming of Christ, the manifestation of the Word in bodily form. Through the sacraments, this embodied Word now penetrates into our bodies, representing the transformation of bodily, creaturely existence through the power of Spirit. Thereby, bodily existence is gradually redeemed, first from sin and finally from mortality itself.

Irenaeus affirms the distinction between a millennium, where the just reign with Christ, and a second eternal age. But, for him, these represent stages in a continuous process. First, through the sacramental power of Christ, all evil is purged from creation, and it returns to its pristine paradisiacal state. There is a millennial age in which the created order can shine forth in its true goodness. Then there is a second stage of regeneration in which mortality itself is overcome. Human and cosmic bodily existence is transformed into glorified flesh capable of reigning together with God eternally. The mystery of redemption is thus a mystery of the intermingling of flesh and spirit whereby spirit descends into flesh and is embodied in it and flesh, in turn, is transformed and becomes capable of eternal life. Redemption is completed when the whole cosmos is transformed into a glorified manifestation of the divine.

Although later orthodoxy discarded the doctrine of the millennium as a dangerous sectarianism that might suggest the overthrow of the present (Christian) sociopolitical order, the vision of a glorified cosmos was never entirely discarded in Eastern and Latin Christian orthodoxy.

This redemption of the flesh of creation (the cosmos as well as human bodies) also suggested an ultimate reconciliation of male and female as symbols of spirit and flesh. The Assumption of Mary the Mother of Christ comes to be seen as the archetype of this mystery of the ultimate redemption of bodiliness, in which the maternal flesh of material existence is transfigured and made capable of manifesting eternal life.

The Assumption of Mary is seen as the "first fruits" of this ultimate reconciliation of flesh and spirit, of female and male. Mary as virginal and hence unfallen flesh is seen as preserved from the effects of sin, which are death. Although she dies, her body does not pass into corruption. Rather, Christ arrives and takes her soul directly to paradise, or, in another version of the story, carries her bodily into heaven.[4]

This doctrine of the Assumption of Mary also allows Catholic Christianity to recover a Queen of Heaven to replace the ancient Goddess who was Queen of Heaven. Christians need not look only at an all-male Trinity when they pray to heaven but now can be assured that they have a Mother in heaven, reigning at the right hand of her Son and his Father, to whom they can direct their prayers. Being maternal, she is more merciful than the male deities, and so one has a better chance to have divine justice tempered with mercy with her help (see chapter VI, reading 8).

In an excerpt from Otto Semmelroth's book on Mary, we see a twentieth-century Catholic theologian reflecting on the Assumption of Mary and identifying it with the ancient vision of the redeemed cosmos. The Church as body of Christ becomes the community that anticipates this redeemed cosmos. Mary's Assumption points forward to this ultimate eschatological unification of Creator with creation.

The final text in this chapter is a poem by feminist sociologist Charlotte Perkins Gilman. In this poem, which appeared in her book *His Religion and Hers*, Gilman questions traditional Christian eschatology. She suggests that the preoccupation with death and the survival of the soul after death comes from a religiosity rooted in male experiences of killing and death, while a female-based religiosity would focus on this-worldly nurturance of the person within society.

Reflection

In the last several centuries, there has been a marked turning away in Western post-Christian culture from expectations of life after death. Modernity has meant a reclaiming of this earth as our home. Even

Christians find it difficult to speak credibly about hopes for life after death and are not sure they should put their energies there. However, as modern civilization is increasingly threatened by its own denouement in technological annihilation, there may be again a desire to turn away from this earth and cultivate the heavenly world. Can we afford to do that?

Do we still dare to hope for such visions as we have seen in this chapter, and, indeed, should we wish to hope for such things? We have seen how eschatological hope has been related to an alienation from and disappointment with bodily life and its processes of seasonal and generational renewal. In seeking an immortal duplication of seasonal and sexual generation, eschatology has also tended to despise these merely finite processes of life renewal and has seen them not as symbols of life but as symbols of death. Sexuality, maternity, the female body become despised as the images of a sinful life whence comes death, that is, merely mortal life.

Is it possible to hope for immortal life without tending to despise and therefore fail to value and cultivate those very life processes by which the cosmos and human beings are sustained from generation to generation? Does feminist theology need, therefore, to call for a rejection of eschatology in favor of cultivating those life processes that can sustain the earth from generation to generation, declaring that this is our true sphere and life as human beings? Perhaps immortal life, if it is possible, can be safely left in the hands of God/ess from which all reality came forth in the beginning?

1. Inanna's Descent to the Underworld[5]

From the Great Above she opened her ear to the Great Below.
From the Great Above the goddess opened her ear to the Great
    Below.
From the Great Above Inanna opened her ear to the Great Below.

My Lady abandoned heaven and earth to descend to the
    underworld.
Inanna abandoned heaven and earth to descend to the
    underworld.
She abandoned her office of holy priestess to descend to the
    underworld.

. . .
She gathered together the seven *me*.
She took them into her hands.
With the *me* in her possession, she prepared herself:

. . .
Inanna set out for the underworld.
Ninshubur, her faithful servant, went with her.
Inanna spoke to her, saying:
  "Ninshubur, my constant support,
  My *sukkal* who gives me wise advice,
  My warrior who fights by my side,
  I am descending to the *kur*, to the underworld.
  If I do not return,
  Set up a lament for me by the ruins.
  Beat the drum for me in the assembly places.
  Circle the houses of the gods.

. . .
If Enlil will not help you,
Go to Ur, to the temple of Nanna.
Weep before Father Nanna.
If Nanna will not help you,
Go to Eridu, to the temple of Enki.
Weep before Father Enki.
Father Enki, the God of Wisdom, knows the food of life,
He knows the water of life;
He knows the secrets.
Surely he will not let me die."
Inanna continued on her way to the underworld.
Then she stopped and said:
  "Go now, Ninshubur —
  Do not forget the words I have commanded you."

When Inanna arrived at the outer gates of the underworld,
She knocked loudly.
She cried out in a fierce voice:
  "Open the door, gatekeeper!
  Open the door, Neti!
  I alone would enter!"

Neti, the chief gatekeeper of the *kur*, asked:
  "Who are you?"

She answered:
>"I am Inanna, Queen of Heaven,
>On my way to the East."

Neti said:
>"If you are truly Inanna, Queen of Heaven,
>On your way to the East,
>Why has your heart led you on the road
>From which no traveler returns?"

Inanna answered:
>"Because . . . of my older sister, Ereshkigal,
>Her husband, Gugalanna, the Bull of Heaven, has died.
>I have come to witness the funeral rites.
>Let the beer of his funeral rites be poured into the cup.
>Let it be done."

Neti spoke:
>"Stay here, Inanna, I will speak to my queen.
>I will give her your message."

Neti, the chief gatekeeper of the *kur*,
Entered the palace of Ereshkigal, the Queen of the Underworld,
>and said:
>"My queen, a maid
>As tall as heaven,
>As wide as the earth,
>As strong as the foundations of the city wall,
>Waits outside the palace gates."

When Ereshkigal heard this,
She slapped her thigh and bit her lip.
She took the matter into her heart and dwelt on it.
Then she spoke:
>"Come, Neti, my chief gatekeeper of the *kur*,
>Heed my words:
>Bolt the seven gates of the underworld.
>Then, one by one, open each gate a crack.
>Let Inanna enter.
>As she enters, remove her royal garments.
>Let the holy priestess of heaven enter bowed low."

Neti heeded the words of his queen.
He bolted the seven gates of the underworld.

Then he opened the outer gate.
He said to the maid:
 "Come, Inanna, enter."
When she entered the first gate,
From her head, the *shugurra*, the crown of the steppe, was
  removed.

Inanna asked:
 "What is this?"
She was told:
 "Quiet, Inanna, the ways of the underworld are perfect.
 They may not be questioned."

[As Inanna passes through the seven gates, she is stripped of her
powers, one by one.]

Naked and bowed low, Inanna entered the throne room.
Ereshkigal rose from her throne.
Inanna started toward the throne.
The Annuna, the judges of the underworld, surrounded her.
They passed judgment against her.

Then Ereshkigal fastened on Inanna the eye of death.
She spoke against her the word of wrath.
She uttered against her the cry of guilt.

She struck her.

Inanna was turned into a corpse,
A piece of rotting meat,
And was hung from a hook on the wall.

When, after three days and three nights, Inanna had not returned,
Ninshubur set up a lament for her by the ruins.
She beat the drum for her in the assembly places.
She circled the houses of the gods.
She tore at her eyes; she tore at her mouth; she tore at her thighs.
She dressed herself in a single garment like a beggar.
Alone, she set out for Nippur and the temple of Enlil.

[Enhil and Nanna both refuse her appeal for help.]

Ninshubur went to Eridu and the temple of Enki.

When she entered the holy shrine,
She cried out:
"O Father Enki, do not let your daughter
Be put to death in the underworld.

Father Enki said:
"What has happened?
What has my daughter done?
Inanna! Queen of All the Lands! Holy Priestess of Heaven!
What has happened?
I am troubled. I am grieved."
From under his fingernail Father Enki brought forth dirt.
He fashioned the dirt into a *kurgarra*, a creature neither male nor
female.
From under the fingernail of his other hand he brought forth dirt.
He fashioned the dirt into a *galatur*, a creature neither male nor
female.
He gave the food of life to the *kurgarra*.
He gave the water of life to the *galatur*.
Enki spoke to the *kurgarra* and *galatur*, saying:
"Go to the underworld,
Enter the door like flies.
Ereshkigal, the Queen of the Underworld, is moaning
With the cries of a woman about to give birth.
No linen is spread over her body.
Her breasts are uncovered.
Her hair swirls about her head like leeks.
When she cries, 'Oh! Oh! My inside!'
    Cry also, 'Oh! Oh! Your inside!'
When she cries, 'Oh! Oh! My outside!'
Cry also, 'Oh! Oh! Your outside!'
The queen will be pleased.
She will offer you a gift.
Ask her only for the corpse that hangs from the hook on the
wall.
One of you will sprinkle the food of life on it.
The other will sprinkle the water of life.
Inanna will arise."
The *kurgarra* and the *galatur* heeded Enki's words.
They set out for the underworld.
Like flies, they slipped through the cracks of the gates.
They entered the throne room of the Queen of the Underworld.

[The creatures share Ereshkigal's pangs and receive various offers of rewards, but they will accept only the corpse of Inanna.]

The *kurgarra* sprinkled the food of life on the corpse.
The *galatur* sprinkled the water of life on the corpse.
Inanna arose. . . .
Inanna was about to ascend from the underworld
When the Annuna, the judges of the underworld, seized her.
They said:
>"No one ascends from the underworld unmarked.
>If Inanna wishes to return from the underworld,
>She must provide someone in her place."

[Inanna is met by her faithful servant, Ninshubur, and then, in turn, by her two children, each of whom has been distraught over Inanna's absence. The demons of the underworld try to take each, but Inanna rebuffs them. But Dumuzi receives her arrogantly, as if a God and not a mere mortal.]

In Uruk, by the big apple tree,
Dumuzi, the husband of Inanna, was dressed in his shining *me*-
>garments.
He sat on his magnificent throne; (he did not move).

The *galla* seized him by his thighs.
They poured milk out of his seven churns.
They broke the reed pipe which the shepherd was playing.

Inanna fastened on Dumuzi the eye of death.
She spoke against him the word of wrath.
She uttered against him the cry of guilt:
>*"Take him! Take Dumuzi away!"*

2. The Hermetic Myth of the Fall and Return of the Soul[6]

"And this is why alone of all the animals on earth man is
twofold, mortal through the body, immortal through the essential
Man. For though he is immortal and has power over all things, he
suffers the lot of mortality, being subject to the Heimarmene;
though he was above the Harmony, he has become a slave within
the Harmony; though he was androgynous, having issued from

the androgynous Father, and unsleeping from the unsleeping one,
he is conquered by love and sleep."

He who has come thus to know himself has come into the
supreme good; he, however, who has cherished the body issued
from the error of love, he remains in the darkness erring,
suffering in his senses the dispensations of death. What then is
the sin of those ignorant ones, that they should be deprived of
immortality? The first cause of the individual body is the hateful
darkness, from which came the humid nature, from which was
constituted the body of the sensible world, from which death
draws nourishment. Thus the lovers of the body actually are *in*
death and deserve death. On the other hand, he who knows
himself knows that the Father of all things consists of Light and
Life, therefore likewise the Primal Man issued from him, and by
this he knows himself to be of Light and Life, and will through
this knowledge return to the Life. The knowing ones, filled with
love for the Father, before they deliver the body to its own death
abhor the senses, whose effects they know; and the Poimandres-
Nous assists them in this by acting as a warder at the gates and
barring entrance to the evil influences of the body. The
unknowing ones are left a prey to all the evil passions, whose
insatiability is their torment, always augmenting the flame that
consumes them.

The soul's ascent after death. First at the dissolution of the
material body you yield up to the demon your sensuous nature
now ineffective, and the bodily senses return each to its source
among the elements. "And thereafter, man thrusts upward
through the Harmony, and to the first zone he surrenders the
power to grow and to decrease, and to the second the
machinations of evil cunning, now rendered powerless, and to the
third the deceit of concupiscence, now rendered powerless, and to
the fourth the arrogance of dominion, drained of [or: now
impotent to achieve] its ambition, and to the fifth the impious
audacity and the rashness of impulsive deed, and to the sixth the
evil appetites of wealth, now rendered powerless, and to the
seventh zone the lying that ensnares. And then denuded of the
effects of the Harmony, he enters the nature of the Ogdoas [i.e.,
the eighth sphere, and that of the fixed stars], now in possession
of his own power, and with those already there exalts the Father;
and those present rejoice with him at his presence, and having
become like his companions he hears also certain powers above
the eighth sphere exalting God with a sweet voice. And then in

procession they rise up towards the Father and give themselves
up to the Powers, and having become Powers themselves, enter
the Godhead. This is the good end of those who have attained
gnosis: to become God.''

3. *The Platonic Myth of the Fall and Return of the Soul*[7]

Of the nature of the soul, though her true form be ever a theme
of large and more than mortal discourse, let me speak briefly, and
in a figure. And let the figure be composite — a pair of winged
horses and a charioteer. Now the winged horses and the
charioteers of the gods are all of them noble and of noble descent,
but those of other races are mixed; the human charioteer drives
his in a pair; and one of them is noble and of noble breed, and
the other is ignoble and of ignoble breed; and the driving of them
of necessity gives a great deal of trouble to him. I will endeavour
to explain to you in what way the mortal differs from the
immortal creature. The soul in her totality has the care of
inanimate being everywhere, and traverses the whole heaven in
divers forms appearing: — when perfect and fully winged she
soars upward, and orders the whole world; whereas the imperfect
soul, losing her wings and drooping in her flight at last settles on
the solid ground — there, finding a home, she receives an earthly
frame which appears to be self-moved, but is really moved by her
power; and this composition of soul and body is called a living
and mortal creature. For immortal no such union can be
reasonably believed to be; although fancy, not having seen nor
surely known the nature of God, may imagine an immortal
creature having both a body and also a soul which are united
throughout all time. Let that, however, be as God wills, and be
spoken of acceptably to him. And now let us ask the reason why
the soul loses her wings!
    The wing is the corporeal element which is most akin to the
divine, and which by nature tends to soar aloft and carry that
which gravitates downwards into the upper region, which is the
habitation of the gods. The divine is beauty, wisdom, goodness,
and the like; and by these the wing of the soul is nourished, and
grows apace; but when fed upon evil and foulness and the
opposite of good, wastes and falls away. Zeus, the mighty lord,
holding the reins of a winged chariot, leads the way in heaven,
ordering all and taking care of all; and there follows him the array

of gods and demi-gods, marshalled in eleven bands; Hestia alone
abides at home in the house of heaven; of the rest they who are
reckoned among the princely twelve march in their appointed
order. They see many blessed sights in the inner heaven, and
there are many ways to and fro, along which the blessed gods are
passing, every one doing his own work; he may follow who will
and can, for jealousy has no place in the celestial choir. But when
they go to banquet and festival, then they move up the steep to
the top of the vault of heaven. The chariots of the gods in even
poise, obeying the rein, glide rapidly; but the others labour, for
the vicious steed goes heavily, weighing down the charioteer to
the earth when his steed has not been thoroughly trained: — and
this is the hour of agony and extremest conflict for the soul. For
the immortals, when they are at the end of their course, go forth
and stand upon the outside of heaven, and the revolution of the
spheres carries them round, and they behold the things beyond.
But of the heaven which is above the heavens, what earthly poet
ever did or ever will sing worthily? It is such as I will describe; for
I must dare to speak the truth, when truth is my theme. There
abides the very being with which true knowledge is concerned;
the colourless, formless, intangible essence, visible only to mind,
the pilot of the soul. The divine intelligence, being nurtured upon
mind and pure knowledge, and the intelligence of every soul
which is capable of receiving the food proper to it, rejoices at
beholding reality, and once more gazing upon truth, is
replenished and made glad, until the revolution of the worlds
brings her round again to the same place.

In the revolution she beholds justice, and temperance, and
knowledge absolute, not in the form of generation or of relation,
which men call existence, but knowledge absolute in existence
absolute; and beholding the other true existences in like manner,
and feasting upon them, she passes down into the interior of the
heavens and returns home; and there the charioteer putting up
his horses at the stall, gives them ambrosia to eat and nectar to
drink.

Such is the life of the gods; but of other souls, that which
follows God best and is likest to him lifts the head of the
charioteer into the outer world, and is carried round in the
revolution, troubled indeed by the steeds, and with difficulty
beholding true being; while another only rises and falls, and sees,
and again fails to see by reason of the unruliness of the steeds.
The rest of the souls are also longing after the upper world and

they all follow, but not being strong enough they are carried
round below the surface, plunging, treading on one another, each
striving to be first; and there is confusion and perspiration and
the extremity of effort; and many of them are lamed or have their
wings broken through the ill-driving of the charioteers; and all of
them after a fruitless toil, not having attained to the mysteries of
true being, go away, and feed upon opinion. The reason why the
souls exhibit this exceeding eagerness to behold the plain of truth
is that pasturage is found there, which is suited to the highest
part of the soul; and the wing on which the soul soars is
nourished with this. And there is a law of Destiny, that the soul
which attains any vision of truth in company with a god is
preserved from harm until the next period, and if attaining always
is always unharmed. But when she is unable to follow, and fails to
behold the truth, and through some ill-hap sinks beneath the
double load of forgetfulness and vice, and her wings fall from her
and she drops to the ground, then the law ordains that this soul
shall at her first birth pass, not into any other animal, but only
into man; and the soul which has seen most of truth shall come to
the birth as a philosopher, or artist, or some musical and loving
nature; that which has seen truth in the second degree shall be
some righteous king or warrior chief; the soul which is of the
third class shall be a politician, or economist, or trader; the fourth
shall be a lover of gymnastic toils, or a physician; the fifth shall
lead the life of a prophet or hierophant; to the sixth the character
of a poet or some other imitative artist will be assigned; to the
seventh the life of an artisan or husbandman; to the eighth that of
a sophist or demagogue; to the ninth that of a tyrant; — all these
are states of probation, in which he who does righteously
improves, and he who does unrighteously, deteriorates his lot.

Ten thousand years must elapse before the soul of each one
can return to the place from whence she came, for she cannot
grow her wings in less; only the soul of a philosopher, guileless
and true, or the soul of a lover, who is not devoid of philosophy,
may acquire wings in the third of the recurring periods of a
thousand years; he is distinguished from the ordinary good man
who gains wings in three thousand years: — and they who choose
this life three times in succession have wings given them, and go
away at the end of the three thousand years. But the others
receive judgment when they have completed their first life, and
after the judgment they go, some of them to the houses of
correction which are under the earth, and are punished; others to

some place in heaven whither they are lightly borne by justice, and there they live in a manner worthy of the life which they led here when in the form of men. And at the end of the first thousand years the good souls and also the evil souls both come to draw lots and choose their second life, and they may take any which they please. The soul of a man may pass into the life of a beast, or from the beast return again into the man. But the soul which has never seen the truth will not pass into the human form. For a man must have intelligence of universals, and be able to proceed from the many particulars of sense to one conception of reason.

4. The Millennium and Eternal Age in the Book of Revelation[8]

Then I saw thrones, and seated on them were those to whom judgment was committed. Also I saw the souls of those who had been beheaded for their testimony to Jesus and for the word of God, and who had not worshiped the beast or its image and had not received its mark on their foreheads or their hands. They came to life again, and reigned with Christ a thousand years. The rest of the dead did not come to life again until the thousand years were ended. This is the first resurrection. Blessed and holy is he who shares in the first resurrection! Over such the second death has no power, but they shall be priests of God and of Christ, and they shall reign with him a thousand years.

And when the thousand years are ended, Satan will be loosed from his prison and will come out to deceive the nations which are at the four corners of the earth, that is, Gog and Magog, to gather them for battle; their number is like the sand of the sea. And they marched up over the broad earth and surrounded the camp of the saints and the beloved city; but fire came down from heaven and consumed them, and the devil who had deceived them was thrown into the lake of fire and brimstone where the beast and the false prophet were, and they will be tormented day and night for ever and ever.

Then I saw a great white throne and him who sat upon it; from his presence earth and sky fled away, and no place was found for them. And I saw the dead, great and small, standing before the throne, and books were opened. Also another book was opened, which is the book of life. And the dead were judged

by what was written in the books, by what they had done. And
the sea gave up the dead in it, Death and Hades gave up the dead
in them, and all were judged by what they had done. Then Death
and Hades were thrown into the lake of fire. This is the second
death, the lake of fire; and if any one's name was not found
written in the book of life, he was thrown into the lake of fire.

Then I saw a new heaven and a new earth; for the first heaven
and the first earth had passed away, and the sea was no more.
And I saw the holy city, new Jerusalem, coming down out of
heaven from God, prepared as a bride adorned for her husband;
and I heard a great voice from the throne saying, "Behold, the
dwelling of God is with men. He will dwell with them, and they
shall be his people, and God himself will be with them; he will
wipe away every tear from their eyes, and death shall be no more,
neither shall there be mourning nor crying nor pain any more, for
the former things have passed away."

And I saw no temple in the city, for its temple is the Lord God
the Almighty and the Lamb. And the city has no need of sun or
moon to shine upon it, for the glory of God is its light, and its lamp
is the Lamb. By its light shall the nations walk; and the kings of
the earth shall bring their glory into it, and its gates shall never be
shut by day — and there shall be no night there; they shall bring
into it the glory and the honor of the nations. But nothing unclean
shall enter it, nor any one who practices abomination of falsehood,
but only those who are written in the Lamb's book of life.

Then he showed me the river of the water of life, bright as
crystal, flowing from the throne of God and of the Lamb through
the middle of the street of the city; also, on either side of the
river, the tree of life with its twelve kinds of fruit, yielding its fruit
each month; and the leaves of the tree were for the healing of the
nations. There shall no more be anything accursed, but the throne
of God and of the Lamb shall be in it, and his servants shall
worship him; they shall see his face, and his name shall be on
their foreheads. And night shall be no more; they need no light of
lamp or sun, for the Lord God will be their light, and they shall
reign for ever and ever.

5. The Resurrected Body in Paul[9]

But in fact Christ has been raised from the dead, the first fruits of
those who have fallen asleep. For as by a man came death, by a

man has come also the resurrection of the dead. For as in Adam all die, so also in Christ shall all be made alive.

But each in his own order: Christ the first fruits, then at his coming those who belong to Christ. Then comes the end, when he delivers the kingdom to God the Father after destroying every rule and every authority and power. For he must reign until he has put all his enemies under his feet. The last enemy to be destroyed is death. "For God has put all things in subjection under his feet." But when it says, "All things are put in subjection under him," it is plain that he is excepted who put all things under him. When all things are subjected to him, then the Son himself will also be subjected to him who put all things under him, that God may be everything to every one.

Otherwise, what do people mean by being baptized on behalf of the dead? If the dead are not raised at all, why are people baptized on their behalf? Why am I in peril every hour? I protest, brethren, by my pride in you which I have in Christ Jesus our Lord, I die every day! What do I gain if, humanly speaking, I fought with beasts at Ephesus? If the dead are not raised, "Let us eat and drink, for tomorrow we die." Do not be deceived: "Bad company ruins good morals." Come to your right mind, and sin no more. For some have no knowledge of God. I say this to your shame.

But some one will ask, "How are the dead raised? With what kind of body do they come?" You foolish man! What you sow does not come to life unless it dies. And what you sow is not the body which is to be, but a bare kernel, perhaps of wheat or of some other grain. But God gives it a body as he has chosen, and to each kind of seed its own body. For not all flesh is alike, but there is one kind for men, another for animals, another for birds, and another for fish. There are celestial bodies and there are terrestrial bodies; but the glory of the celestial is one, and the glory of the terrestrial is another. There is one glory of the sun, and another glory of the moon, and another glory of the stars; for star differs from star in glory.

So is it with the resurrection of the dead. What is sown is perishable, what is raised is imperishable. It is sown in dishonor, it is raised in glory. It is sown in weakness, it is raised in power. It is sown a physical body, it is raised a spiritual body. If there is a physical body, there is also a spiritual body. Thus it is written, "The first man Adam became a living being"; the last Adam became a life-giving spirit. But it is not the spiritual which is first but the physical, and then the spiritual. The first man was from the earth, a man of dust; the second man is from heaven. As was the man of dust, so are those who are of the dust; and as is the man of heaven, so are those who are of heaven. Just as we have borne the image of the man of dust, we shall also bear the image of the man of heaven. I tell you this, brethren: flesh and blood cannot inherit the kingdom of God, nor does the perishable inherit the imperishable.

Lo! I tell you a mystery. We shall not all sleep, but we shall all be changed, in a moment, in the twinkling of an eye, at the last trumpet. For the trumpet will sound, and the dead will be raised imperishable, and we shall be changed. For this perishable nature must put on the imperishable, and this mortal nature must put on immortality. When the perishable puts on the imperishable, and the mortal puts on immortality, then shall come to pass the saying that is written:

"Death is swallowed up in victory."

6. The Trimorphic Protennoia and the New Eon in Gnosticism[10]

[I] am [Protennoia, the] Thought that [dwells] in [the Light. I] am the movement that dwells in the [All, she in whom the] All takes its stand, [the first]-born among those who [came to be, she who exists] before the All. [She (Protennoia) is called] by three names, although she exists alone, [since she is perfect]. I am invisible within the Thought of the Invisible One. I am revealed in the immeasurable, ineffable things. I am intangible, dwelling in the intangible. I move in every creature.

I am the life of my Epinoia that dwells within every power and every eternal movement and (in) invisible Lights and within the Archons and Angels and Demons and every soul dwelling in [Tartaros] and (in) every material soul. I dwell in those who came to be. I move in everyone and I delve into them all. I walk uprightly, and those who sleep I [awaken]. And I am the sight of those who dwell in sleep.

I am the Invisible One within the All. It is I who counsel those who are hidden, since I know the All that exists in it. I am numberless beyond everyone. I am immeasurable, ineffable, yet

whenever I wish, [I shall] reveal myself. I [am the movement of]
the All. I exist before the [All, and] I am the All, since I [exist
before] everyone.

I am a Voice [speaking softly]. I exist [from the first. I dwell]
within the Silence [that surrounds every one] of them. And [it is]
the [hidden Voice] that [dwells within] me, [within the] intangible,
immeasurable [Thought, within the immeasurable Silence.]

Now the Voice that originated from my Thought exists as
three permanences: the Father, the Mother, the Son. A Sound
that is perceptible, it has within it a Word endowed with every
glory, I am the Image of the Invisible Spirit and it is through me
that the All took shape, and (I am) the Mother (as well as) the
Light which she appointed as Virgin, she who is called Meirothea,
the intangible Womb, the unrestrained and immeasurable Voice.

I am the Voice that appeared through my Thought, for I am
"He who is syzygetic," since I am called "the Thought of the
Invisible One." Since I am called "the Unchanging Sound," I am
called "She who is syzygetic."

I am a single one (fem.) since I am undefiled. I am the Mother
[of] the Voice, speaking in many ways, completing the All. It is in
me that knowledge dwells, the knowledge of things everlasting.
[It is] I [who] speak within every creature and I was known by the
All. It is I who lift up the Sound of the Voice to the ears of those
who have known me, that is, the Sons of the Light.

Now I have come the second time in the likeness of a female
and have spoken with them. And I shall tell them of the coming
end of this Aeon and teach them of the beginning of the Aeon to
come, the one without change, the one in which our appearance
will be changed. We shall be purified within those Aeons from
which I revealed myself in the Thought of the likeness of my
masculinity. I settled among those who are worthy in the Thought
of my changeless Aeon.

For I shall tell you a mystery [of] this Aeon that is, and tell
you about the forces that are in it. The birth cries [out; hour]
begets hour, [and day begets day]. The months made known the
[month. Time] has [gone round] succeeding [time]. This Aeon that
is was completed in [this fashion], and it was estimated, and it
(was) short, for it (was) a finger that released a finger and a joint
that was separated from a joint. Then when the great Authorities
knew that the time of fulfillment had appeared — just as in the
pangs of the parturient it (the time) has drawn nigh, so also had
the destruction approached — all together the elements trembled,

and the foundations of the underworld and the ceilings of Chaos
shook and a great fire shone within their midst, and the rocks and
the earth were shaken like a reed shaken by the wind. And the
lots of Fate and those who apportion the domiciles were greatly
disturbed over a great thunder. And the thrones of the Powers
were disturbed since they were overturned, and their King was
afraid. And those who pursue Fate paid their allotment of visits to
the path, and they said to the Powers, "What is this disturbance
and this shaking that has come upon us through a Voice
[belonging] to the exalted Sound? And our entire habitation has
been shaken, and the entire circuit of our path of ascent has met
with destruction, and the path upon which we go, which takes us
up to the Archigenetor of our birth, has ceased to be established
for us." Then the Powers answered, saying, "We too are at a loss
about it since we did not know what was responsible for it. But
arise, let us go up to the Archigenetor and ask him." And the
Powers all gathered and went up to the Archigenetor. [They said
to] him, "Where is your boasting in which [you boast]? Did we
not [hear you say], 'I am God [and I am] your Father and it is I
who [begot] you and there is no [other] beside me? Now behold,
there has appeared [a] Voice belonging to that invisible Sound of
[the Aeon] that we know not. And we ourselves did not recognize
to whom we belong, for that Voice which we heard is foreign to
us, and we do not recognize it; we did not know whence it was.
It came and put fear in our midst and weakening in the members
of our arms. So now let us weep and mourn most bitterly! As for
the future, let us make our entire flight before we are imprisoned
perforce and taken down to the bosom of the underworld. For
already the slackening of our bondage has approached, and the
times are cut short and the days have shortened and our time has
been fulfilled, and the weeping of our destruction has approached
us so that we may be taken to the place we recognize. For as for
our tree from which we grew, a fruit of ignorance is what it has,
and also its leaves, it is death that dwells in them, and darkness
dwells under the shadow of its boughs. And it was in deceit and
lust that we harvested it, this (tree) through which ignorant Chaos
became for us a dwelling place. For behold, even he, the
Archigenetor of our birth, about whom we boast, even he did not
know this Sound."

So now, O Sons of the Thought, listen to me, to the Sound of
the Mother of your mercy, for you have become worthy of the
mystery hidden from the Aeons, so that [you might be perfect].

And the consummation of this Aeon [that is and] of the life of
injustice [has approached, and there dawns the] beginning of the
[Aeon to come] which [has no change forever].

7. The Redemption of the Cosmos in Irenaeus[11]

Vain indeed are they who say that God [the Son] came to things
not his own, . . . Nor would he have truly redeemed us by his
blood if he had not been truly made man, restoring again to his
own creation what was said [of it] in the beginning, that man was
made according to the image and likeness of God — . . .

Vain above all are they who despise the whole dispensation of
God, and deny the salvation of the flesh and reject its rebirth,
saying that it is not capable of incorruption. For if this [mortal
flesh] is not saved, then neither did the Lord redeem us by his
blood, nor is the cup of the Eucharist the communion of his
blood, and the bread which we break the communion of his body.
For blood is only to be found in veins and flesh, and the rest of
[physical] human nature, which the Word of God was indeed
made [partaker of, and so] he redeemed us by his blood. . . . For
since we are his members, and are nourished by [his] creation —
and he himself gives us this creation, making the sun to rise, and
sending the rain as he wills — he declares that the cup, [taken]
from the creation, is his own blood, by which he strengthens our
blood, and he has firmly assured us that the bread, [taken] from
the creation, is his own body, by which our bodies grow. For
when the mixed cup and the bread that has been prepared receive
the Word of God, and become the Eucharist, the body and blood
of Christ, and by these our flesh grows and is confirmed, how can
they say that flesh cannot receive the free gift of God, which is
eternal life, since it is nourished by the body and blood of the
Lord, and made a member of him? . . . He does not say this
about a [merely] spiritual and invisible man, for the spirit has
neither bones nor flesh, but about [God's] dispensation for the
real man, [a dispensation] consisting of flesh and nerves and
bones, which is nourished by his cup, which is his blood, and
grows by the bread which is his body.

And just as the wooden branch of the vine, placed in the
earth, bears fruit in its own time — and as the grain of wheat,
falling into the ground and there dissolved, rises with great
increase by the Spirit of God, who sustains all things, and then by

the wisdom of God serves for the use of men, and when it receives the Word of God becomes the Eucharist, which is the body and blood of Christ — so also our bodies which are nourished by it, and then fall into the earth and are dissolved therein, shall rise at the proper time, the Word of God bestowing on them this rising again, to the glory of God the Father. It is he who indeed grants to this mortal immortality, and gives to the corruptible the gracious gift of incorruption, . . .

For the righteous must first rise again at the appearance of God to receive in this created order, then made new, the promise of the inheritance which God promised to the Fathers, and will reign in this order. After this will come the judgment. It is right, for this created order to be restored to its pristine state, and to serve the just without restraint. . . .

(This prophecy) undoubtedly refers to the times of the Kingdom, when the just, rising from the dead, will reign, when the created order will be made new and set free, and will produce an abundance of all kinds of food, from the dew of heaven and of the fertility of the earth. . . .

Since men are real, they must have a real existence, not passing away into things which are not, but advancing [to a new stage] among things that are. Neither the substance nor the essence of the created order vanishes away, for he is true and faithful who established it, but the pattern of this world passes away, that is, the things in which the transgression took place, since in them man has grown old. Therefore God, foreknowing all things, made this pattern of things temporary. . . . But when this pattern has passed away, and man is made new, and flourishes in incorruption, so that he can no longer grow old, then there will be new heavens and a new earth. In this new order man will always remain new, in converse with God. This state of things will remain without end. . . .

In all and through all these things the same God the Father is manifest, who formed man, and promised to the Fathers the inheritance of the earth, who brings this [promise] forth at the resurrection of the just, and fulfills the promises in the Kingdom of his Son, afterwards bestowing with paternal love those things which eye has not seen, nor ear heard, nor have they entered into the heart of man. Then there is one Son, who accomplished the Father's will, and one human race, in which the mysteries of God are accomplished, which angels long to behold. For they cannot search out the wisdom of God, by which what he had fashioned

is perfected by being conformed and incorporated with the Son —
or how that his offspring, the first-begotten Word, could descend
into his creature, that is, into what he had fashioned, and be
contained within it — and that the creature again should lay hold
on the Word and should ascend to him, passing beyond the
angels, and be made [anew] according to the image and likeness
of God.

8. The Assumption of Mary in Christian Apocrypha[12]

And the apostles, carrying Mary, came to the place of the Valley
of Jehoshaphat which the Lord had showed them; and they laid
her in a new tomb, and closed the sepulchre. And they
themselves sat down at the door of the tomb, as the Lord had
commanded them; and, behold, suddenly the Lord Jesus Christ
came with a great multitude of angels, with a halo of great
brightness gleaming, and said to the apostles: Peace be with you!
And they answered and said: Let Thy mercy, O Lord, be upon
us, as we have hoped in Thee. Then the Saviour spoke to them,
saying: Before I ascended to my Father I promised to you, saying
that you who have followed me in the regeneration, when the
Son of man shall sit upon the throne of His majesty, will sit, you
also, upon twelve thrones, judging the twelve tribes of Israel. Her,
therefore, did I choose out of the tribes of Israel by the command
of my Father, that I should dwell in her. What, therefore, do you
wish that I should do to her? Then Peter and the other apostles
said: Lord, Thou didst choose beforehand this Thine handmaid to
become a spotless chamber for Thyself, and us Thy servants to
minister unto Thee. Before the ages Thou didst foreknow all
things along with the Father, with whom to Thee and the Holy
Spirit there is one Godhead, equal and infinite power. If,
therefore, it were possible to be done in the presence of the power
of Thy grace, it had seemed to us Thy servants to be right that,
just as Thou, having vanquished death, reignest in glory, so,
raising up again the body of Thy mother, Thou shouldst take her
with Thee in joy into heaven.

Then the Saviour said: Let it be according to your opinion.
And He ordered the archangel Michael to bring the soul of St.
Mary. And, behold, the archangel Michael rolled back the stone
from the door of the tomb; and the Lord said: Arise, my beloved
and my nearest *relation*; thou who hast not put on corruption by

intercourse with man, suffer not destruction of the body in the sepulchre. And immediately Mary rose from the tomb, and blessed the Lord, and falling forward at the feet of the Lord, adored Him, saying: I cannot render sufficient thanks to Thee, O Lord, for Thy boundless benefits which Thou hast deigned to bestow upon me Thine handmaiden. May Thy name, O Redeemer of the world, God of Israel, be blessed for ever.

And kissing her, the Lord went back, and delivered her soul to the angels, that they should carry it into paradise. And He said to the apostles: Come up to me. And when they had come up He kissed them, and said: Peace be to you! as I have always been with you, so will I be even to the end of the world. And immediately, when the Lord had said this, He was lifted up on a cloud, and taken back into heaven, and the angels along with Him, carrying the blessed Mary into the paradise of God.

9. Mary's Assumption: Archetype of the Redeemed Cosmos and Church[13]

The material world's completed redeemed state must also shine forth in Mary as Archetype of the Church. The essential point of view by which Mary is seen as the Type of the Church is as follows: Mary typifies the essence of the Church, a community of men and the Mystical Body of Christ, in whom the Divine Life of Christ dwells. This life is to be given to everyone who has been incorporated into this Body as a living member. The Church has performed her receptive co-redemption in Mary, her representative. It is in Mary that the Church has fully received her Redemption.

It follows, therefore, that the body must be seen in its perfected redeemed state in Mary. This does not mean that her body could have avoided passing through the dark portal of death. Every human being assumes completely the work of Redemption and its fruits of grace when, by dying, he gives his whole existence back to God the Father. Mary fulfilled this subjective, receptive and co-redeeming role of the Church when, by dying, she made Christ's redemptive death her own and subjectively co-enacted it.

Mary died too, as Archetype of the co-redemptive Church. The Church day by day has to make Christ's death her own. It is she who constantly, continually dies with Christ and therefore

rises with Him to eternal life. Mary is the perfect expression of the
Church's co-redemptive work. Therefore it is most fitting that she
should have died as did her Redeemer, both by her constant
moral affirmation and by a physical, bodily death.

At the same time the redeemed state of the physical cosmos at
the end of time shines forth in her body. In her body she co-
enacted subjectively Christ's death. In her, as Archetype, her body
shows the Church's fully redeemed body. Her body lights the
way for the body of the Church and shows that the
transfiguration dwells like a seed within her corporeality.

10. *His Religion and Hers: A Poem by Charlotte Perkins Gilman*[14]

Man the hunter, Man the warrior,
Slew for gain and slew for safety,
Slew for rage, for sport, for glory —
    Slaughter was his breath;
So the man's mind, searching inward,
Saw in all one red reflection,
Filled the world with dark religions
    Built on Death.

Death, and the Fate of the Soul; —
The Soul, from the body dissevered,
Through the withering failure of age,
Through the horror and pain of disease,
Through raw wounds and destruction and fear; —
In fear, black fear of the dark,
Red fear of terrible gods,
Sent forth on its journey alone,
To eternity, fearful, unknown —
    Death, and the Fate of the Soul.
. . .
Woman, bearer; Woman, teacher;
Overflowing love and labor,
Service of the tireless mother
    Filling all the earth; —
Now her mind awakening, searching,
Sees a fair world young and growing,
Sees at last our real religion —
    Built on Birth.

Birth, and the Growth of the Soul; —
The Soul, in the body established,
In the ever-new beauty of childhood,
In the wonder of opening power,
Still learning, improving, achieving,
In hope, new knowledge, and light,
Sure faith in the world's fresh Spring, —
Together we live, we grow,
On the earth that we love and know —
    Birth, and the Growth of the Soul.

To create new texts from WomanChurch, we must draw from our own experience and also learn to joust with the guardians of male texts and break their lances.

A Duel Between a Woman and a Dominican. Miniature from the codex of Lancelot du Lac, Beinecke Rare Book and Manuscript Library, Yale University, Yale Manuscript, f. 100v.

12

New Beginnings

DOCUMENTS

1. The Parable of the Naked Lady
2. The Journey

Neither revelation nor the telling of stories is closed. Every new up-surge of the liberating spirit must challenge the efforts of fossilized re-ligious authority to "close the canon," to declare that God has spoken once and for all in a past time and "his" words are enshrined in a final and definite form in a past collection of texts, and therefore, that all true theology is confined to circumscribed commentaries on these past texts. It is ironic that Christianity particularly has attempted to cut off all further revelatory experience and declare that God's final word is spoken in Jesus, even to the exclusion of any word from God spoken before Jesus. Jesus alone becomes the one word from God. This is ironic because it was key to Jesus' own message that revelation was not closed and that he spoke "with authority," as a prophet, and not "as the scribes and the Pharisees," those who were confined merely to commentary on past texts.

So feminism, too, recognizing that patriarchal texts deform the lib-erating spirit for women, rejects a theology confined to commentary on past texts. We are not only free to reclaim rejected texts of the past and put them side by side with canonized texts as expressions of truth, in the light of which canonized texts may be criticized; but we are also free to generate new stories from our own experience that may, through community use, become more than personal or individual. They may become authoritative stories, for it is precisely through community use in a historical movement of liberation, which finds in them paradigms of redemptive experience, that stories become authoritative. Woman-Church, too, as church may, through its use of stories and parables generated through its struggles, raises some of these stories to the level of authoritative texts.

What follows in this concluding chapter are two stories that arose from classes in feminist theology in which we have used the texts of this collection. The members of the class were authorized to write their own parables, *midrashim*, and stories. The two stories presented here, ''The Parable of the Naked Lady'' by Anne Spurgeon and ''The Journey'' by Beth Hamilton, are both intensely personal. They represent profound crises and turning points in their authors' lives. But these crises have been translated into story form that may become paradigmatic for many women, for the community of women as Woman-Church.

The message with which I close is this: The Spirit blows where it will. The Spirit is not confined to past institutions and their texts. It leads us into new futures. We don't know the path, for we make the path as we go. But it is through generating stories of our own crisis and hope and telling them to one another that we light the path.

1. THE PARABLE OF THE NAKED LADY

by Anne Spurgeon

The young women gathered round him and one of them asked, ''Master, tell us what is the best image of womanhood that we can become? We feel uncertain about the ways of our mothers.'' And Jesus said to her, ''Women, what you ask is something I can not decide for you.'' And he told them a parable, saying: A naked woman sat at the crossroads where the road that went north and south met the road going east and west. People passed her; some were ashamed, some were angry, but most looked upon her with disapproval. Some threw clothes at her — all different types, colors and sizes. The woman knew she was naked, but did not lift a finger to cover herself.

There was a woman in a golden gown who stopped her journey and went to the naked woman saying, ''Take my dress. See how beautiful it is, a golden brocade covered with pearls and diamonds.'' She took off the garment and handed it to the naked woman, who instantly felt its weight. ''This is very heavy,'' said the naked woman. The elaborate woman nodded. ''The wearer of that gown must always look beautiful, must always act charming, must remain still and maintain beauty for her husband. She must constantly display her husband's wealth no matter what its cumbrance. She must not lose her figure nor grow old. She must put up with her husband's temperament, appetites, and decisions."

"I do not want this dress," said the naked woman. "Here, take it back." But instead, the elaborate woman threw the dress in a heap by the side of the road. She sat down next to the naked woman.

There was a woman in a simple gray dress who stopped her journey and went to the naked woman saying, "Take my dress. See how simple it is; it takes no special care and is easy to move in." She handed the dress to the naked woman, who felt that its burden was also great.

"What causes the weight of this dress?" she asked.

"Thankless toil," said the simple woman. "Years of washing, scrubbing, vacuuming, diapering, cooking, chauffeuring, arguing, punishing, remembering, organizing and catering. The wearer of that dress is forever the backbone of her home — she can never tire, get sick, leave, be alone or cultivate her own interests. She loses her color and her youth and watches as her man's eye looks elsewhere for beauty."

"Here, take back your dress," said the naked woman. But the simple woman put her dress with the golden dress by the side of the road. She sat down next to the elaborate woman and the two began to argue about whose garment had been the heaviest. The three women sat at the crossroads.

There was a woman in a short red dress who stopped her journey and went to the naked woman. "My dress might suit you. It is easy to get in and out of and is very soft and alluring. Here." She handed the dress to the naked woman. "Don't be deceived," said the sensuous woman. "It too is heavy laden."

"Why?" asked the naked woman.

"The wearer of this dress must bear the burden of frigid wives. She must always be available for the sexual demands of men. She is the keeper of lies and deceits, and must endure the hate of women who do not like what she does, but wish they had her power. The woman who wears this dress must open her legs to feed herself, to clothe herself, to house herself, and to care for any misbegotten offspring. She must always be soft and sensuous, bold and enterprising, calculating and owned. She lives with the knowledge that she must always welcome men who never stay."

"This dress will not do either," said the naked woman. "Take it back." But the sensuous woman tossed the red dress among the others at the side of the road and sat down next to the simple woman. She joined in the argument that had not let up.

There was a woman in a long black habit who stopped her journey and went to the naked woman. "My child," she said, "you are naked, let me clothe you. Here, take my habit. It is warm and safe."

"Safe?" questioned the naked woman. "It's weight is very great."

"Yes," said the holy woman. "It holds the secrets of a hundred thousand souls. One must be very strong to wear it, but must show that strength in silence and servitude. The wearer of this habit must understand birth, but never bear; must understand the cravings of the flesh, but never experience them; must understand the ways of the world, but never be part of it. The woman who wears this must sacrifice herself constantly for the needs of others and never fill her own. She must punish herself for thoughts and longings that extend beyond the confines of cloistered walls."

"I am neither cold nor fearful," said the naked woman. "Take back your habit." But the holy woman placed the habit with the other dresses at the roadside and sat and entered into the argument that continued between the elaborate woman, the simple woman and the sensuous woman.

There was a woman in a grey suit who stopped her journey and went to the naked woman saying, "Here, this tweed would look smart on you. Its lines are professionally tailored to give a serious appearance." She handed the suit to the naked woman.

"Now why does *this* garment carry so much weight?"

"Don't be fooled by its professional appearance. The wearer of this suit must live in the sterile world and must never be part of any of the worlds you have seen so far. This woman must never be beautiful and artistic, for that would distract people from the business at hand; she must never bear children or have any relationship that would slow her progress to the top of her field. She must never be sensuous, for she would then be the mark of wolves who would find any way to destroy her and her power. She must also endure being mocked as a dyke by those who fail to understand the purposes behind her sexlessness. She must never be holy, for the world of the spirit weakens the power of the world of the rational. It is seen as foolishness and gets in the way of advancement with its silly notions of ethics and morality. So the wearer of this dress must remain closed like a prison against all outside forces that would drain her of her power."

"Your world is frightening," said the naked woman, "take back your suit." But the professional woman tossed her suit among the other garments, sat and joined in the argument, insisting that of all the other garments, hers had been the heaviest.

The women argued beside the naked woman far into the night. At some point their argument changed from self-pity to blame upon the other. As each experienced the pointed finger of the others, she began to see that there were things about her dress that were worthy and good. There were things that each was not ashamed of or encumbered by.

"I know how to enjoy my body, to feel the pleasure of physical love," said the sensuous woman.

"Oh, teach me that," said the holy woman, "and I will teach you the wonder of the quest for union with God."

"I know how to organize a large business and make it run smoothly, and how to handle many things in the face of emergency," said the professional woman.

"Oh, teach me," said the elaborate woman, "and I will teach you how to make yourself beautiful so that you can enjoy the appearance of your body."

"Teach me my attraction also," said the simple woman, "and I will teach you how to bear and love a child."

New life sprang up among the women and they fashioned for themselves garments out of the clothing that had piled at the side of the road, each unique and sharing parts of each. As they taught and worked, the naked woman got up and walked to the next intersection east of them; and sat down.

And Jesus said to the young women, "Those who have ears to hear, let them hear."

2. THE JOURNEY

by Beth Hamilton

Once upon a time, a group of people who called themselves "the Christians" lived on the plains of certainty. Those who lived beyond their borders were referred to as "the non-Christians."

Since they had never gone beyond the plains of certainty, they did not know the names of those who inhabited the strange regions off of the way.

In this land, the people knew what was wrong and right, what they should and should not do and believe. They did not need to know themselves because they existed in the mirror of the other. What is yet to be, they said, was ordained in the past. They went forward in reverse. The Christians focused their attention on the unseen Father King who supposedly lived up above and ordered what was seen down below. They traveled on the way, a circular narrow road with clear signs and landmarks that copied His divine plan. Some of the signs were "absolute truth," "God's will," and "knowing that you know." Everyone had their place, both men and girls. There was no need for change, that is, except for the digging of ditches for deviants, the digging of ruts for ministers, and the digging of graves for all. These exceptions occurred on the edge of the plains and were seldom noticed by the group.

Those who did not follow the way were lost on the plains. It was rumored that they fell to the underlands where all was darkness and pain. These words were, of course, meaningless to the plains people. They only knew the sunlit happiness of the surface. There were a few who had come up from the underlands, but their past was quickly forgotten in the sunlit regions of testimony. The plains people were fulfilled as long as they continued to follow the way in the land of certainty.

One day, a spirit of experience blew in the land. A few felt the cold gust blow across the sunlit way. They wondered whether they were falling off the way into the underland. Many of the plains people ignored experience and turned their faces to the sunlight. They built strong walls to protect themselves from the spirit. They knew that they were right regardless of what they felt and heard. Some of the seemingly most daring believed that the wind came from enemies beyond the way. They shouted in the name of the way that the breezes cease. Experience left.

But not alone. A handful of those who wondered began to wander. These few realized that the darkness and pain were just as real as the sunlight. To leave the way was terrifying. Perhaps they were condemned to the underland. They began to shout as well — not for experience to leave but for an explanation. There was no answer. The chilly breezes enfolded them, tore through them, and they followed. To their surprise, the way had

disappeared in the mist. Occasionally the sunlit regions of
certainty could be glimpsed, but they looked like shadows that no
longer made any sense. Rage increased. They could hardly go
back now that they were uncertain, but they did not know what
lay ahead. Beyond the way, the signs, the sunlit wall, experience
blew unreason. Mirrors shattered. Feelings overwhelmed. Each
faced the terror of themself alone, divided within. And the
whirlwind drew them on.

One such wanderer came to the edge of the cliff. The cliff had
been a vague rumor even in the land of certainty. It was the
chasm of despair in the land of nonbeing. Endless eons of
darkness whirled beyond the edge.

Freezing gusts of experience were flung from the depths. The
sunlit regions were mere dreams, confusing memories of the
distant past. She was alone. Some of those who had wandered
with her had tried to return to the plains of certainty. Others had
jumped into the chasm because it was too painful to go back or to
go on. She hoped that there was a way out for those who had
fallen below. There came the moment of decision.

She leapt. In despair and hope she hurtled into the chaos.
Without assurance or certainty, she did what she had to do to go
on. It was ages or an instant later that she landed. She had, in
fact, been standing for some time before she was aware of the
other side. Slowly, ever so slowly, the darkness began to lift. The
twilight hung in expectant suspense beyond the chasm. Wrapped
in grey in-between, she took a step forward. She was in the land
of the journey.

The land was both familiar and unknown. She could not go
back now even if she had wanted to, and yet there was
continuity. She thought she had left the way. A road stretched
before her that was so new and so old that she could hardly
recognize it. The grass looked purple. New forms had old names
from the plains of certainty, while other names were left behind.
She would not have trusted the land except that darkness and
light were joined in the names. The terrain was beautiful and
dreadful, comforting and offensive. She named herself, "I am."

There were actually many roads that branched out from where
she landed. They all headed roughly in the direction of the
beyond. Glimpses of the end, if there were an end, could be seen
in the now. Through valley and over mountains, the journey
stretched on to the unknown new earth. Some joined and
welcomed her on the way which she had chosen, while others

journeyed on different roads. She was surprised to find others who had left certainty behind. "I am. You are. We are." They went on alone and together.

She did not live happily ever after. At times she traversed valleys that were so deep that she wondered if she had ever left the chasm. A number of times she had to risk short leaps. When the road was long and difficult she felt like giving up. But the valleys were never as deep as the chasm. When she leaped, she now hoped and believed there was another side. And there were moments of sunlight and of connection with others. The journey was worthwhile. She had found herself. She was a woman.

NOTES
BIBLIOGRAPHY
INDEX

Notes

1. Gender Imagery for God/ess

1. Psalm 19 (RSV).
2. Isaiah 42:13–16 (RSV).
3. Prayer of Lamentation to Ishtar, from *Religion in the Ancient Near East, Sumero-Akkadian Religious Texts and Ugaritic Epics*, ed. Isaac Mendelsohn (New York: Liberal Arts Press, 1955), 155–159.
4. Apuleius, *The Golden Ass*, trans. Robert Graves (New York: Pocket Library, 1954), 236–239.
5. Mary Baker Eddy, *Science and Health with Key to the Scriptures* (Boston: Christian Science Publishing Co., 1890), 16–17.
6. *Gifts of Power: The Writings of Rebecca Jackson, Black Visionary, Shaker Eldress*, ed. and intro. Jean McMahon Humez (University of Massachusetts Press, 1981), 152–154. In a four-month preaching tour west of Philadelphia, Pennsylvania, in the summer of 1834, Jackson preached sixty-nine sermons. The trustees were the legal governance of the African Methodist Episcopal Church who forbade Jackson to preach in their church. She was also "published" or banned in three quarterly meetings of the AME congregations at Bush Hill, West Chester, and West Town, but other, friendly Methodists invited her into their homes and churches to preach.

2. The Divine Pleroma

1. Wisdom of Solomon 6:13–22, 24–27; 7:7–11, 22–30; 8:1–16.
2. *The Odes of Solomon*, ed., with translation and notes, James H. Charlesworth (Oxford: Clarendon Press, 1973), 82–83, 126–217.
3. From the account of Ptolemaeus' system in Irenaeus, *Adversus Haereses*, vol. 1, translation from *Gnosticism: A Source Book of Heretical Writings from the Early Christian Period*, ed. Robert M. Grant (New York: Harper and Brothers, 1961), 163–164.
4. The Athanasian Creed, fourth century A.D.
5. From *Testimony of Christ's Second Appearing*, the Shaker Bible, 4th ed., published by the United Society called Shakers (Albany, N.Y.: Van Benthuysen, 1956), 503–504.

3. Stories of Creation

1. The literacy of women, both queens and priestesses, in the Old Babylonian period is attested to in the female correspondence from Mari. See Bernard Frank Batto, *Studies on Women at Mari* (Baltimore: Johns Hopkins University Press, 1974).

2. Samuel Noah Kramer, *History Begins at Sumer* (Garden City, N.Y.: Doubleday, 1956), 83–84.

3. S. H. Hooke, "The Babylonian New Year's Festival," *Journal of the Manchester Egyptian and Oriental Society* 13 (1927): 29–38; also S. A. Pallis, "The Babylonian Akitu Festival," *Historisk-filologiske Meddelelsen* (Copenhagen) 12, no. 1 (1926).

4. See Phyllis Bird, "Male and Female, He created Them: Gen. 1:27b in the Context of the Priestly Account of Creation," *Harvard Theological Review* 74, no. 2 (1981): 129–159.

5. "Enki and Ninhursag: A Paradise Myth," in *Religions of the Ancient Near East, Sumero-Akkadian Religious Texts and Ugaritic Epics,* ed. Isaac Mendelsohn (New York: Liberal Arts Press, 1955), 4–11.

6. "The Creation Eic," in Mendelsohn, *Religions of the Ancient Near East,* 19–20, 23–24, 33–37.

7. *Hesiod's Theogony* (New York: Library of Liberal Arts, 1953), 56–58, 66–67.

8. Genesis 1:1–31; 2:1–4 (RSV).

9. Plato, *Timaeus,* from *The Dialogues of Plato,* vol. 2, ed. B. Jowett (New York: Random House, 1937), 14–20, 23.

4. Humanity: Male and Female

1. Samuel Noah Kramer, *History Begins at Sumer* (Garden City, N.Y.: Doubleday, 1956), 107.

2. Phyllis Trible, "Departriarchalizing in Biblical Interpretation," *Journal of The American Academy of Religion* (March 1973): 35–42.

3. Theodor Reik, *The Creation of Woman: A Psychoanalytic Inquiry into the Myth of Eve* (New York: McGraw-Hill, 1960).

4. Thomas Aquinas, *Summa Theologica,* pt. 1, q. 92, art. 1.

5. "The Making of Man by the Mother Goddess," in *Religions of the Ancient Near East: Sumero-Akkadian Religious Texts and Ugaritic Epics,* ed. Isaac Mendelsohn (New York: Liberal Arts Press, 1955), 116–118. The Old Babylonian text is fragmentary and has been combined here with the Assyrian version.

6. Genesis 2:4b–24.

7. Philo, "On the Creation of the World," XLVI, LIII, from *The Essential Philo,* ed. Nahum Glatzer (New York: Schocken, 1971), 28, 34.

8. Alfa Beta di Sira, from *Gates to the Old City: A Book of Jewish Legends,* ed. Raphael Patai (Detroit: Wayne State University Press, 1981), 407–408.

9. Louis Ginzberg, *The Legends of the Jews,* vol. 3 (Philadelphia: Jewish Pub-

lication Society of America, 1913), 66–68. Ginzberg's account combines several different rabbinic commentaries; see his notes.

10. Judith Plaskow, "The Coming of Lilith," originally written at the Feminist Theologizing Conference, Grailville, Ohio, 1972, with help from Karen Bloomquist, Margaret Early, and Elizabeth Farians. Published, among other places in *Religion and Sexism: Images of Women in the Jewish and Christian Traditions*, ed. Rosemary Ruether (New York: Simon and Schuster, 1974), 341–343.

11. Aristotle, *Generation of Animals*, 729b, 738b, 737a, 775a.

12. Aristotle, *Politics*, 1254a–b.

13. Plato, *Symposium*, 190–192, from *The Dialogues of Plato*, vol. 1, ed. B. Jowett (New York: Random House, 1937), 318–320.

5. The Origins of Evil

1. Louis Ginzberg, *The Legends of the Jews*, vol. 3 (Philadelphia: Jewish Publication Society of America, 1911), 121–122.

2. Bernard P. Prusak, "Women: Seductive Siren and Source of Sin?" in *Religion and Sexism: Images of Women in the Jewish and Christian Traditions*, ed. Rosemary Ruether (New York; Simon and Schuster, 1974), 89–107.

3. See Denis R. MacDonald, *The Legend and the Apostle: The Battle for Paul in Story and Canon* (Philadelphia: Westminister, 1983).

4. Elisabeth Schüssler Fiorenza, *In Memory of Her: A Feminist Theological Reconstruction of Christian Origins* (New York: Crossroads, 1983), 243–270.

5. Belief in a hereditary sin affecting all humans that descends from the sin of Adam is found already in Jewish apocalyptic writings contemporary with Paul. See *IV Ezra* 3:20–23, in R. H. Charles, *Apocrypha and Pseudepigrapha of the Old Testament*, vol. 2 (Oxford: Clarendon Press, 1913). But this idea is not generally accepted by Jewish writers of the period. In *II Baruch*, from the same period, the idea is vigorously rejected: "Adam is not the cause, save of his own soul, but each of us has been the Adam of his own soul" (*II Baruch* 54:19).

6. Milton, *Paradise Lost*, bk. 9, 11.901–960.

7. See Stevan Davies, *The Revolt of the Widows: The Social World of the Apocryphal Acts* (Carbondale, Ill.: Southern Illinois University Press, 1980), 50–69 and passim.

8. The European and English Renaissance saw a lively new literature by women defending the female sex against its traditional attacks in male Christian culture. See, for example, Christian de Pisan, *Book of the City of Ladies* (1450); Jane Anger, *Her Protection for Women* (1589); Ester Sowerman, *Ester Hath Hanged Haman: Answer to the Arraignment of Women* (1617); and Mary Astell, *An Essay in Defense of the Female Sex* (1693).

9. The classical text for this nineteenth-century matriarchal theory of origins is J. J. Bachofen, *Myth, Religion and Mother Right* (1861). Engels himself drew upon the work of Lewis H. Morgan, *Ancient Society* (1877).

10. Exodus 32:1–35.

11. *Testimony of Reuben*, chs. 5, 6, 1–4, from *Testimony of the Twelve Patriarchs*, in R. H. Charles, *Apocrypha and Pseudepigrapha of the Old Testament*, vol. 2, 299.

12. Hesiod, *Works and Days*, chs. 5–6.

13. Genesis 3:1–24.

14. *The Hypostasis of the Archons*, 88.12–91.12, in *The Nag Hammadi Library in English* (New York: Harper and Row, 1977), 154–156.

15. 1 Timothy 2:9–14.

16. Elizabeth Cady Stanton, ed., *The Woman's Bible*, I (1895; rpt. New York: Arno Press, 1972), 26–27.

17. Sigmund Freud, *Moses and Monotheism* (New York: Vintage, 1962), 102–105.

18. Friedrich Engels, *The Origin and History of the Family, Private Property and the State* (1885; rpt. New York: International Publishers, 1942), 49–50.

6. Redeemer/Redemptrix: Male and Female Saviors

1. "Acts of the Martyrs of Lyons and Vienne," in *The Acts of the Christian Martyrs*, ed. Herbert Musurillo (Oxford: Clarendon Press, 1912), 75.

2. See Elisabeth S. Fiorenza, "Word, Spirit and Power: Women in Early Christian Communities," in *Women of Spirit: Female Leadership in the Jewish and Christian Traditions*, ed. R. Ruether and E. McLaughlin (New York: Simon and Schuster, 1979), 44–51.

3. Caroline Bynum, *Jesus as Mother: Studies in the Spirituality of the High Middle Ages* (Berkeley: University of California Press, 1982).

4. Eleanor McLaughlin, "Equality in Souls: Inequality in Sexes: Women in Medieval Theology," in *Religion and Sexism: Images of Women in the Jewish and Christian Traditions*, ed. Rosemary Ruether (New York: Simon and Schuster, 1974), 250.

5. Isaac Mendelsohn, ed., *Religions of the Ancient Near East: Akkadian Religious Texts and Ugaritic Epics* (New York: Liberal Arts Press, 1955), 246–248, 253, 255–256.

6. Zechariah 9:9–10; 14:1–19 (New English Bible).

7. Revelation 19:11–21; 20:1–3 (New English Bible).

8. Matthew 20:17–28; 23:1–12; Philippians 2:6–11 (New English Bible).

9. John 1:2–5, 9–13; Colossians 1:15–20 (New English Bible).

10. "The Gospel of the Egyptians," from Clement of Alexandria, *Stromateis, Alexandrian Christianity*, ed. J. E. L. Oulton and Henry Chadwick (Philadelphia: Westminster, 1954), 69–70. "The Gospel of Thomas," 112 (99.18–26), from *The Secret Sayings of Jesus*, ed. Robert McQueen Grant (Garden City, N.Y.: Doubleday, 1961), 197. "The Gospel of Philip," 111, 118, trans. and comm. Robert McL. Wilson (London: A. R. Mowbray, 1962), 39, 46.

11. Julian of Norwich, *Revelations of Divine Love*, trans. John Walsh (New York: Harper and Row, 1961), chaps. 58–59, pp. 159–161.

12. Alfonso de Liguori, *The Glories of Mary* (New York: P. J. Kennedy, 1852), 279.

13. Auguste Comte, *A General View of Positivism* (Paris, 1848; rpt. Stanford, Calif.: Academic Reprints, n.d.), 286–288.

14. *The Testimony of Christ's Second Appearing* (United Society (Shakers), 1856), 506, 514–518.

15. Nancy Ore, 1983, unpublished.

16. Nancy Ore, 1983. Winner of Sierra Poetry Guild Fall Poetry Contest, 1983, and published in *The Monthly Communicator* 2, no. 4 (Nov. 1983): 2.

7. Repentance, Conversion, Transformation

1. C. Kraeling, *John the Baptist* (New York: Scribner's, 1951).

2. L. Finkelstein, "The Institution of Baptism for Proselytes," *Journal of Biblical Literature* 52 (1933): 203–211; H. H. Rowley, "Jewish Proselyte Baptism," *Hebrew Union College Annual* 15 (1940): 313–334.

3. Morton Scott Enslin, *Christian Beginnings* (New York: Harper Brothers, 1938), 149–153.

4. See Hans Jonas, *The Gnostic Religion: The Message of the Alien God and the Beginning of Christianity* (Boston: Beacon, 1963), 153–173, for interpretation and commentary.

5. Catherine Romano, "A Psychic-Spiritual History of Teresa of Avila: A Woman's Perspective," in *Western Spirituality: Historical Roots, Ecumenical Routes*, ed. Matthew Fox (Notre Dame, Ind.: Fides/Claretian, 1979), 274–278.

6. Jonah 3:1–15, 10 (RSV).

7. Matthew 3:1–3, 7–10 (RSV).

8. Romans 6:3–23 (RSV).

9. "The Hymn of the Pearl," Acts of Thomas, from Jonas, *Gnostic Religion*, 113–116.

10. Augustine, *Confessions*, VIII.

11. Augustine was reading Athanasius' life of the first monk, St. Anthony, which describes how Anthony gave up all his possessions after hearing the gospel read in which Jesus told the rich young man that if he would be perfect he must sell what he possessed and give to the poor (Matt. 19:16–30).

12. Teresa of Avila, *The Interior Castle*, tr. E. Allison, Peers (Garden City, N.Y.: Doubleday, 1961), 207–208, 213–214.

13. *Gifts of Power: The Writings of Rebecca Jackson, Black Visionary, Shaker Eldress*, ed. and intro. Jean McMahon Humez (Amherst: University of Massachusetts Press, 1981), 71–72, 107–108.

14. Nancy Ore, "Untitled," previously published in *Rough Edges*, Garrett-Evangelical Theological Seminary Women's Caucus publication, May 1983.

8. Redemptive Community

1. Neither the French or the American Revolutions included women in their constitutions, which guaranteed equal rights to "all men." The French Revolutionary Republican Olympe de Gouges (1745–1793) argued for women's

rights in her *Declaration des droits de la Femme et de la Citoyenne* (1791), but her efforts were suppressed by the radicals of the Revolution and she herself was executed two years later. *Woman as Revolutionary*, ed. Frederick Griffin (New York: New American Library, 1973), 46–49. During the American Constitutional Convention, Abigail Adams wrote to her husband, John Adams, a delegate at the convention, and told him to "remember the ladies" and to include them in the rights that the convention delegates were fashioning for the new republic, but her husband scoffed at her suggestion. See *Feminism: Essential Historical Writings*, ed. Miriam Schneir (New York: Random House–Vintage, 1972), 2–4. In the twentieth century, Black and Latin American liberation movements have been equally male-dominated and unwilling to take feminism seriously until pressed by women revolutionaries in their own ranks. See *Theology in the Americas*, ed. Sergio Torres and John Eagleson (Maryknoll, N.Y.: Orbis Press, 1976), 361–376.

2. The theme of God's preferential option for the poor has been developed in Latin American liberation theology as the interpretation of this biblical tradition. See particularly Gustavo Gutierrez, *The Power of the Poor in History* (Maryknoll, N.Y.: Orbis Press, 1983).

3. R. Gryson, *The Ministry of Women in the Early Church* (Minneapolis: University of Minnesota Press, 1976).

4. Elisabeth Schüssler Fiorenza, *In Memory of Her: A Feminist Theological Reconstruction of Christian Origins* (New York: Crossroads, 1983), 285–293.

5. Fiorenza, *In Memory of Her*, 243–269.

6. Jerome, *Adversus Jovinianum* 20.

7. Cyprian of Carthage's treatise on the *Unity of the Church*, 251 A.D., speaks of Peter's apostolic leadership as the source of episcopal authority. He probably means this not in the sense of a special priority of the Bishop of Rome as heir of Petrine authority but as the whole episcopal office as heir of Petrine authority.

8. This confrontation scene between Peter and Mary appears in several places in gnostic texts. See, for example, *The Gospel of Thomas* (ch. 6, reading 4).

9. Elaine Pagels, *The Gnostic Gospels* (New York: Random House, 1979), 28–47. Pagels points out the controversy between gnostic and orthodox Christians on matters of Church polity, showing that gnostics adhere to a more spiritualist concept of the Church as a small intentional community without elaborate institutional structure and see the developing episcopacy as a departure from the intention of Christ.

10. Exodus 19:1, 2b–11, 13b–19; 20:1–3 (RSV).

11. Hosea 2:1–20 (RSV).

12. Luke 1:31–55 (RSV).

13. 1 Timothy 2:1–6a, 8, 11–12; 3:1–5, 8–13 (RSV).

14. Ephesians 5:1–4, 18b–33 (RSV).

15. Cyprian, *On the Unity of the Church*, ch. 6 in *Ante-Nicene Fathers*, ed. Alexander Roberts and James Donaldson (New York: Scribner's, 1899), V, 423.

16. Methodius, *Symposium: Ancient Christian Writers* (Westminster, Md.: Newman Press, 1958), no. 27, pp. 65–66.

17. *The Gospel of Mary*, in *The Nag Hammadi Library in English*, ed. John

Robinson et al. (New York: Harper and Row, 1977), 471–474.

18. Rosemary Ruether, address at the WomanChurch Speaks Conference, Chicago, November 1983.

9. Foremothers of WomanChurch

1. Raphael Patai, *The Hebrew Goddess* (Philadelphia: Ktav, 1967), 284.

2. Leonard Swidler, *Biblical Affirmations of Women* (Philadelphia: Westminster, 1979), 87.

3. Patai, *Hebrew Goddess*, 49–50.

4. Stevan Davies, *The Revolt of the Widows: The Social World of the Apocryphal Acts* (Carbondale, Ill.: University of Southern Illinois Press, 1980), 95–109.

5. Denis R. MacDonald, *The Legend and the Apostle: The Battle for Paul in Story and Canon* (Philadelphia: Westminster, 1983), passim.

6. "Acts of the Martyrs of Lyons and Vienne," in *The Acts of the Christian Martyrs*, ed. Hebert Musurillo (Oxford: Clarendon Press, 1912), 75.

7. The struggle of Bishop Cyprian of Carthage with the charismatic confessors during the Decian persecutions (250 A.D.) represents the classic confrontation in early Christianity between episcopal and charismatic authority. See Cyprian's *On the Lapsed* and *On the Unity of the Church*, in ch. 8, note 15.

8. Didache 15:1–2.

9. Acts 2:17–18, from Joel 2:28–32.

10. Exodus 15:20–21.

11. Numbers 12:12–16.

12. Judges 4:4–10, 13–15, 17–21.

13. Judges 5:1, 3, 6–7, 12–15, 24, 27, 31.

14. 2 Kings 22:11–20.

15. John 20:1–18.

16. *Acts of Paul and Thecla*, vol. 8 in *Ante-Nicene Fathers*, ed. Alexander Roberts and James Donaldson (New York: Scribner's, 1885–1897), 487ff.

17. *The Passion of Saints Perpetua and Felicitas*, vol. 3, app., in Roberts and Donaldson, *Ante-Nicene Fathers*.

18. Epiphanius, *Haer.* 48:2, 12–13, 49, 1.

10. The New Earth: Visions of Redeemed Society and Nature

1. See Albert Nolan, *Jesus Before Christianity: The Gospel of Liberation* (Capetown, S.A.: David Philip, 1976), 44–49.

2. The chief source of matriarchal anthropology is J. J. Bachofen, *Myth, Religion and Motheright* (1861; rpt. Princeton, N.J.: Princeton University Press, 1967).

3. See chapter 8, reading 1, in this book.

4. Condorcet pleaded for the Citizenship of women before the French Revolutionary Assembly, but lost. His address can be found in *Journal de la Société de 1789*, 3 July 1790. Translated into English in *The Fortnightly Review* 13, no.

42 (June 1870): 719–720.

5. John Stuart Mill's classical treatise on the emancipation of women, *The Subjugation of Women*, was originally published in 1869 and has been frequently reprinted (Cambridge, Mass.: MIT Press, 1970).

6. Miriam Schneir, *Feminism: Essential Historical Writings* (New York: Random House–Vintage, 1972), offers a good sampling of the writings of these classical liberal feminists.

7. Zillah Eisenstein, *The Radical Future of Liberal Feminism* (New York: Longman, 1981), is a recent expression of Marxist feminism.

8. See Charlotte Perkins Gilman, *Herland* (1923; rpt. New York: Pantheon, 1979).

9. Leviticus 25:10–12, 13–14, 17, 23–28, 39–42 (RSV).

10. Isaiah 2:1–4; 11:6–9; 40:3–5; 65:17–25 (RSV).

11. Luke 4:14–21 (RSV).

12. Antoine-Nicholas de Condorcet, *Sketch for a Historical Picture of the Progress of the Human Mind*, trans. June Barraclough (London: George Weidenfeld and Nicolson, 1955), 196–202.

13. Pierre Teilhard de Chardin, *The Future of Man*, trans. Norman Denny (New York: Harper and Row, 1964), 76–81.

14. Friedrich Engels, *Socialism, Utopian and Scientific* (1882; rpt. New York: International Publishers, 1935), 69–73.

15. Murray Bookshin, *Post-Scarcity Anarchism* (San Francisco: Ramparts Press, 1971), 69–70, 80–82.

16. Elizabeth Gould Davis, *The First Sex* (Baltimore, Md.: Penguin, 1971), 68–69, 331–339.

11. The New Heaven: Personal and Cosmic Eschatology

1. Franz Cumont, *Astrology and Religion Among the Greeks and Romans* (New York: Dover, 1912), esp. ch. 6.

2. *The Great Bundahis*, vol. 5, ch. 30 in *The Sacred Books of the East: Pahlavi Texts*, ed. F. Max Miller (Oxford: Clarendon Press, 1897).

3. Walter Bauer, *Orthodoxy and Heresy in Earliest Christianity*, ed. Robert Kraft and Gerland Krodel (Philadelphia: Fortress, 1971), passim.

4. Pseudo-Melito, "The Passing of Mary," in vol. 8, *Apocrypha of the New Testament*, in *Ante-Nicene Fathers*, ed. Roberts and Donaldson (New York: Scribner's, 1897), 592–598.

5. "The Descent of Inanna," in Diane Wolkstein and Samuel Noah Kramer, *Inanna: Queen of Heaven and Earth: Her Stories and Hymns from Sumer* (New York: Harper and Row, 1983), 52–71. The text goes on to suggest that Dumuzi escapes the sentence of death by appealing to Utu, God of Justice. In a complementary text on Dumuzi's Return from the Underworld (85–89), Dumuzi (like Persephone, in the Greek Demeter myth) must stay in the underworld half a year. So his cycle of yearly descent to and ascent from the underworld represents the dying and rising vegetation.

6. "The Poimandres of Hermes Trismegistus," in Hans Jonas, *The Gnostic Religion: The Message of the Alien God and the Beginning of Christianity* (Boston: Beacon, 1963), 152–153.

7. Plato, *Phaedrus* 246–249, from *The Dialogues of Plato*, vol. 1, ed. B. Jowett (New York: Random House, 1937), 250–254.

8. Revelation 20:4–15; 21:1–4, 22–27; 22:1–5 (RSV).

9. 1 Corinthians 15:20–54 (RSV).

10. *The Trimorphic Protennoia*, from *The Nag Hammadi Library in English*, ed. John Robinson et al. (New York: Harper and Row, 1977), 461–467.

11. Irenaeus, *Adv. Haer.* V, from vol. 1, *Early Christian Fathers*, ed. Cyril Richardson (Philadelphia: Westminster, 1953), 387–398.

12. "The Book of John Concerning the Falling Asleep of Mary," from Roberts and Donaldson, *Ante-Nicene Fathers*, 587–591.

13. Otto Semmelroth, *Mary: Archetype of the Church*, trans. Maria von Eroes and John Devlin (New York: Sheed and Ward, 1963), 166–168.

14. Charlotte Perkins Gilman, *His Religion and Hers: A Study of the Faith of the Fathers and the Work of Our Mothers* (New York: Century, 1923), vii–viii.

Bibliography

J. J. Bachofen. *Myth, Religion and Mother Right*. 1861. Reprint. Princeton, N.J.: Princeton University Press, 1967.

Richard A. Baer. *Philo's Use of the Categories Male and Female*. Leiden: Brill, 1970.

D. S. Bailey. *The Man-Woman Relationship in Christian Thought*. London: Longman, 1959.

Bernard Frank Batto. *Studies on Women at Mari*. Baltimore: Johns Hopkins University Press, 1974.

Walter Bauer. *Orthodoxy and Heresy in Earliest Christianity*. Translated by Robert Kraft and Gerland Krodel. Philadelphia: Fortress, 1971.

Phyllis Bird. "Male and Female, He Created Them: Gen. 1:27b in the Context of the Priestly Account of Creation." *Harvard Theological Review* 74, no. 2 (1981).

Murray Bookshin. *The Ecology of Freedom: The Emergence and Dissolution of Hierarchy*. Palo Alto, Calif.: Cheshire, 1982.

Kari Børreson. *Subordination and Equivalence, the Nature and Role of Women in Augustine and Aquinas*. Translation from French. Washington, D.C.: University Press of America, 1981.

John Boswell. *Christianity, Social Tolerance, and Homosexuality*. Chicago: University of Chicago Press, 1980.

Caroline Bynum. *Jesus as Mother: Studies in the Spirituality of the High Middle Ages*. Berkeley: University of California Press, 1982.

Carol Christ and Judith Plaskow, eds. *Womanspirit Rising: A Feminist Reader in Religion*. San Francisco: Harper and Row, 1979.

Linda Clark, Marian Ronan, and Eleanor Walker. *Image Breaking–Image Making: A Handbook for Creative Worship for Women of Christian Tradition*. New York: Pilgrim Press, 1981.

Franz Cumont. *Astrology Among the Greeks and Romans*. 1912. Reprint. New York: Dover, 1960.

———. *The Mysteries of Mithra*. 1902. Reprint. New York: Dover, 1956.

———. *Oriental Religions in Roman Paganism*. 1911. Reprint. New York: Dover, 1956.

Mary Daly. *Beyond God the Father: Toward a Philosophy of Women's Liberation*. Boston: Beacon, 1973.

———. *Gyn/Ecology: The Metaethics of Radical Feminism*. Boston: Beacon, 1979.

_____. *Pure Lust: Elemental Feminist Philosophy.* Boston: Beacon, 1984.

Stevan Davies. *The Revolt of the Widows: The Social World of the Apocryphal Acts.* Carbondale, Ill.: University of Southern Illinois Press, 1980.

Elizabeth Gould Davis. *The First Sex.* Baltimore, Md.: Penguin, 1971.

Dorothy Dinnerstein. *The Mermaid and the Minotaur: Sexual Arrangements and Human Malaise.* New York: Harper and Row, 1976.

Zillah Eisenstein. *The Radical Future of Liberal Feminism.* New York: Longman, 1981.

Elizabeth Schüssler Fiorenza. *In Memory of Her: A Feminist Theological Reconstruction of Christian Origins.* New York: Crossroads, 1983.

Charlotte Perkins Gilman. *Herland.* 1923. Reprint. New York: Pantheon, 1979.

_____. *His Religion and Hers: A Study of the Faith of the Fathers and the Work of Our Mothers.* New York: Century, 1923.

Lynda M. Glennon. *Women and Dualism: A Sociology of Knowledge Analysis.* New York: Longman, 1979.

Norman K. Gottwald. *The Tribes of Yahweh: A Sociology of the Religion of Liberated Israel, 1250–1050 B.C.* Maryknoll, N.Y.: Orbis Press, 1979.

Frederick Griffin, ed. *Woman as Revolutionary.* New York: New American Library, 1973.

Susan Griffin. *Woman and Nature: The Roaring Inside Her.* New York: Harper and Row, 1978.

R. Gryson. *The Ministry of Women in the Early Church.* Minneapolis: University of Minnesota Press, 1976.

Robert Hamerton-Kelly. *God the Father: Theology and Patriarchy in the Teachings of Jesus.* Philadelphia: Fortress, 1979.

Susan Ashbrook Harvey. "Women in Early Syriac Christianity." In *Images of Women in Antiquity,* ed. Averil Cameron and Amelia Kuhrt. London: Croon Helm, 1983.

Sharon Kelly Heyob. *The Cult of Isis Among Women in the Greco-Roman World.* Leiden: Brill, 1975.

Carter Heyward. *A Priest Forever: The Formation of a Woman and a Priest.* New York: Harper and Row, 1976.

Joyce Irwin. *Womanhood in Radical Protestantism, 1525–1675.* New York: Mellen, 1979.

E. O. James. *The Cult of the Mother Goddess: An Anthropological and Documentary Study.* New York: Barnes and Noble, 1959.

_____. *The Worship of the Sky God: A Comparative Study of Semitic and Indo-European Religion.* London: Athlone Press, 1963.

Hans Jonas. *The Gnostic Religion: The Message of the Alien God and the Beginning of Christianity.* Boston: Beacon, 1963.

Carol Karlsen. "The Devil in the Shape of a Woman." Diss., Yale University, 1980.

Samuel Noah Kramer. *History Begins at Sumer.* Garden City, N.Y.: Doubleday, 1956.

Samuel Laeuchli. *Power and Sexuality: The Emergence of Canon Law at the Council of Elvira.* Philadelphia: Temple University Press, 1972.

Denis R. MacDonald. *The Legend and the Apostle: The Battle for Paul in Story and Canon*. Philadelphia: Westminster, 1983.

Sally McFague. *Metaphorical Theology: Models of God in Religious Language*. Philadelphia: Fortress, 1982.

George MacRae. "The Jewish Background of the Gnostic Sophia Myth." In *Novum Testamentum* 12.

Carolyn Merchant. *The Death of Nature: Women, Ecology and the Scientific Revolution*. San Francisco: Harper and Row, 1980.

Giovanni Miegge. *The Virgin Mary*. London: Lutterworth, 1955.

Robert Murray. *Symbols of Church and Kingdom: A Study of Early Syriac Christianity*. Cambridge: University Press, 1975.

Albert Nolan. *Jesus Before Christianity: The Gospel of Liberation*. Capetown, S.A.: David Philip, 1976.

Carol Ochs. *Behind the Sex of God*. Boston: Beacon, 1977.

Judith Ochshorn. *The Female Experience and the Nature of the Divine*. Bloomington: Indiana University Press, 1980.

John H. Otwell. *And Sarah Laughed: The Status of Woman in the Old Testament*. Philadelphia: Westminster, 1977.

Elaine Pagels. *The Gnostic Gospels*. New York: Random House, 1979.

Raphael Patai. *The Hebrew Goddess*. Philadelphia: Ktav, 1967.

Judith Plaskow. *Sex, Sin and Grace: Women's Experience and the Theologies of Reinhold Niebuhr and Paul Tillich*. Washington, D.C.: University Press of America, 1980.

Marjorie Reeves. *The Influence of Prophecy in the Later Middle Ages: A Study in Joachimism*. Oxford: Clarendon Press, 1969.

_____. *Joachim of Fiore and the Prophetic Future*. New York: Harper and Row, 1976.

Theodor Reik. *The Creation of Woman: A Psychoanalytic Inquiry into the Myth of Eve*. New York: McGraw-Hill, 1960.

Katherine Rogers. *The Troublesome Helpmate: A History of Misogyny in Literature*. Seattle: University of Washington Press, 1966.

Catherine Romano. "A Psychic-Spiritual History of Teresa of Avila: A Woman's Perspective." In *Western Spirituality: Historical Roots, Ecumenical Routes*, ed. Matthew Fox. Notre Dame, Ind.: Fides/Claretian, 1979.

Sheila Rowbotham. *Women, Resistance and Revolution: A History of Women and Revolution in the Modern World*. New York: Random, 1974.

Rosemary Radford Ruether. *Mary: The Feminine Face of the Church*. Philadelphia: Westminster, 1977.

_____. *The New Woman/New Earth: Sexist Ideologies and Human Liberation*. New York: Seabury, 1975.

_____. *Religion and Sexism: Images of Women in the Jewish and Christian Traditions*. New York: Simon and Schuster, 1974.

_____. *Sexism and God-Talk: Toward a Feminist Theology*. Boston: Beacon, 1983.

Rosemary Ruether and Rosemary Keller. *Women and Religion in America: The Nineteenth Century: A Documentary History*. San Francisco: Harper and Row, 1981.

_____. *Women and Religion in America: A Documentary History: The Colonial and Revolutionary War Periods*. San Francisco: Harper and Row, 1983.

Letty Russell. *Human Liberation in a Feminist Perspective*. Philadelphia: Westminster, 1974.

Letha Scanzoni. *All We're Meant to Be: A Biblical Approach to Women's Liberation*. Waco, Tex.: Word Books, 1974.

Anne Wilson Schaef. *Women's Reality: An Emerging Female System in the White Male Society*. Minneapolis: Winston Press, 1981.

Miriam Schneir. *Feminism: Essential Historical Writings*. New York: Random House–Vintage, 1972.

G. C. Stead. "The Valentinian Myth of Sophia." In *Journal of Theological Studies* 20 (1969).

Leonard Swidler. *Biblical Affirmations of Women*. Philadelphia: Westminster, 1979.

George Tavard. *Women in the Christian Tradition*. West Bend, Ind.: Notre Dame University Press, 1973.

Elizabeth M. Tetlow. *Women and Ministry in the New Testament*. New York: Paulist Press, 1980.

Phyllis Trible. "Depatriarchalizing in Biblical Interpretation." *Journal of the American Academy of Religion* 41, no. 1 (March 1973).

_____. *God and the Rhetoric of Sexuality*. Philadelphia: Fortress, 1978.

Index

Rosemary Radford Ruether is Georgia
Harkness Professor of Applied Theology
at the Garrett-Evangelical Theological
Seminary in Evanston, Illinois, and a
faculty member in the joint doctoral pro-
gram with Northwestern University. A
contributing editor to *Christianity and
Crisis* magazine, she is also the author of
*Mary: The Feminine Face of the Church,
Religion and Sexism,* and *New Woman/
New Earth.*